THE WHIG MYTH
of
JAMES FENIMORE COOPER

BY

DOROTHY WAPLES

ARCHON BOOKS
1968

FIRST PUBLISHED 1938 BY YALE UNIVERSITY PRESS

REPRINTED 1968 WITH PERMISSION
IN AN UNALTERED AND UNABRIDGED EDITION
[*Yale Studies in English, Vol. 88*]

LIBRARY OF CONGRESS CATALOG CARD NUMBER: 68-12528
PRINTED IN THE UNITED STATES OF AMERICA

CONTENTS

PREFACE

ONE might almost say that Mr. H. W. Boynton and Professor R. E. Spiller in *James Fenimore Cooper* and *Fenimore Cooper, Critic of His Times* have not merely reinterpreted but even reconstructed Cooper in the general conception of him. This was a reconstruction certainly well founded and greatly needed.

The present work explores a field untouched by those two books, neither repeating what Mr. Boynton and Professor Spiller have performed so much more ably than I could do it, nor, as I see it, necessarily entering into conflict with their essential interpretations. It is offered in the hope merely of extending our knowledge of American literary history in one more interesting direction. It tells the neglected story of Cooper's association with the Democratic party, and of revenges taken upon the novelist by the offended Whigs, revenges which later generations have misinterpreted and which, indeed, have persisted in our day so vigorously as to have produced just those misunderstandings which caused the crying need for Mr. Boynton's and Professor Spiller's books. It adds some further facts and further interpretations.

The list of sources at the end of this book records the names of libraries which have contributed help to me, and to all of them I feel deeply indebted. The Morgan Library and the Library of the New York Historical Society were especially kind. The Yale University Library has been both generous and long-suffering in its assistance, especially in trusting me in the use of the Cooper collection. All who have studied at Yale admire the Yale Library for its liberal policies and its union of human qualities with efficiency, and I have many particular reasons for sharing the general gratitude. Yale would not be Yale without Miss Emily Hall, and to this book perhaps Miss Hall contributed as much as the Cooper collection.

It is characteristic of Lawrence College that my colleagues in the Department of English there and Dr. Henry Merritt Wriston, then our President, generously and cheerfully made it possible for me to visit the Cooper collection when it was delivered at Yale during a college term.

Professor Homer E. Woodbridge of Wesleyan started me on this work long ago, when he was my first great teacher, and assisted me again with his encouragement in 1926. It was written under the direction of Professor S. T. Williams, as part of a doctoral thesis at Yale. There is no way to explain or to thank Professor Williams; besides the ungrudging helpfulness which he gives so readily to his students at Yale, he continues his loyal and wise advising for years after that association, even in times, places, and offices thoroughly inconvenient to him. The publication of this book has depended heavily upon those characteristics.

Professor Dorothy Bethurum and Mrs. Rachel W. Stevenson gave me criticism which always proved right. Besides this, they and Mrs. F. A. Waples have contributed hours of labor so hard that no one else would have performed it, and I feel that I can not write any acknowledgement of assistance at all without mentioning the services of Miss M.R. Stevenson.

DOROTHY WAPLES.

APPLETON, WISCONSIN
JANUARY, 1938

CHAPTER I

Cooper's Unpardonable Sin

IN the days of Henry VIII, Johan Johan amused himself, while approaching his cottage door, by garrulous anticipation of the beating he would soon be giving his wife. He reminds one, at times, of the American public talking about its artists. Of course, Johan admitted a drawback:

> The more I bete her, the worse is she:
> And wors and wors make her I shall!

But then, as he said:

> That is a poynt of an honest man
> For to bete his wyfe well nowe and than,
> Therefore I shall bete her. . . .
> And I ought to bete her. . . .
> And why? By God, bicause it is my pleasure!

It happens that we have on the rolls of our history one notable literary man who for twenty years was belabored by a powerful political party until even Johan Johan, who had heroic ideas of beatings, might have said of him that

> There is never a wyfe betwene heven and hell
> Which was ever beten halfe so well.

The politicians, though they did not break his spirit, ruined his reputation and his fortune in the prime of his life; indeed, they so blackened his character that for almost a hundred years we have had a damaged remembrance of him.

James Fenimore Cooper exposed himself to this treatment by being a Democrat. We do not attack him for this alliance now, but various critics do appear to dread discovering or admitting that the alliance existed. It is implied, now, that if a man works with a political party he is by that working decreased in spiritual stature. Whether Cooper's political interest impaired his artistic production would be a true literary question, worthy of discussion. But instead of discussing this question, we are unwilling to think of Cooper as a Democrat at all. Thus we have been prevented from seeing certain political attacks on him for what they were. If we can bring ourselves to shake off the fear of discovering that Cooper had a political party, I believe we need fear no damage to his character thereby, and can even be rewarded by finding that he was a man more generously built than the Whigs have allowed us to suppose. In other words, it can be demonstrated that a myth promulgated by hostile politicians has seriously affected the American conception of Cooper.

Lounsbury began the tradition of minimizing the novelist's political connections. His biography, which set the nation's feelings for fifty years, was characteristic of Professor Lounsbury in its high quality. But as everybody knows, Lounsbury was hindered by lack of biographical material because the family would not authorize a biographer or furnish information. The family took this attitude because Cooper requested it, perhaps because he had been so falsely represented in his lifetime that he could not bear a perpetuation of the old mistakes. But this action left Lounsbury to write whatever he could learn of Cooper from men's conversations, and men's conversations at that time were still busy with the Whig myth. Therefore it happened that Lounsbury established in American thinking this Cooper of the Whigs' invention, a Cooper widely advertised for political purposes; and Lounsbury did not discover what he had done, because he was taken up with denying that Cooper had any politics at all. He took pains to say that the novelist's political connections were merely nominal; indeed, he mentioned them only twice, and then very briefly, in his whole book.[1] Not ascribing sufficient importance to political animosities, Lounsbury found that in 1883 Cooper was a nationally unpopular figure, and he sought the cause of the trouble in Cooper's character. His book became an analysis of Cooper's personality to find in it the germs of discord. Almost three-fourths of the biography is devoted to the subject of Cooper's difficulties with enemies,[2] though the same space might equally well have been devoted to his friendships; and within these pages, wherever Cooper's charm of personality or nobility of character is mentioned (these things are spoken of so frequently by Cooper's contemporaries that a biographer is forced to let some notice of them creep in), it is referred to only concessively, subordinated to the exposition of Cooper's unpleasant behavior or experiences.[3] Lounsbury himself was conscious, when he reached the close of his book, that he had developed a false emphasis; for he admitted that although America has among all her authors "no manlier nature, and no more heroic soul," and that Cooper's nature was essentially sweet, yet he declared that in his book he had deliberately veiled the best side of Cooper, while on the other hand he had "not sought to hide his foibles and his faults, his intolerance and dogmatism, the irascibility of his temperament, the pugnacity of his nature, the illiberality and injustice of many of his opinions, the unreasonableness as well as the imprudence of the course he often pursued."[4] The "illiberality," "injustice," and "unreasonableness" Lounsbury chose to stamp into his final impression of Cooper are hardly to be seen in the real man. Of course, the Whigs

[1] *James Fenimore Cooper*, Boston, 1883, pp. 133, 171.

[2] Pp. 78-286.

[3] *E.g.*, pp. 127, 133, 136. Chapter V seeks to demonstrate that Cooper invited dislike. Chapters XI and XII, which deal with the last years of Cooper's life, ostensibly were planned to say that these years were not embittered, but actually they do not so much dwell upon this fact as reiterate how bitter the earlier quarrels might have made him; the effect is still to emphasize the quarrels.

[4] *Ibid.*, p. 285.

had been applying adjectives like these to Cooper for many years, but I think it can be demonstrated that the adjectives mean nothing more than that Cooper was a Jackson man.

Lately, critics are much friendlier than Lounsbury was. Professor Robert E. Spiller has given careful attention to Cooper's social criticism and has shown warm appreciation of Cooper's generous and persistent patriotism. But he dismisses very lightly the whole matter of politics[5] and seems as anxious as other critics to ignore that subject as if for Cooper's sake. Perhaps we ought to free ourselves from such phrases as "tie Cooper down to party affiliation." Why

[5] For instance, in his introduction to *Gleanings in Europe*: *France*, Oxford, 1928, xxii, Mr. Spiller quotes Cooper: "The polity of the United States is that of a confederated republic, but the power of the federal government acting in most instances on the body of the community, without the intervention of the several states, it has been better styled a Union." Mr. Spiller comments: "In emphasizing this principle as the basis of his discussion, Cooper alligns himself with the position of the federalists rather than with that of the Jeffersonian democrats, and in doing so he anticipates the issues of the Civil War." This comment is consistent with Professor Spiller's course in his excellent introduction, for his purpose there is to discuss Cooper's social criticism in general terms. Yet it is a comment on political platforms, and as such we must admit that it is misleading. By 1830, the Federalist and Jeffersonian parties were defunct, and there could be no question of Cooper's thinking or voting with either of them. Whigs and Jacksonians were contesting the field. Moreover, the quoted passage is not so much Whig as Jacksonian, and at least is entirely consistent with Cooper's constantly Jacksonian utterances on the subject of State's Rights wherever he speaks positively. In the quotation, Cooper emphasized that the nation was actually in *polity* a confederation, and simply remarked that the country "has been better styled a Union" because in actual operation the *powers* of the government act directly. Cooper always insisted without deviation that every one of these centrally and directly operated powers is strictly a power delegated by the states. Cooper's patriotic passion for keeping the nation undivided accompanied this belief in State Sovereignty, and that combination of desire and principle gave him, as it gave other Democrats, much anxiety. This point of Cooper's Jacksonism is discussed, with documentation, in Chapter II.

should a literary critic assume that party affiliation must be a tying down? Milton, Swift, Addison, Burns, Wordsworth, Byron, Carlyle all had it; and where can we find an exact science of imagination which can assure us so positively that any of these great men would have been nobler if things had been different and he in particular had been a man without a party? American authors, unlike the English, are expected to keep themselves immaculate from the vote, democratic but not Democrats, liberal but not Liberals, social but not Socialists; America assumes that it ties a man down to give his principles instrumentation through a party. But I can not help thinking that the essential question of whether partisanship in literature is a narrowing agent, must be kept separate from the issue of whether a man may have a party and be large-minded.

Cooper's latest biographer, Mr. H. W. Boynton, has shaken off Lounsbury's grip and restored Cooper to us as a hearty, active, attractive man, inclined to argue, certainly, and loving to shine, but thoroughly kind, gay, and attractive. He sees the political situation a little more realistically, too, even going so far as to say: "Cooper was a Democrat—not a reliable party man, but still unmistakably on the Democratic side."[6] I believe there is evidence that Cooper was a staunchly reliable party man. Moreover, I think this evidence does not destroy Mr. Boynton's characterization but drives one to carry it farther than he does—to the conviction that Cooper's later years were not corroded by biliousness and petty quarrelings, but that the Cooper of Otsego was not so different from the Cooper of the Bread and Cheese Club.

Cooper was always a brusque man; he was an active man who loved physical pleasures and physical jokes. He loved an argument, too, and could carry one into minute detail, rejoicing in a labyrinth which exhausted other men. He was too quickly moved to indignation when he thought he saw

[6] *James Fenimore Cooper*, New York, 1931, p. 275.

injustice or dishonesty, and he was equally bad about this whether he was the victim or another was. But the sweetness which so strongly attached all who knew him stayed with him through his life. In fact, his dearest friendships—those with Bryant, Greenough, Morse, and Shubrick—closed into firmer bonds during his hardest years. It has not been the fashion to think of Cooper in this way, and yet I am convinced that we must think thus if we will examine the evidence.

Then let us turn the necessary stones, whatever they are hiding. We can comfort ourselves by knowing that political partisanship is not necessarily smallness, any more than nonpartisanship is universally bigness. If the Whig press, as a Whig organization, called Cooper mean, let us estimate its attack justly by seeing that he was nothing worse than a Jacksonian. Now that the Cooper family has transferred to Yale University the great wealth of the novelist's correspondence, including hundreds of unpublished letters, the documents for such an estimation are in part provided. There are abundant clues in this correspondence pointing to Whig misrepresentation. These clues must be followed up in contemporary newspapers and magazines. The files of American newspapers published between 1821 and 1842[7] reveal ample corroboration of the suspicion. So do the magazine reviews. The more one reads of this material, the plainer the pattern grows; the Whig press, which between 1830 and 1842 was just gathering its forces and launching them in battering assaults upon the Democrats, for some reason turned out in full hue and cry against the novelist.

One of the difficulties in dealing with this periodical material is the necessity of following the party affiliations of the journals. As everyone knows who has wandered in this morass, this is slippery ground. The statements herein made

[7] I used those at the Library of Congress, Boston Public Library, New York Public Library, Harvard, and Yale.

that certain papers in certain years were Whig or were allied with the Bank press are based upon all the information to be gleaned from histories of journalism, biographies of editors, and the much ampler witness of the papers themselves. To be certain of a paper's allegiance, I often had to note the tenor of its statements for years. This material is too extensive even to be mentioned in footnotes. A questioner must be referred to the papers themselves; there is no easier way to test the classifications I have made than by repeating the operations which led to them.

It is on record, for instance, that James Watson Webb "aided in consolidating, and gave the name of Whig to the party that sprang into existence in opposition to democracy;" that Weed established the Albany *Evening Journal* in 1830 to give leadership to the Whig press in opposition to the patronized Jackson press; that after getting control of the New York legislature by spending $8000 in Democratic districts, Weed made a successful stroke by securing Greeley's assistance on a new Albany Whig sheet, the *Jeffersonian*; and that Greeley bought the *Tribune* in 1841 on money lent by a Whig friend to support the Whig movement in that year;[8] and we discover for ourselves that Webb, Weed, and Greeley were Cooper's hottest enemies. But more detailed information must be gathered from the sheets themselves.

A reader who will adventure into this nineteenth century journalism must be prepared to find this "the darkest period in the history of American journalism . . . a time truthfully characterized as the 'period of black journalism,' when a greater depth of degradation was reached than was ever touched in the so-called 'yellow period' of recent times. Those who look over the papers of this era will find that all of the customary courtesies of life were put aside; that the papers of both parties employed the vilest, grossest epithets found in

[8] *National Cyclopaedia of American Biography*, New York, 1893, III, 31; George Henry Payne, *History of Journalism in the United States*, New York, 1920, pp. 275-277.

the English language. . . The coarseness, the shallowness, the distortion of news, the use of the press to avenge private wrongs, all this and much more could be excused, but no reason can be found to justify the papers which so often during this period were little short of being blackmailers and blackguards."[9] The journalistic habits of these years must be remembered by a person to whom they are foreign, lest he erroneously suppose that where a journal sent up a column of smoke there must have been some fire.

It would be too long and tedious a process to retell all the versions of Cooper's story now extant and to discuss their differences from mine at every step. I have therefore assumed the right to retell the narrative of Cooper's struggle, using the emphasis which seems to me warranted by the facts I have derived from the sources mentioned.

In James Fenimore Cooper, then, America seems to have had a novelist who took his political responsibilities with great seriousness, even with an inbred sense of *noblesse oblige*. His father was an inveterate politician. All of Cooper's biographers enjoy writing of this father as a great landed proprietor, one of an Empire Stateful of landed proprietors, who lived a life of manorial aristocracy reminiscent of England. But this frontier adaptation of the English country gentleman's life included that political activity which proprietorship enforced, in both countries, as a civic duty and as a business interest. We hear much of the Cooper family hall, and we ought to hear as often that that hall was not merely a social center, but "a citadel of Federalism and the council place of party methods for the Otsego country."[10]

[9] James Melvin Lee, *History of American Journalism*, New York, 1923, pp. 143, 144. These statements refer to the period beginning "at the close of the second war with England." Conditions were as bad in the 1830's; see the same authority, pp. 197-198.

[10] Dixon Ryan Fox, *The Decline of Aristocracy in the Politics of New York*, Columbia University Studies LXXXVI, New York, 1919, p. 31.

The novelist has himself described William Cooper's vigorous partisan activity, not withholding examples of his father's piquant political language.[11] He quotes a letter to the elder Cooper from Philip Schuyler which gives an idea of Judge Cooper's campaign methods:

> I believe fasting and prayer to be good, but if you had only fasted and prayed I am sure we should not have had seven hundred votes from your country—report says that you was very civil to the young and handsome of the sex, that you flattered the old and ugly, and even embraced the toothless and decrepid, in order to obtain votes. When will you write a treatise on electioneering? Whenever you do, afford only a few copies to your friends.

Like most politicians of the day, William Cooper was accused of gerrymandering his county and of exercising undue influence on voters. One day when a certain James Cochran attacked him at fisticuffs for his politics, he defended himself so ably that Cochran had to say, "I acknowledge you are too much of a buffer for me." Thereupon the worldly wise Judge Cooper had a legal deposition made of this confessed defeat.[12]

Another version of this or of a second fight with Cochran gives Cooper's fisticuffs less glory. Levi Beardsley says Cochran and Cooper were both Federalists but ran against each other one year for a seat in Congress. Cochran took his violin on his campaign trip and at Canandaigua played for a dance. He defeated Cooper in the election, and then word reached him that Cooper had said he had fiddled himself into office. He got on a horse and rode right up to Cooperstown and the Court of Common Pleas. He told Cooper he had come from the Mohawk to chastise him. "Judge Cooper treated it lightly, and remarked that Cochran could not be in earnest, who answered by a cut with his cowskin. Cooper

[11] Introduction to William Cooper, *A Guide in the Wilderness*, Rochester, 1897, v-vii.

[12] D. R. Fox, *op. cit.*, pp. 140-141.

closed in with his adversary, but Cochran being a large strong man, they were pretty well matched for the scuffle, and the judge did not throw him as he intended; the bystanders interposed and the parties were separated." Cochran was fined. Cooper, of course, was elected to Congress later, and "He was present at those ballottings in congress, between Mr. Jefferson and Col. Burr, and with others of the Federal party, voted for the latter. He was so unwell at the time; that I believe he had to be carried into congress to give his votes."[13] A story of Cooper's being accused of dishonest practices is told by a New York Democratic politician, Jabez Delano Hammond, who says a charge of dishonesty in getting votes for Jay was probably trumped up against him to offset charges that had been made against Democrats. The charges were dismissed as "frivolous vexations."[14] But it is not a surprise to learn that Cooper was known as a hard man on his opponents.[15]

Yet William Cooper was a man of dignity and power in politics. He was First Judge of the Court of Common Pleas of Otsego County for nine years, and he served two terms in Congress. He paid a high price for his successes, and his death was a kind of martyrdom to the party methods of his time; in 1809, only a year before his son James became a voter, he was killed by a political opponent who struck him a blow from behind his back as he left a political meeting.

Such was James Cooper's baptism of party. Moreover, while James was growing up, the boy seldom left the atmosphere of politics when he left his father's "citadel." Passivity towards politics simply was not in the philosophy of any of Cooper's early associates. New York State seethed with passionate Federalism, and the leaders of the party in the counties adjoining Otsego were natural associates of the

[13] Levi Beardsley, *Reminiscences*, New York, 1852, pp. 89-90.

[14] Jabez Delano Hammond, *The History of Political Parties in the State of New York*, Cooperstown, 1846, I, 76-77, 82.

[15] *Ibid.*, pp. 131-132.

Coopers.[16] Young James so adored Moss Kent that for a while in boyish fashion he signed himself James Kent Cooper;[17] and Moss Kent was an important leader in the Federalist party.[18] James's schoolfellows in Albany were a Jay, a Hillhouse, and a van Rensselaer; sons respectively of John Jay, whose politics the whole nation knows; James Hillhouse, whose politics Connecticut knows;[19] and John J. Rensselaer of Greenbush,[20] whose family helped to keep New York Federalist, as New York knows.[21] This brood of Federalist nestlings were confided to the care of a violent and indefatigable Tory, the Reverend Thomas Ellison. In later years, when James was a seasoned Democrat, he described with relish the incorrigible partisanship of his old schoolmaster, who "detested a Democrat as he did the devil; cracked his jokes daily about Mr. Jefferson and Black Sal, never failing to place his libertinism in strong relief against the approved laurels of George III, of several passages in whose history, it is charity to suppose he was ignorant . . ."[22]

The Tory schoolmaster was not the only man in New York State who associated Democrats, Jefferson, and immorality. Society, propriety, and divinity were all with the Federalist party. Two years after James Cooper's coming of age, there was a riot at the Commencement exercises of Columbia because the provost withheld the diploma from a young man who uttered anti-Federalist statements in his graduation speech. There on the platform was the diploma, signed and sealed, and there was the bold young man with his college

[16] D. R. Fox, *op. cit.*, p. 31; James Fenimore Cooper, *op. cit.*, v.

[17] *Correspondence of James Fenimore-Cooper*, edited by James Fenimore Cooper, New Haven, 1922, I, 77.

[18] D. R. Fox, *op. cit.*, p. 134.

[19] Federalist member of Congress, 1791-1795; senator, 1797-1810.

[20] Letter, William Jay to Susan Fenimore Cooper, New York, April 15, 1854. Unpublished. Cooper collection, Yale.

[21] D. R. Fox, *op. cit.*, pp. 44ff.

[22] J. F. Cooper, *Gleanings in Europe: England*, Philadelphia, 1837, I, 264-265.

credits receipted in full; but there was the speech, too, the surprise of it still vibrant in the hall; and a respectable New York college had to make Federalism a prerequisite. Why should it not, when there were New York banks which refused to do business with Democrats, factories which would not sell stock to them, and even a parson in a county familiar to Cooper who declined to christen an infant Thomas Jefferson? Democrats even lived under a sort of quarantine (perhaps voluntary), for there were definite Federalist residential sections in New York City.[23]

Catharine Sedgwick, the novelist, came of a strongly Federalist family whom Cooper knew well. Looking back upon her childhood, she wrote:

I heard my father's conversation with his political friends, and in the spontaneous expressions of domestic privacy, and I received the impression then (and . . . I feel assured of its correctness) that the Federal party loved their country, and were devoted to it, as virtuous parents are to their children. It was to my father what selfish men's private affairs are to them, of deep and ever-present interest. . . .[24]

It is not to be supposed that the Federalist love of country was non-partisan; rather, the Federalists identified the safety of the country with the domination of their party, and the more patriotic they were, the more partisan: "I remember well looking upon a Democrat as an enemy to his country, and at the party as sure, if it prevailed, to work its destruction."

Let no one suppose that when James Cooper grew to manhood in another generation from Judge William's and thought of his father's Federalist associates as having been actual monarchists in their Toryism, he was the only person who thought in that way. If in 1830 he was too nervous in his fears that the Whigs were monarchists, his idea that the

[23] D. R. Fox, *op. cit.*, pp. 162-163, 55-56, 24.

[24] *The Life and Letters of Catharine Maria Sedgwick*, edited by Mary E. Dewey, New York, 1871, pp. 34-35.

Federalists had been monarchists was well founded. In fact, Jabez Hammond, in James Cooper's maturity, cautioned Americans against forgetting this fact; he reminded them that in the elections of 1798 the opponents of Adams thought that his followers were guilty of "almost treasonable partiality for the British government" and a desire "if not in name in spirit" for "a limited monarchical government similar to that of Great Britain. These charges may seem to us at this day, entirely extravagant. . . . But in my judgement, we should do injustice to a large portion of the intelligent and best informed part of the republicans, who led on the attack upon the federal administration, in arriving at such a conclusion." Many of the most intelligent federalists, Hammond reminded us, thought a "pure representative government" impossible. They looked either to revolution or gradual reversion to some form of monarchy.[25] When we find Cooper's friend, Horatio Greenough, then, declaring to his brother in 1843 that his idea of old-fashioned federalism is that it was nothing but "a desire for monarchy or aristocracy,"[26] with a hint in his phrasing that the same spirit was still a danger, we are not surprised. When, in turn, we find James Cooper in the 1830's striking about him at the old serpent, we still are not surprised; as for Cooper's fighting on the side that was not his father's, that was a common enough experience, then as now.

In such a society, where political partisanship was so absorbing, so necessary, and, although connected with much that was trivial, so nobly associated with the finest patriotism our country has seen, how could a vigorous man like Cooper have lived as a man without a party? Many of us would not wish him to have done so. A non-partisan James Cooper would have been almost a freak of nature, and it is surprising that we have believed for so long that such a thing once

[25] Jabez D. Hammond, *op. cit.*, pp. 116-117, 120.

[26] *Letters of Horatio Greenough to his brother, Henry Greenough,* Boston, 1887, pp. 145-146.

existed. His daughter[27] and his wife[28] have left us written testimony that he had strong interest in politics. Politics, not literature, is the recurrent theme of his correspondence. This interest was no mere temporary flame. As early as 1823, an enemy referred to him as a disappointed politician.[29] In 1834, at the prime of his life, he was said by a friendly journal to be immersed in politics.[30] Only four years before his death he was visited by N. P. Willis, who found him hale and youthful, apparently fit to live on for several decades unless "plethora or politics" should take him off.[31] Neither was his political enthusiasm a private indulgence or a non-partisan spectatorship. It was practical and public enough for the Democrats to consider how he ought to be rewarded for his services. Jacob Sutherland suggested to President Van Buren a political appointment:

> The Democratic tendency of Mr. Cooper's later Publications has drawn upon him attacks of Various Kinds from the Federal Press. They have attempted to depreciate and undervalue his writings both literary & political and he thinks he has not been Sustained by the Democratic Press & the Country, in the manner he had a right to expect. Such a Mark of Public Confidence & Consideration, as would be implied in this appointment, would undoubtedly under existing circumstances be peculiarly Gratifying to him.[32]

"Sustained by the Democratic Press & the Country in the manner he had a right to expect." Cooper's service to his

[27] Susan Fenimore Cooper, "A Glance Backward, *Atlantic Monthly*, LIX (February, 1887), 199; letter to Mrs. Cooper, Paris, September 14, 1831. Unpublished. Cooper collection, Yale.

[28] Letter, Mrs. Cooper to her sister, Martha De Lancey, Vevay, Switzerland, September 11, 1832. Unpublished. Cooper collection, Yale.

[29] S. B. H. Judah, *Gotham and the Gothamites*, New York, 1823, xlix, note.

[30] *New York Mirror*, XII (August 2, 1834), 39.

[31] N. P. Willis, *Rural Letters*, New York, 1849, pp. 321-322.

[32] Letter, Jacob Sutherland to President Martin Van Buren, Geneva, New York, April 12, 1837. Van Buren correspondence, Library of Congress.

party was perfectly conscious, evidently. He did not think of such a thing as being ashamed of it. Rather, he expected his party to recognize it.

He did not, however, seek political office. He practiced quixotic principles in that respect, as when he resigned his consulship of Lyons because he had come to disapprove of administering such an office through a *chargé des affaires*.[33] He declined an appointment as Minister to Sweden,[34] and discouraged his friends from advocating his appointment as Secretary of the Navy.[35] He did have political influence, for his friends asked his assistance in gaining appointments, and his efforts on their behalf met with success.[36] But for himself, he wanted from his party something other than office, defence; and that was something which the party for various reasons was not able to give at the time.

The Whigs were aware that Cooper was a force in Democratic politics. They knew, for instance, that he was in the field to assist this same Martin Van Buren, and they attacked and derided him for it. Read, for example, a paragraph in a Whig paper, linking him with William Cullen Bryant:

> The poets and romancers are smitten with him [Van Buren], and the 'tuneful nine' seem to have entwined themselves into a 'cat-o'-nine-tails' to lash down all opposition. The *Evening Post* [the leading Democratic journal] is edited by a Poet; 'Cooper the Novelist' is a zealous defender of the administration. . . .[37]

[33] James Fenimore Cooper, *A Letter to His Countrymen*, New York, 1834, p. 34.

[34] Susan Fenimore Cooper, "Small Family Memories," *Correspondence of James Fenimore-Cooper*, I, 59.

[35] *Correspondence of James Fenimore-Cooper*, I, 361, II, 402.

[36] *E.g.*, letters, Isaac Cooper to Cooper, New York, September 26, 1845; Anthony J. Bleeker to Cooper, New York, February 3, 1845; James K. Paulding to Cooper, Washington, January 20, 1840. Unpublished. Cooper collection, Yale; William Jay to Cooper, *Correspondence of James Fenimore-Cooper*, I, 88.

[37] *Hartford Courant*, July 13, 1840.

Manifestly, there is more here than has recently met the American eye. To search out systematically just how much there is, we need, first, to establish a clear outline of what the tenets of Democracy were in Cooper's time. This is not at all a simple thing to do, and it is no wonder if readers of Cooper are in a state of some confusion as to what a Jacksonian or a National Republican or a Whig might have been in any given year, since issues are very shifty in a period when old parties are breaking up and new ones are forming; but if we are to draw any conclusions as to whether Cooper was a Democrat or not, we must have before us some definition of Democracy against which to try his opinions. Our next business will be to see how many Jacksonian tenets Cooper held and incorporated in his writings. Then we can observe the effect of this Jacksonism of his upon the Whigs, and I think we shall discover in the origin and growth of their hostility the origin and growth, also, of the Whig myth of the disagreeable Mr. Cooper.

CHAPTER II

Those Shocking Jacksonians

IN 1832, little Paul Cooper, playing in the lakes of Switzerland with the toy boat that his father had made for him, was troubled whether to name his craft General Jackson, the Constitution, or Guillaume Tell.[38] His father must have done more to create the boy's quandary than to help him out of it, for James Fenimore Cooper was himself committed to all three, and a choice would have gone hard with him. Fortunately, political allegiance did not require a choice in this commitment, as did the naming of vessels. To love "liberty," Jackson, and the Constitution, all three, was to be an orthodox Democrat.

To establish oneself as a Jacksonian Democrat between 1824 and 1840, a person subscribed to five tenets.[39] He must believe in strict construction of the Constitution; he might desire a protective tariff, and then struggle against the concomitant annoyance of Southern nullification; he must believe in Jackson's method of collecting the French spoliation indem-

[38] Mrs. Cooper to her sister, Martha De Lancey, Vevay, Switzerland, September 11, 1832. Unpublished. Cooper collection, Yale.

[39] Authorities consulted on the politics of this period are: De Alva S. Alexander, *A Political History of the State of New York*, New York, 1906-1909; John S. Bassett, *The Life of Andrew Jackson*, New York, 1911; Levi Beardsley, *Reminiscences*, New York, 1852; Claude G. Bowers, *The Party Battles of the Jackson Period*, Boston, 1922; Edward Channing, *A History of the United States*, volume VI, New York, 1928-1930; Dixon Ryan Fox, *op. cit.*; George Pierce Garrison, *Westward Extension, The American Nation: a History*, XVII; Jabez D. Hammond, *The History of Political Parties in the State of New-York*, Cooperstown, 1846-1847; Albert Bushnell Hart, *Slavery and Abolition, The American Nation: a History*, XVI; William Macdonald, *Jacksonian Democracy*, New York, 1906; F. A. Ogg, *The Reign of Andrew Jackson*, New Haven, 1919; Theodore Clarke Smith, *Parties and Slavery, The American Nation: a History*, XVIII.

nity; he had to oppose the United States Bank; and he would have been enthusiastic for the exercise against Congress of strong executive power. Slavery hung ominously over campaigns after the Missouri Compromise of 1820, but was not a clear party issue.

In addition to these topics of dissent, there was another cause of division between Whigs and Democrats which was still more pervasive in American life, being diffused like air over every field of sentiment as well as through the temples of government. This was a divergence of feeling towards what was called "aristocracy." The Democrats throughout the period applied this term to Whiggism as an epithet of opprobrium, because the Whigs were suspected of sympathizing with English Tories and French Doctrinaires, and of maintaining also an attachment for England and English institutions which sometimes approached idolatry. Anyone hoping to understand Cooper must bring himself to realize that a stand against Whig "aristocrats," English Tories, and French Doctrinaires was a definitely partisan attitude; it marked a person as a Democrat just as plainly as any vote he could cast on the National Bank, and it figured as prominently in election campaigns. The Whigs maintained their attitude of Tory and Doctrinaire sympathy with diligence. They displayed, in fact, great ingenuity in declaring themselves supporters of American republican institutions, and at the same time defending conservatism in European affairs. They might declare, for instance, that though Americans believed in free institutions, yet Europe was not used to freedom, and changes there must be made to take generations for their consummation; that, hence, the late Reform Bill in England had gone much too far.[40] But before Cooper's connection with politics was over, these so-called aristocrats were forced in self-defense to turn the tables upon the Democrats by averring that it was they and not the Whigs who had shot the good bird of republicanism. The Democrats, they cried,

[40] *Commercial Advertiser*, December 2, 1831 (a Whig paper).

were the true supporters of tyranny; raising shouts of "King Andrew" and "Down with Van Buren," they managed at length to chock up a log-cabin campaign and to huzzah a candidate into the Presidency. So in 1841 a newspaper writer could say, "the Whigs have of late years repeatedly declared themselves true Jeffersonian Democrats."[41] It was perfectly true. Until the late 1830's, the Whigs were more or less admitted by both sides to be "aristocrats," and the Democrats, "the people." After that, to go on making this discrimination was the sign of a Democrat. When the discrimination was linked with a belief that England was, in general, a Tory nation definitely hostile to America, the sign was all the more surely that of an Anti-Whig.

Now we have reached the end of the spring board, and can no longer postpone the plunge into the dreadful waters of Cooper's Jacksonian partisanship.

The first admission must be that Cooper believed in strict construction from the beginning. This matter was, of course, the rock on which the old parties split and reorganized as Democratic and Whig. Demands for internal improvements in the 1820's sharpened the question of the government's power to engage in such enterprises. Jackson ran for the Presidency in 1824 on the strict construction side of this issue, and in 1828 he was of the same mind. His followers took the name of "Jackson Men" at first, considering themselves a variety of Republican; but at length they adopted the title of Democrats. On the other side, Clay and Adams, being drawn to each other by their common policy of loose construction, styled their sect first National Republicans and, in 1835, Whigs. All this time, Cooper was a strict constructionist, and therefore something of a charter member of Jacksonism.

In 1828, a crucial year for Jackson, Cooper expounded the strict construction theory in *Notions of the Americans.*[42] In

[41] *New World*, III (September 25, 1841), 205.

[42] *Notions of the Americans*, London, 1828, II, 199-204.

Homeward Bound (1838), he went out of his novel's way to say that "The general government . . . is purely a government of delegated powers."[43] One of the cleverest passages in *The Monikins* ridicules liberties taken by the parliament of Leaplow with their Great National Allegory (the Constitution).[44]

On the tariff question, Cooper spoke so decidedly for protection that Professor Lounsbury actually acquired the belief that tariff was the only subject of partisan dispute on which Cooper took a consistent stand.[45] Lounsbury supposed that Cooper's protectionist attitude antagonized the Democratic party, but there is no indication of any such antagonism in the Democratic reviews; and the fact is that under Jackson the tariff question divided the country on sectional rather than party lines. Even Old Hickory was forced by his party to support a protective tariff, and in 1833 he signed a notorious "Bloody Bill" in its defense. At a National Convention of Protectionists that was held in Harrisburg, Pennsylvania, July 30, 1827, northern Democrats leagued with National Republicans to promote protective tariff. Cooper's tariff arguments are not original enough to be quoted, but they are clearly and sometimes epigrammatically stated. Good examples may be found in *Notions of the Americans*[46] and *England*.[47] In *The American Democrat* he asserted that the doctrine of free trade was promulgated in this country by England on purpose to injure our industries;[48] a remark so extreme and yet so like a Jacksonian that it almost brings hilarity to read it, now. No remark on tariff could have

[43] *Homeward Bound*, New York, G. P. Putnam's Sons (Mohawk Edition, n. d.), pp. 100-101. See also *The American Democrat*, Cooperstown, New York, 1838, pp. 18-27, 166.

[44] *The Monikins*, New York, G. P. Putnam's Sons (Mohawk Edition, n. d.), pp. 340 ff.

[45] *Op. cit.*, p. 133.

[46] Chapter II, 434-439.

[47] I, 221.

[48] *The American Democrat*, pp. 160-161.

been better calculated to infuriate the Whig Anglophiles, then.

Old Hickory's policy of enforcing tariff collections embroiled him in the nullification turmoil. Just as Jackson managed to be a strict constructionist and yet to oppose nullification, so did Cooper. Cooper's point was that the Constitution did not, as it stood, provide for secession. If the South procured an amendment granting them such right, he would, he said, be with them.[49] But for expediency's sake, as well as for legality, he devoutly hoped secession would not be attempted. The secession of the Southern states was a cherished desire of America's enemies, he discovered when he was abroad;[50] and he felt it to be a patriotic and Jacksonian duty to spread this news at home.

The discomfiture of the Whigs was greatest, however, over Cooper's championship of Jackson's treatment of the French spoliation claims. This episode is a stirring drama, moving in one's heart an unusual mixture of emotions for Cooper's sake. Cooper seems throughout the story a generous, courageous patriot, painfully worried about our safety because of disillusioning counter revolutions he had seen take place abroad. Like American travelers who are terrified by some harsh experience of communism in Russia, totalitarianism in Germany, or militarism in Japan, he thought of democracy at home with an intensely anxious and cherishing love. Such anxiety must be sharp in any moment of surrounding revolutions, and for Cooper it was the sharper in that the American plan was so new that it was in the first stages of proving itself. When he found Europeans considering our republican government a mere experiment, he was overcome with

[49] *Correspondence of James Fenimore-Cooper*, I, 188, 207; *Gleanings in Europe*: *France*, Philadelphia, 1837, II, 165, note; C. K. Tuckerman, "James Fenimore Cooper on Secession and State Rights," *Continental Monthly*, VI (July, 1864), 79-83.

[50] *Sketches of Switzerland*, Part Second, Philadelphia, 1836, II, 178; *England*, I, 239, note.

the passion for defense, for advertisement, for exhibition of success. He felt every American toryism to be a treacherous delivering over of our republican cause to foreigners who hoped for our failure, and he felt it like a wound. Americans thought, often, that this passion of his was quixotic; he said they thought so because, with all their sycophancy, they were blind to the real foreign opinion. And so the more he met with disbelief, the more anxious he grew and the more he felt himself to be a lone voice crying ever louder and louder in a more and more deserted wilderness.

In France, Cooper moved in circles where fears of liberal monarchies were not considered chimeras. When the republicans there began to see, soon after the revolution of 1830, that they had been duped by Louis-Philippe, "*çe républicanisme commençant réunit dans son idéalisme toutes les republiques, de Washington à Babeuf, et tous les républicains, qu'ils souffrent dans leurs espérances retardées ou dans leur misère materielle, c'est-a-dire toutes les déceptions qui ont suivi la gloire de juillet. La République donne à la foule des idéalistes et des pauvres le sentiment, la conscience qu'ils forment une classe, que cette classe a des intérêts, qu'elle doit avoir un programme, qu'elle représente un droit éternel, absolu, supérieur, auprès duquel tous les autres droits sont inférieurs, passagers et périssables.*" Besides this, "*L'autre opposition, l'intellectelle, ne forme pas un parti, mais elle sépare du gouvernement toute une élite sociale.*" A large part of this "*élite sociale*" was composed of French authors and artists; the historian who used the phrase reminds us that Hugo, Dumas, and Stendhal were all received as being protagonists for republicanism in their works, and that Stendahl's *Le Rouge et le Noir* (published in 1831, when Cooper was trying to accomplish something with *The Bravo*) became the ancestor of a host of books which represented the nineteenth century novelists' ambition to perform in their works the " '*fonction' de medicin, de physiologiste social,*" a role resembling that of *vates* which the poets had been claiming "*depuis que tout devient 'serieux' dans les lettres.*"[51] As a novelist, Cooper belonged in this *élite sociale*, and must have felt its corroboration in the political efforts of his fiction. As a friend of Lafayette, he was the intimate of a man who still lived in the eyes of the active republicans as the symbol of all the liberal ideas that had supported and yet had been defeated by the revolution of July, 1830.[52] It is not difficult, when we consider Cooper's European environment, to find ourselves admiring the simple-hearted patriot who sacrificed so much of private profit in order to plead for a fair trial for republicanism in the years before the twentieth century disillusionment blurred democratic enthusiasm. The French republicans talked and agitated for a republic like the United States, as they said.

Nor is it surprising that Cooper's defense of republican institutions was bound up with his Democratic partisanship, as the earlier patriotism had been wedded to Federalism. Since the event which called him into his most spectacular demonstration against toryism was the trouble over the French spoliation claims, it is in this controversy that we find the key to much of his writing and to most of the persecution he suffered.

The full narrative of Cooper's part in the French controversy should be told in its chronological place in Cooper's career. It is appropriate here merely to show that the quarrel was a political one, and to give the setting and characters. The actors certainly were a dramatic medley; Napoleon, Andrew Jackson, Lafayette, George Washington Lafayette, Louis Philippe, and James Fenimore-Cooper. When two nations meet through such a selection of characters, almost anything may happen. Napoleon's part was characteristic. He had destroyed some American property. Andrew Jackson's part was to discover, when he came into office, that

[51] Ernest Lavisse, *Histoire de France Contemporaine*, 1921, XV, 38-39, 42, 53-54.

[52] *Ibid.*, XV, 20.

claims for indemnity were still pending. Then Old Hickory, when he could, began to do something about it. In 1829 negotiations were opened through W. C. Rives and Polignac, reactionary French minister. With the French people at this date, old claims against Napoleon were exceedingly unpopular. Americans therefore looked to the monarchists as their only hope; but when the king seemed willing to negotiate, his enemies raised a cry to stir sentiment against him in the people's party. On such a seesaw the bickering continued through the Revolution of 1830 and into the reign of Louis Philippe. Feeling ran high in both France and the United States, with the Americans trusting in the Doctrinaire party. But Louis Philippe, of course, continued to do nothing. At last some of the liberals, in particular Lafayette and his son George Washington, managed to get a treaty signed. Ratification, however, was another thing, and for this Lafayette had to labor indefatigably for months longer. On February 2, 1832, ratification was obtained, but not a cent of money.

Now the high comedy of this situation is the behavior of the Whigs at home. They were the American commercial party, and they emphatically wanted the indemnity paid. However, their distrust of liberals in France was as great as their contempt for Democrats at home, and they caviled at every move that was made. Instead of rejoicing at Lafayette's success and deserting their vain hopes of the Doctrinaire party which had given no inch that Lafayette had not wrested from it, they showed a marvelous restiveness and kept crying nervously that one must not, no, must not offend the party of Louis Philippe, whatever one did.

Cooper was in France while events were taking this course, and in France he was a very close friend of Lafayette. What is laughable in party conduct at the end of a hundred years can be extremely exasperating while it is going on. The time arrived when Lafayette found himself repudiated in France by both parties because of his activity on America's behalf, and yet painfully discountenanced in America, where the Whigs began to blame the Democratic party, Andrew Jackson, and Lafayette for all delays in French payment. Lafayette wrote sadly to Cooper about his unpleasant position.[53]

In the meantime, Cooper had already been unwillingly drawn into a political controversy in defense of Lafayette when, in 1831, *La Revue Britannique* had published a monarchist article implying that the American government was financially inefficient and suggesting that Lafayette had been a fool or a liar in presenting our republic in a favorable light. At the request of Lafayette and others, Cooper had undertaken to give his friend, as he said, "what is due to even a criminal—the benefit of the truth."[54] He had published a series of letters in the *National* attempting to prove by statistics that our government was economical. They were all transmitted to Lafayette for approval before being printed.

Thereupon wheels began to turn within wheels. The Whigs began to bark at Cooper to frighten him away from the French Doctrinaires, whom they wished to mollify. Cooper began to explain to the Whigs the rightness of General Jackson, of the Democrats, and of Lafayette, and the general unreliability of Louis Philippe and his Doctrinaires. For a while, Cooper was afraid that his old idol, Jackson, would be led by national timorousness into a weakness of action contradictory to the "formidable character for decision and an inclination to make the flag respected" with which he had entered office. He hated to give up faith in Old Hickory; he believed it might have been either Jackson or his friends who were at fault, and he wished these friends had "left the man a character for the only quality by which he was at all honored on this side of the water." He feared Jackson had only made "supererogatory professions," and yet he hoped the President might still be himself; "Will King Andrew

[53] *Correspondence of James Fenimore-Cooper*, I, 315-316.

[54] *A Letter to His Countrymen*, p. 10. See letter from Lafayette, *Correspondence of James Fenimore-Cooper*, I, 245-246.

fight, think you?"[55] In the autumn of 1833, Jackson was true to himself and to Cooper's hope. He sent a determined message to Congress on the subject of the execution of the treaty, and he hinted at war. The French made a great stir about his having impeached their national honor, and demanded an apology. The Whigs became frantic, supposing their worst fears to have come true. Until 1835, France waited for the apology from Old Hickory and gave no sign of payment. In 1834 Cooper came home, delighted at Jackson's firmness. He walked up and down Wall Street every day, talking war to all who would listen; as Paulding said, "my old friend . . . declaims against Louis Philippe, and pricks on the merchants."[56] In April of the next year he published a letter in the Democratic *Evening Post*,[57] declaring that France would never pay without a war, that President Jackson had taken a noble stand, but that the loud opposition to him in the United States had given the Duc de Broglie and the Chambers an idea that they need not frame provisions for payment. Of course, the Whigs retorted vehemently that Cooper was estranging Louis Philippe and losing everything for America. Finally Jackson inserted in his message of 1835 a phrase which the French accepted as sufficient restoration of their honor, and payments began to move. For three years Cooper cherished so great an admiration for Jackson's conduct of this affair that he introduced praise of it into his books.[58] All this time, the real struggle seemed to Cooper to be, so far as his share in it was concerned, an attempt to awaken Americans to the danger and

[55] Letter to [William Branford] Shubrick, May 1, 1831, quoted by R. E. Spiller, *Fenimore Cooper: Critic of His Times*, New York, 1931, p. 213.

[56] Letter, J. K. Paulding to Martin Van Buren, New York, December 6, 1834. Van Buren correspondence, Library of Congress.

[57] April 14, 1835.

[58] *England*, II, 233, note; *Home as Found*, New York, G. P. Putnam's Sons (Mohawk Edition, n. d.), p. 104; *Gleanings in Europe: Italy*, Philadelphia, 1838, II, 30; *The American Democrat*, Cooperstown, 1838, 161-162.

delusion in trusting to a monarchical party, as the French liberals had done in 1830—a monarchical party which would have rejoiced at the failure of the annoying American example of republicanism.

Really, in the last years of the indemnity contest, when Cooper was in America, this particular difficulty with the United States was the center of an eleven-month struggle between Louis Philippe and the Duc de Broglie as to whether or not the former could dispense with the office of *président du Conseil*; thus the King's opposition to the payments became a vital issue in connection with his monarchical encroachments. The measure was defeated as an excuse to force the proud Duc de Broglie to resign in April, 1834, and the months of delay which followed are the months during which the King tried to avoid recalling him and also to act as his own *président*. When Broglie was recalled, in February, 1835, his position demanded that he force the measure through to save his face. Meanwhile, Jackson's behavior had created antagonism; hence the task was harder than ever.[59]

This had been an affair of secret cabal, and Cooper seems not to have understood the hidden complications any better than Jackson had. He seems, therefore, to have been wrong in his judgment of Jackson's conduct but right about Louis Philippe. The Whigs violently disagreed with him on both counts, and at the end of the three years Cooper and the Whig party were permanently estranged.

One of the most obvious tests to apply to a Jacksonian Democrat would have been a question on the United States Bank. But the Jacksonian's answer would have entangled him also in another issue, loyalty to Jackson in the contest he waged for the executive's supremacy over Congress. In 1832 a newspaper[60] complained that the two parties had come to hold so many principles in common that they could no longer be distinguished by such old standard tests as protec-

[59] Ernest Lavisse, *op. cit.*, XV, 112-117. Cooper tells the story of Lafayette's activity in *Sketches of Switzerland*.

[60] *Niles' Weekly Register*, XLIII (October 13, 1832), 97-101.

tion or loose construction, but were marked instead by the degree of their devotion to General Jackson. Personal loyalty (so ran the complaint) had become such a fetish that "every man in Pennsylvania . . . (the 'great Jackson state' . . .), *before the veto*, being an acknowledged democrat, was a friend of the bank; but, *after the veto*, to support the bank was to be a federalist—*the entire character and principles ! ! ! of parties being changed as gen.* JACKSON said YEA or NAY."

Cooper was one of Jackson's inordinate admirers, and he did not conceal his sentiments from the public. Even as early as Jackson's first contests for the Presidency, he accorded the General a degree of praise which indicated his partiality.[61] A Democratic as well as a Federalist friend deprecated this warm attachment.[62] He tilted, also, for his hero against false reports of King Andrew's character which had been circulated abroad by the "electioneering trash of the opposition prints at home."[63]

Of course, then, Cooper ran true to Democrat form and served on King Andrew's side in the United States Bank war. Cooper's private opinion certainly was opposed to the Bank as a business venture:

> Your big bank makes but an indifferent figure in the report of the Government directors, and I begin to believe that hickory will prove to be stronger than gold.[64]

A Letter to His Countrymen gave considerable space to maintaining the unconstitutionality of the Senate's vote of censure against Jackson's removal of the officer in charge of the

[61] *Notions of the Americans*, II, 227-232; 242, 243. Compare with these enthusiastic descriptions of the defeated candidate the colorless announcement of Adam's victory, II, 224-225.

[62] William Dunlap, *Correspondence of James Fenimore-Cooper*, I, 240-241; Charles Wilkes, *ibid.*, I, 181.

[63] *Gleanings in Europe*: *Italy*, Philadelphia, 1838, I, 238-239.

[64] *Correspondence of James Fenimore-Cooper*, I, 331.

Bank;[65] that was enough to arouse Whig ire when the book became prey to the reviewers, for this removal was an important inroad upon the Bank. In *The Monikins,*[66] Cooper wrote on the subject in his best satiric form, ridiculing those men of commercial interests who attributed the financial depression of the thirties to Jackson's destruction of the Bank. Sir John Goldencalf receives a letter from the United States,

> where it would seem the president, by a decided exercise of his authority, had drawn upon himself the execrations of a large portion of the commercial interests of the country; since the effect of the measure, right or wrong, as a legitimate consequence or not, by hook or by crook, had been to render money scarce.

John Goldencalf's American correspondent goes through another thought process which was common among his Whig fraternity. When the struggle over the Bank forced Jackson and Congress to come almost to blows, Democrats protested against "congressional encroachments" upon the executive powers, and Whigs set up a hue and cry against "tyranny" in the White House.[67] So the American letter to Goldencalf reads:

> 'alas! there is an end of the much boasted liberty of America! The executive has swallowed up all the other branches of the government, and the next thing will be to swallow up us. Our altars, our firesides, and our persons will shortly be invaded; and I much fear that . . . we . . . shall be precluded from writing, by being chained like beasts of burden to the car of a bloody tyrant.'

The Monikins makes short shrift of this Whiggery.

It was, indeed, one of Cooper's favorite tenets that Americans ought not to deceive themselves by a superficial resem-

[65] Pp. 75, 89-90.

[66] P. 94.

[67] *E.g., Morning Courier and New York Enquirer,* April 26, 1832, May 1, 1832; *New York Daily Advertiser,* June 6, 1834.

blance between our three departments of government and England's. English government, he maintained, had lost all possibility of democracy, and not to the monarch but to the legislative body, which had absorbed all the powers of government. (See, for instance, *A Letter to His Countrymen*, *The Monikins*, and the A. B. C. Letters.) He seemed not to be able to say often enough that the American government preserved its democratic character because the legislature was subject to checks from two other departments. He stubbornly insisted that if American democracy should ever be endangered, the danger would proceed from legislative encroachment, not executive. Thus it was that in *A Letter to His Countrymen* Cooper could state that Jackson had made an unconstitutional diplomatic appointment and that Congress had made an unconstitutional censure of Jackson, and yet that Jackson's act was not dangerous, while the behavior of Congress was: "God forbid that Congress should ever have power to do that which parliament does daily; and, on the other hand, God forbid that the president should not do daily that which the king of England (of his own will) cannot do at all!"[68] This passage has been cited as a proof that Cooper was not consistently a supporter of Jackson. What could be more Jacksonian, as a matter of fact? And what, just at the moment, could have been so flaming a party topic?

Now, the most important result of Cooper's concern for the finance controversy, the spoliation claims, the discontinuance of the Bank, and the importance of the executive office as a guarantee of democracy was that it involved him in that national quarrel about "aristocracy" which I have said was really a political partisanship. It was Cooper's fate, as I have already indicated, to come to the real grip of controversy first with the Doctrinaires and, because of this

[68] *A Letter to His Countrymen*, pp. 67-87. Cf. *The American Democrat*, pp. 29, 32, 34-42.

struggle, to find himself next involved with their American admirers, the Whigs.

These French Doctrinaires, who called themselves the party of the "*juste milieu*," he once defined as "gentry that believe in the possibility of having Monarchy, Aristocracy and Democracy all at once."[69] But his serious definition of the party, written near the time when his controversy with it began, was printed in *Sketches of Switzerland*:

> The crisis which drove the cabinet of Charles X. to the extreme measures that overturned the throne, had been produced by a legislative combination . . . many, even of those who were personally attached to the Bourbons, resisting their project of re-establishing the *ancien regime*. Most of the capitalists, in particular, and more especially those who were engaged in pursuits that were likely to be deranged by political convulsions, were secretly disposed to support the dynasty, while they were the most zealously endeavoring to reduce its power. The object of these men was to maintain peace, to protect commerce and industry, more especially their own, and, at the same time to secure to property the control of affairs. In short, England and her liberty were their models, though some among them had too much good sense to wish to retrograde, as is the case with a party in America, in order to make the imitation more perfect. Those who were for swallowing the English system whole, were called the *doctrinaires*, from their faith in a theory. . . .[70]

This definition comprises three significant statements; that the Doctrinaires were largely composed of the nation's commercial interests; that the capitalists were secretly monarchists, and desired a government like the English because it gave control of affairs to property; and that there was a party in America like the Doctrinaires but even more extreme, a party willing even "to retrograde . . . in order to make the imitation [of England] more perfect." These

[69] *Correspondence of James Fenimore-Cooper*, I, 304.
[70] *Sketches of Switzerland*, Part Second, I, 119.

are the features in Doctrinairism which always seemed most prominent to Cooper, and when he saw sentiments like these in America he actually feared lest Doctrinairism establish a monarchy here as it had performed the restoration in France. Lafayette and his circle of liberals talked to him of their fear of French monarchy. What might not happen in America? He had had no dread of monarchy when he had written *Notions of the Americans,* but American talk had altered.[71] He believed that jealousy would be sufficient motive for the Doctrinaires to attempt to influence the new world.[72] If they succeeded, the Republic was lost, and if they succeeded it would be through the Whigs. Of course, he did what he could to save America, and that meant saving us from Whiggery.

He composed at least one satire on the Doctrinaire party, and printed it, in the French language, at Paris in *Le Livre des Cent et Un*[73] in 1832. It was a fantastic allegory entitled *"Point de bateaux a vapeur. Une vision."* Cooper has explained his purpose in writing it:[74] "The Doctrinaires . . . in their jealousy of us, have let loose the curs of abuse upon us for the last twelvemonth. I have personified this theory under the name of The Three Ideas, and have made them the organs of proclaiming their own nonsense as respects us, by giving their facts and arguments a little coloured, and, by George, not much coloured either." In Cooper's tale, Monarchy, Aristocracy, and Democracy enter the novelist's study and introduce themselves. Their conversation reveals Europe's bigoted ignorance of America, touches upon the finance controversy, and exemplifies what Cooper believed

[71] *England,* II, 238, note.

[72] *The Bravo,* G. P. Putnam's Sons (Mohawk Edition, n. d.), Preface, iv-v; *Sketches of Switzerland,* Part Second, II, 219.

[73] *Paris, ou Le Livre des Cent et Un,* IX, 221-250. Paris: Chez L'Advocat, Libraire de S. A. R. Le Duc D'Orleans, 1832. A copy of this book is in the Cooper collection, Yale.

[74] *Correspondence of James Fenimore-Cooper,* I, 304.

was the fallacious reasoning upon which Europeans based their advocacy of government by aristocracy, which they called the *juste milieu.* A fragment of manuscript in the Yale University Library, called "America: a vision," is evidently a preliminary draft in English of part of this article, which Cooper himself rendered into French. Two quotations will illustrate its humor: "'The antiquity of the trois pouvoirs, might be illustrated by other examples. Let us look at France. In that illustrious kingdom the equilibrium of the wheel of State has always been preserved by such a contre-poid. Under the Carlovingian race, there was the King, the main du Palais, and the rebels. This kept each other constantly on the alert, and promoted healthful circulation in the views of the public. Later, we find the . . . Cardinals, the fronde and the mistresses; Louis XIV—' 'Called himself the state.' 'Oh, Mr. Cooper, that was only in appearance. Look at it, as you will, you find the trois pouvoirs always in activity. Maintenon, père le chaise, and Louvres; glory, women and the arts; victory, defeat and repose. Turn it on every side you please, there are always two influencing powers pulling in contrary directions, and a third to preserve the equilibrium.'" "'Mon cher, Mr. Cooper reflect on the effects which democracy is producing on your polity, morals, and character. Nay, we see, by Capt. B. Hall, that even your climate is getting to be detestable.' 'I shall not deny that M. Hall would probably have found the climate better, had he found less democracy.'" In other words, Cooper was representing that if the *juste milieu* is the party of Louis Philippe or of the Whigs, republicanism and Democracy are better than that oligarchic middle ground.

These ideas of Cooper's had formed themselves by 1832 into a belief that actual monarchy was dead in Europe. The semblance of monarchy was kept presentable by a commercial oligarchy which, at the same time that they preserved it, drew off all its power to themselves. His hatred for the English aristocracy, who seemed to him as cold as marble, united with this conviction to make him fear not so much kingship as the aristocratic, secretly monarchic political parties themselves.[75] Most of his work from this date until after 1840 in one way or another exposed Whig aristocracy as he indirectly defined it through the Doctrinaire. And always the Whigs and Democrats knew perfectly well what he was doing.

Perhaps he might be satirizing stock-jobbers, or complaining of the habits of commercial men.[76] Well, it was definitely a political right of a Democrat to hate merchants. The *Evening Post*, for instance, would refer to the Whig party as "The U. S. Bank, and its aristocracy of stock-jobbers," and thus infuriate the *New York American* (Whig).[77] He might be exercising his well-known dislike for New Englanders.[78] Well, the Democrats shared the feeling. The Whig *New York American* once got out an appeal to all the "sons of New England" living in New York to arise and put down a faction who were "circulating a hand bill of HUZZA FOR GEN. JACKSON, and DOWN WITH THE YANKEES ! ![79] He might be merely championing the intelligence and orderliness of Democrats against the Whig aspersions of "the mob"; turning the tables, for instance, upon a traveler who claimed that the "talent, property, and respectability" of America were not ranged behind Jackson's administration,[80] or demonstrating in a novel that a man can know

[75] *The Bravo*, Preface, iii, p. 13.

[76] *E.g.*, *The Monikins*, pp. 360-361, 365-366; *Sketches of Switzerland*, Second Part, II, 24, 108; *England*, I, 165; *Italy*, II, 26-31, 156-157; *Homeward Bound*, pp. 289-290.

[77] For epithet and retort see *New York American*, November 24, 1836.

[78] *E.g.*, *Notions of the Americans*, I, 73; *England*, II, 133; *Homeward Bound*, *passim*.

[79] November 6, 1827.

[80] *Sketches of Switzerland*, Part Second, II, 110, note.

his own social station although he is a Democrat and the husband of a woman who tries to shame him into invading the parlors of his betters by crying, "Mr. Jarvis! . . . and you, too, one of the committee of Tammany Hall!"[81] Well, the Democrats of the better class knew what that meant, and so did the Whigs.

Cooper's position on party politics after Martin Van Buren's political demise was uncertain. This does not mean that Cooper altered, but that the parties themselves were in commotion. When such time-tried allies as Andrew Jackson and Van Buren split over the question of annexing Texas with its slavery, it is evident that no Democrat could be very certain of his party. But if a Democrat might be uncertain, the Whigs were even less certain; for the Whigs had never had existence except as a negation of Democracy. The period from 1835 to Cooper's death may be described by a series of statements from American historians.

> But to follow Jackson after he became president meant the adoption of a positive and aggressive policy and a set of principles which could not be misunderstood. With the Whigs, however, the common bond was not in their uniformity of political faith, but in their opposition to Jackson, which was carried over to Van Buren as 'following in the footsteps of his illustrious predecessor.' The name of the party was given it by James Watson Webb, in 1834, through his newspaper, the New York *Courier and Enquirer*, and it was intended to suggest opposition to the encroachments of the executive. A more accurate name would have been the Anti-Jackson party.[82]

Albert Bushnell Hart has called our attention to the fact that as we look back, slavery seems to have been the most important problem in 1837, but that to the people actually

[81] *Home as Found*, p. 376.

[82] George Pierce Garrison, *Westward Extension, The American Nation: a History*, XVII, 43-44.

living then, several things seemed more important; commercial and financial questions and mere party "manoeuvers" formed the issues.[83] Between 1840 and 1850, he reminds us, the abolitionists tried to wring concessions from both the major parties, and Whigs and Democrats alike tried to sidestep the whole matter and to keep it out of their programs.[84] Van Buren in his inaugural address of 1837 declared he would oppose the "slightest interference" with slavery in the states where it existed, and would also quell all mob violence offered against abolitionists.

Between 1840 and 1860, the differences between extremists and conservatives within each party exceeded the differences between parties. Party leaders, both Whig and Democrat, sought primarily to keep their parties clear from the rocks of Northern and Southern sectional division. They therefore attempted to divert the public from such alignment by keeping non-sectional questions agitated as being Whig and Democratic. What they insisted upon, as a life and death necessity, was strict party loyalty, so that men should not vote between 1840 and 1850 on principles, but on party lines. This party "loyalty" was openly proclaimed as a political virtue.[85]

Edward Channing says:

In the general commingling of parties and issues that centered around the election of Taylor in 1848, it would seem that even the astute politicians of that day would sometimes have been hard put to it to define the principles of the Whig or the Democratic party or to give any reason for themselves belonging to one party or another.[86]

[83] Albert Bushnell Hart, *Slavery and Abolition*, New York, 1906, *The American Nation: a History*, XVI, 296.

[84] *Ibid.*, p. 319.

[85] Theodore Clarke Smith, *Parties and Slavery, The American Nation: a History*, XVIII, 5-13.

[86] Edward Channing, *A History of the United States*, New York, 1928-1930, VI, 138.

He describes the decade which followed Taylor in these words:

The Whig party was born of opposition to Jacksonism and died in the effort to 'swallow the Fugitive Slave Act.' It had no reason for existence other than its devotion to things that were past. It attracted to itself the rich and well-born and many of those who were on the way to wealth. It had no principles, other than opposition to the Democratic control of the government. Whenever a new political principle developed, its supporters formed themselves into a new party, and if they showed strength, the Democrats or the Whigs would take them into their fold. The sixth decade of the nineteenth century proved to be a time of political flux in which the advocates of one thing or another grouped themselves around some hoped-to-be popular designation or around some name that might attract voters. The trouble was that there were too many issues: there was temperance reform, there was abolitionism, or the milder free-soilism, and there was hostility to the white new-comer. On these various topics the Whig party in the several states and the Democrats also did not feel at all sure as to what position would be the wisest to take. The result, the final result, was the death of the Whig party, the abandonment by all other anti-Democrats of temperance reforms and hostility to foreigners and the coming together on the platform of opposition to the extension of negro slavery.[87]

Cooper did not live until this coalition of Anti-Democrats on the clear issue of slavery expansion took place. He died in 1851, a time when the state of affairs was such that:

The passage of the Compromise of 1850 was the signal for the disruption of the Whig party and the revival of the Democratic party. . . . The Democrats, having assented to the Compromise, stood for its 'finality.' The Whigs were now to dabble with all kinds of reformations and movements with Know-Nothingism, with Free-Soilism, and with Temperance![88]

[87] *Ibid.*, VI, 124-125.
[88] *Ibid.*, VI, 138.

This agitation of the people over false issues disturbed not only the Democrats but many of the Whigs; so much so that in 1850 a coalition of Democrats and Fillmore Whigs promoted a great meeting in Castle Garden, calling for vigorous enforcement of the fugitive slave law, and making "a great popular protest against demagoguery" on the ground that the demagogues were inciting dangerous controversy. Weed and Greeley bitterly attacked this meeting and Fillmore's administration.[89] Thus we see that a protest against "demagoguery," which in ordinary times would be considered a protest against any party's low politics, might, in 1850, have been particularly a mark of a Democrat or a Fillmore Whig; a mark, therefore, of a person sympathetic to enforcement of the fugitive slave act, and in general unsympathetic to the elements which the leaders of the Whig press were trying to call the Whig party.

What Cooper thought of these conditions is set down in clearest form in *Men of Manhattan*, which is merely a preface to a projected but unwritten study of New York.[90] In this essay, Cooper denounced in colorful language the bitter partisanship then raging; the practice then advocated of voting by party loyalty; the obstinate opposition maintained in both of the major sects, an opposition which he declared would ruin the country if persisted in; and the whole race of demagogues. Then he discussed slavery, and while positively denying all party membership, he proceeded, as he had so often done before, to expound doctrines held rather by Democrats than by Whigs, or at least by Democrats and those Whigs like Fillmore who, agreeing with their old opponents, were attacked by the Whig political journals and the Weed-Greeley group. (Perhaps when Cooper said he was non-partisan he meant, as of old, that there was only one tenable position and Whigs should make that position

[89] De A. Stanwood Alexander, *op. cit.*, II, 151.

[90] Republished in book form as *New York*, edited by Dixon Ryan Fox, New York, 1930.

non-partisan by joining the Democrats upon it.) He wanted peace to be kept in the country, and he said the center of friction was not the right to secede, but the return of fugitive slaves. To keep the South from wishing to secede, slaves simply must be returned. The North, he said, "still owes the South a great deal more [than the compromises then in effect], though it may be questioned if the machinations of demagogues and the ravings of fanaticism will permit it to discharge the obligation." He made a strong plea for the policy (which I have given authority for calling Democratic) of working by compromise, preferably by enforcing the compromises already adopted, until natural causes could produce peaceable emancipation. Cooper had a well-defined view of secession, though secession was not then recognized as an issue by either party. It was a view held by many Democrats and Whigs, Northerners and Southerners. Whether secession was legal or not (he did think it was illegal, though he still maintained States' Rights; for while he said the States retained all rights not specifically surrendered, he believed sovereignty had been delegated) he was willing to arrange secession anyway, provided the South earnestly desired it and the arrangement would be a permanently peaceful and profitable settlement. That such an arrangement could ever be made, he doubted; sentimental and economic ties would prevent it. Therefore, our only practical procedure was to muzzle inflammatory demagogues and trust to natural emancipation.

This opinion shows no change from his position in 1828 (*Notions of the Americans*, II, 340-367) except that in that earlier year he had not seen so clearly that natural causes are exceedingly slow. The Cooper who seemed such a firebrand in considering war with England or France is placed in a newly revealing light when we consider his patient forbearance in this internal struggle.

The *Notions of the Americans* had maintained that the institution of slavery was undoubtedly bad—both unchristian and unsuited to a liberal nation. It repeated in several places that the physical and moral well-being of the slaves, "the name of liberty alone excepted," was quite equal if not above that of an equal proportion of the population of Europe. Yet "God has planted in all our spirits secret but lasting aspirations after a state of existence, higher than that which we enjoy, and no one has a right to say that such are the limits beyond which your reason, and, consequently your mental being, shall not pass."

But Cooper perceived even in 1828 that many Southern slave holders were of the same liberal opinion, and that the number was increasing. The Southerner was born into "an unfortunate predicament," professing equal rights and keeping slaves. But, wrote Cooper, "this does not involve quite so great an absurdity as one would at first imagine." The Southerner was as innocent of the creation of slavery as a man in New York, Connecticut, London, or Paris; yet he was faced with an inherited problem of government. "The black man in the southern states . . . is not considered a citizen at all. It would not be safe to consider him a citizen . . . since he is far too ignorant, and must for a generation at least, remain too ignorant to exercise, with sufficient discretion, the privileges of a citizen in a free government." In the North, minors, women, and other individuals who were considered incompetent were not allowed to vote. The Southerner found himself forced to do "exactly what his northern countryman has done, and no more."

The very thought of sudden emancipation Cooper abhorred. "I feel confident that no discreet father, or husband, or brother, could ask a Carolinian, who was living in a state of highly polished society, and who enjoyed all the advantages of great moral improvement, to admit, at once, a body of men who had been nurtured in the habits of slavery, with all their ignorance and animal qualities, and who are numerically superior, to a participation of equal political rights." Such a condition, he said, would induce the Southerner to abandon his country and his property, leaving the South to blacks, or else to live in "a degradation, and abuses that are horrible to reflect on." Some individuals had made a sacrifice and freed their slaves, but we could not expect such a sacrifice of wealth from communities, he declared, and moreover "discreet individuals" would not emancipate if such action became general, for a "disorganization of society" would be "an inevitable consequence." As far as emancipation by law is concerned, he assured his reader that no one had a right to free slaves but their masters. Cooper was no John Brown. In case of a black rebellion, he said, "It would not only be the duty of the northern men, but it would be a duty readily performed, to fly . . . to the assistance of their southern neighbors." As for the principle that a nation of liberal doctrine should not countenance slavery, Cooper said there were many unanswerable reasons why abolition could not take place "or reasons that will be deemed unanswerable, by that portion of mankind who regard life as it actually exists, in its practical aspects and influences."

What Cooper dreaded in 1828 was impatience and rabid abolitionism. Impatience, he said, is "a characteristic of zeal" but in this case it was a destructive force. It might "retard the very consummation" the abolitionist wished. "Although I am an ardent wisher for the happy moment of general emancipation, I always turn with disgust from those cold and heartless paragraphs which occasionally appear in the northern journals of this country, and which, under a superficial pretension to humanity, trifle with the safety and happiness of two of their fellow citizens in order to give an affected aid to the undoubtedly righteous cause of one black man." The worst of this was, in Cooper's mind, that such paragraphs not only were destructive but tended to harden the South.[91]

[91] In order that the press might not feel this as a rebuke to them, Cooper added the remark that "The general tone of the press, however, is sufficiently amicable." He was very kind to the American press throughout this book.

The strongest agency for promoting emancipation, Cooper thought, was the combination of growing liberal sentiment in the South and the demonstration, by years of experience and comparison, that slavery was economically less satisfactory than free labor. He placed great hope in the border states, which would be best able to make the comparison, and he actually was bold enough to say that it was fortunate Pennsylvania lay between New England and the South, for the steady and quiet Pennsylvanians would afford a better opportunity for untroubled observation than the "ever busy" Yankees would have given. When we consider that in 1828 New England was the retreat of the Anti-Jackson men and Pennsylvania was the stronghold of Jacksonians, we perceive that if Cooper was cautious not to offend the South he was equally incautious about offending the members of a hostile party.

It is like reading farther in the same book to turn again to *Men of Manhattan*. Here the insistence upon return of fugitive slaves is followed by an outburst: "Penal laws should be passed, punishing those who meddle with this grave interest out of the limits of the States in which the parties reside; and energy should be shown in rendering such an act of justice effective and sure." Meddling, he said, had not advanced emancipation "a single foot" and had thrown the south into "hostile defiance." A "numerous and respectable" body of people in the North were disgusted at such behavior and "could be induced to adopt a wiser mode of procedure, were it not that dissolute politicians, who care only for the success of parties, and who make a stalking-horse of philanthropy . . . interpose their sinister schemes to keep agitation alive for their benefit."

The agitators here described were not leaders of the Democratic party, and though Cooper wrote in *Men of Manhattan* like an honest citizen he wrote not unlike a Democrat. He described conditions as he saw them in 1850 and 1851, when the Democrats were rallying around the Compromise and the *status quo*.[92]

A consideration of Cooper's relation to politics between 1840 and 1850 must include a reference to state politics. Here confusion was worse confounded, and one needs to follow a mass of detail. Comparing Cooper's publications and his letters with the network of intrigues which the politicians were weaving in the state, we can discern in Cooper's remarks a pattern of conscious adherence to such Democratic party as there was.

He was opposed to the Anti-Rent party, we know from the Chainbearer series. But to make such opposition as this was not to leave his party, for the issue tore both machines asunder. Anti-Renters in districts where there was no Anti-Rent party candidate voted for either a Whig or a Democrat, whichever seemed, as an individual, friendlier to their cause.[93] Jabez D. Hammond, who was in the thick of the politics which he helped both to make and to record, tells us:

> Although in the end the democrats suffered quite as much from the anti-rent excitement, and perhaps more than the Whigs, yet the appearance in the political field of the anti-rent party, in addition to the Native Americans and abolitionists, was calculated to confuse and derange both parties, and especially the Whigs, who were not so well organized as the democrats.[94]

[92] Another interesting comment which Cooper made in this preface, and one not unrelated to Cooper's twenty-year-old faith in the President as the choice of the people, is his objection to the new method of nominating the Executive, so that parties, rather than the Constitution, dictated the method of choice. Between 1835 and 1850 the caucus gave place to the nominating convention and party platforms made their appearance. (Edward Channing, *op. cit.*, VI, 121ff.).

[93] J. D. Hammond, *The History of Political Parties in the State of New-York*, Cooperstown, 1846, III, 506, 578.

[94] *Ibid.*, III, 481.

As for references to Cooper's continuance as a Democrat, we have a number of statements recorded between 1840 and his death in 1851 which keep us informed that his affiliation was still firm. During the elections in 1840, he made an ambiguous confession of mixed feelings about the choice of President. "I fear Martin must win," he said, "but I hope Seward will be beaten." Seward, of course, was the Whig candidate for governor of New York. Cooper's reserve towards Van Buren might have been caused by Van Buren's Barn Burner tendency, which had already been indicated; Cooper seems not to have been of that sect. According to several anecdotes and references in his published correspondence, he was intimate with Hamilton Fish when Fish was living in Albany after defeating John A. Dix in the 1848 campaign for governor's office. Dix had been a loyal Democrat until he allied himself with the Whigs as a Barn Burner. Cooper had been interested in the question enough to write Dix on the issue which split Barn Burners and Hunkers; namely, the advisability of admitting Texas as a slave state.[95] In 1848 he hoped for Cass's election, when Cass as the Democratic nominee was running against Taylor, the Whig, and Martin Van Buren, the Barn Burner. John Van Buren, it is said, took up his Barn Burner leadership because his father had stepped in that direction in 1840. (A farm boy furiously pitching hay from an overturned load was asked the reason for his haste; "Stranger, *dad's under there*," came the answer—with this story John Van Buren explained his allegiance.)[96] If Taylor should be successful in 1848, Cooper prophesied, the nation faced bad days indeed,[97] and perhaps this Hunkerism in Cooper is sufficient to explain his "fear" of Martin in 1840; if not, it is evidence enough that Cooper was a Democrat in 1848.

[95] *Correspondence of James Fenimore-Cooper*, II, 579.

[96] D. S. Alexander, *A Political History of the State of New York*, II, 129.

[97] *Correspondence of James Fenimore-Cooper*, II, 598.

Between 1840 and 1848 he gave other evidence of the same conviction. He was delighted, for instance, with Tyler's disappointing the Whigs as he did after Harrison's death. In June he was writing that he had "hopes of the President"; again, that at Washington Whiggery was "tumbling to pieces" and "old Quincy Adams" was "a general tormentor."[98] In September, after a summer in which Tyler had tried his party's patience further, "Mr. Tyler enjoys the choicest benediction of the Whigs. It is thought he will veto the new bank law, in which case there is to be a Whig manifesto showing him up."[99] In 1844, he laughed at the Whigs for being furious over the elections and referred with satisfaction to the Democrats as "our people."[100] "Our people" continued, evidently, to think him theirs, for the Tammany Society invited him the next month to their annual ball.[101]

Therefore we are not surprised to find that in 1848 Cooper showed other Democratic tendencies than wanting Cass to win. He thought, at that time, that "peace must follow our successes" in Mexico if the Whigs would allow it, and "If the Whigs make their alliance with Mexico a little more active, the war may yet last five years. If *they* will be neuter, six months will bring it to a close."[102] In that year, too, he repeated once again his ideas about the necessity of a free use of the Presidential veto in a republic, where the threat of tyranny came from the legislature.[103] Such an opinion would have been as malodorous to Whigs at that date as it had been under Jackson. In fact, the same letter expounds Cooper's disapproval of Taylor's belief that a

[98] *Ibid.*, II, 442, 444.

[99] *Ibid.*, II, 447. For details of Tyler's offenses to the Whigs, see Alexander, *op. cit.*, II, 47, 52.

[100] *Ibid.*, II, 527.

[101] *Ibid.*, II, 529.

[102] *Correspondence of James Fenimore-Cooper*, II, 741 (entry in the Journal); II, 582.

[103] *Ibid.*, II, 594ff.

President should not veto but should let Congress rule; a stand which Cooper could only consider indicative of that oligarchic despotism which he had been tilting against for so many years.

During the last spring before Cooper's death, Shubrick wrote him that disaffection to the Union was so strong in South Carolina that in an election for members of a State Convention to meet in 1852 the result had been "mortifying to the democrats" but the latter had been "much pleased with an extract, published in their papers, from your answer to the New York invitation."[104]

But for Cooper the outlook was sad in 1851. He was sick, and he was poor, too. He had been trying to sell his paintings, but had had difficulty in raising any cash by this means. The nation also seemed in a desperate case. The plans he had made for his country were inadequate, now. He could not even guess at the future. "Separate we cannot, yield so far as to make any new bargains with guarantees for slavery we will not, and fights must come." He was sure of nothing about the outcome except that it would not be a happy one for the man with his neck under the window sash.[105] He had thought, the year before, that a peaceable separation would be preferable to war if that were possible, but it would be impossible with the West demanding control of the Mississippi.[106] "*Nous verrons,*" he had said then, but now he seemed almost to doubt that we ever should. One day in November of 1850 he lost patience and even wanted a display of force to bring respect for the Union as he had wanted it in the old days, to enforce respect for America in Europe. Now in 1851, "fights must come," but they would do no one any good.

Yet Cooper's letters were strikingly cheerful. He had written his wife in 1849, concerning their own lives, not the

[104] *Ibid.*, II, 704.
[105] *Ibid.*, II, 701.
[106] *Ibid.*, II, 675. Compare the similar attitude in *Men of Manhattan.*

nation's, "Keep up your heart, my well beloved; we have seen darker hours, and are in merciful hands. My tenderest love to all."[107] From this to the end, his letters are marked by courage, gayety, and unflagging interest in gossip, people, and the nation. There were honest men and courageous patriots who died Whigs in 1851, and other men, as honest and courageous, who died Democrats. Cooper happened to be one of the latter.

There is a remarkable series of political essays by Cooper which deserves individual mention in connection with this review of the novelist's political opinions. Their existence seems to have been totally forgotten since Cooper's day, and they have lain neglected since 1835 among the ordinary ephemera of the New York press. These papers are an interesting revelation of Cooper's power in political debate, and they commit him unequivocally to Jackson's party. One letter is that, already mentioned, which praised Jackson's conduct of the French indemnity affair, and the others are a sequence of legal arguments attacking Daniel Webster's theories of the President's constitutional powers of removal (*i.e.*, removal in connection with the Bank). When they were printed, they received appropriate partisan reception by Whig and Democratic papers, including complimentary notices by William Cullen Bryant as editor of the sheet. These notices assist us in recognizing the anonymous letters as Cooper's, and the language and style are everywhere his.[108] Their argument is thoroughly Jacksonian.

[107] *Ibid.*, II, 640.

[108] The letter on the French payment was published in the *Evening Post*, April 14, 1835. The letters on Webster's interpretation of the constitution appeared March 14, 21, 25, 28, and 31, 1835. After the first of the letters in reply to Webster was printed, the Whig New York *American* published an editorial ridiculing its logic. Bryant defended his correspondent with an editorial which informed the *American* "that our correspondent A. B. C. is quite as distinguished a man as Mr. Webster; that he has done far more to advance the interest, fame, and honour of his country; that his name is better

Yet why, the ghost of the redoubtable Judge William Cooper may have asked his son, why should a son of the Federalist Judge Cooper devote himself to Jacksonian democracy? Of course, James Cooper did try to be a Federalist; at first, he did join the party which had been his father's before him. But that party fell into decay, and he was forced to choose between Whigs and Jacksonians. He made the choice without hesitation, as did a circle of New York literary men and intellectuals. Professor Fox has used for the frontispiece in his book on New York politics portraits of John Jay and Thurlow Weed, with the legend, "Party Leaders—Old and New." The parties these men led were the Federalist-Whig succession of "aristocrats." Now, Jay and Weed were men of such different characters that this juxtaposition of their faces on a frontispiece is a fit introduction to a book on *The Decline of Aristocracy.* John Jay, the Federalist and the true aristocrat, was an old ally of William Cooper, and James Cooper's children looked upon him as a

known and more highly prized by his countrymen, and not by his countrymen only, but is as familiar as household words in every quarter of Europe, where there is scarcely a hamlet, however obscure, into which some production of his master-mind has not penetrated. The name of our correspondent, we can further assure the American, is imperishably associated with the literature of our country, and will be frequent in men's mouths, and always with honour, when that of Daniel Webster, forgotten with the factions of the hour which have given it a temporary importance, will be heard no more." See the *Evening Post,* March 17, 1835. The Whig *Courier and Enquirer* immediately recognized these remarks as a description of Cooper, and on March 18 printed an editorial which quoted the passage and said: "The idea of comparing Daniel Webster, who is unquestionably the first statesman and greatest jurist of the age, with James Fenimore Cooper the author of some very good and several very execrable novels, is so perfectly ridiculous in itself and so evidently the conception of a *madman,* that we give the paragraph a place as affording such conclusive evidence of the *lunacy* of the editor of the Post, that even his political followers can no longer question his mental alienation." Bryant did not deny this identification of A. B. C.

grandfather.[109] Thurlow Weed, leader of the Whig press, master of journalistic vilification, became Cooper's loudest enemy. The parties had undergone a realignment. The Whig party was not the Federalist. The Adamses, the Jays, and many of the old aristocrats went with it, but there were Federalists who saw more of their real ideas of American aristocracy in Jackson's principles.

At any rate, Cooper made his choice unequivocally. For him, the Democrats became "our people," whom he rejoiced to see triumphant, and Whiggery was a sore and insolent body which he was not sorry to see tumbling to pieces.[110] His Democratic friends sent him best wishes for unmerciful beatings of the Whigs,[111] and his still loyal Whig friends wrote grumblingly about "you democrats who are a pretty set of fellows."[112] Being interested in politics was not always a matter of facing bitter choices or low enemies, and working furiously at patriotism. There was a great deal of easy zest in it for Cooper. Before he ever wrote a novel, he composed campaign songs, long remembered, about such notables as:

> Sheriff J—m, sheriff J—m,
> You're tall and you're slim.[113]

His correspondence shows that he loved Bryant and Dunlap, Morse and Greenough the better for their being Democrats

[109] Susan Fenimore Cooper, "Small Family Memories," I, 29-40, *passim.*

[110] *Correspondence of James Fenimore-Cooper*, II, 527.

[111] *Ibid.*, I, 345-346.

[112] Letter, J. R. Ingersoll to Cooper, Washington, July 22, 1846; H. C. Carey to Cooper, Philadelphia, April 29, 1836; James De Peyster Ogden to Cooper, New York, August 15, 1845. Unpublished. Cooper collection, Yale.

[113] See *American Quarterly Review*, XVIII (June, 1835), 411, note. In 1841 Cooper still enjoyed the gift; he was requested to send a song that he had been singing to the Democratic meeting in Castle Garden. See letter, J. Oakley to Cooper, n. d. [1841?]. Unpublished. Cooper collection, Yale.

as well as artists and authors. He let himself grow old in what he thought was a good tradition. The year before Cooper died, a gentleman was introduced to him as an editor of the Albany *Argus*, and the gentleman's report of the meeting is that Cooper "very pleasantly remarked: 'Then of course you are a Democrat, Mr. Shaw. I also am one, and I suppose for the reason that it takes a first-class aristocrat to make a first-class Democrat.' "[114] Thus he believed in such a thing as personal aristocracy without political aristocracy, and in the possibility of expressing the belief through the Democratic party. He was loyal to the idea all his life. Andrew Jackson indulged himself in aristocratic tastes while he founded his own kind of Dèmocracy. Cooper might have enjoyed a visit at *The Hermitage*.[115]

[114] Isaac N. Arnold, "James Fenimore-Cooper," *A Centennial Offering, Being a Brief History of Cooperstown*, edited by S. M. Shaw, Cooperstown, New York, 1886, p. 206.

[115] Better than the reading of the chapter just concluded, for gaining a knowledge of the political bearing of many of Cooper's frequently reiterated ideas, would be the consecutive reading of the general articles in a strongly Jacksonian organ such as the *United States Magazine and Democratic Review*. Here one finds agreement with Cooper on specific points, as, for instance, an editorial note saying that according to the policy of the paper the editor must dissent from some praise of England and of Louis Philippe which had occurred in an otherwise acceptable description of France (the praise had included a statement that the King had been helpful in the indemnity affair); but also ideas similar to Cooper's about American literature, "stock-jobbing aristocracy," England, France, the old Federalists, and many other topics, all presented in connections patently partisan. (The editorial note here mentioned may be found in VII (May, 1840), 443-444.)

CHAPTER III

How Cooper Was Received before 1830

BOSTON once pronounced Cooper to be vulgar because he wrote, "perspiring effects of toil," and to be shocking because he wrote, "buries his weapon in the heart of one of the enemy."[116] But a twentieth-century reader need not pride himself on his own superior ruggedness and say that such criticism explains, somewhat, why Cooper's characters had to be so stiff when they got into a parlor. Discrepancies between critical opinions on Cooper were hemispheric in breadth even in those times, and while Boston was calling him vulgar there were cities that were calling him parlor-conscious. Of the same novel, one critic might complain that it was not realistic enough, and another that it was not Gothic enough.

Cooper appears to have been highly amused at these differences. At any rate, he laughed at them, said they left him standing like an ass between two bundles of hay, and declared that the best thing for an author to do was to try to please himself. He said, on the same occasion, that he was more touched by the approval of the American people than by that of the critics, and we know from a letter to a friend that in saying this he actually meant American approval, not financial profits.[117]

When Cooper complained about the American reception of his work it was later than this, at the time of his valedictory in *A Letter to His Countrymen*, and the complaint was not that people had failed to appreciate his art; it was that they had not properly supported his Americanism, or as he said always, his American principles. Americans, he repeatedly lamented, were ready enough to praise him or any man for

[116] *North American Review*, XVIII (April, 1824), 314-329.

[117] *The Pioneers*, New York, 1823, Preface, xi; Letter to W. B. Shubrick quoted by W. B. S. Clymer, *James Fenimore Cooper*, Boston, 1900, pp. 136-38.

writing of American things, such as scenery, but they were blind or even cowardly in their reception of books which defended American principles. The demonstration of these principles, he believed, was an American author's major duty, whereas the treatment of local color was only a minor achievement.

There is a morbid feeling in the American public . . . which will even uphold an inferior writer, so long as he aids in illustrating the land and water, which is their birthright. This weakness has been publicly charged upon them, here [in England] as resembling the love of property. The latter accusation is probably urged a little too much in an inimical spirit, but the press has fairly laid itself open to the imputation, for while it has betrayed a total and a most culpable indifference to the maintenance of American *principles*, and even of American character, it has manifested a rabid jealousy of the credit of American *things*![118]

Concerning the importance of American principles, Cooper said that they were both the source of the only possible nationalism in our literature and also the force by which our literature will exert power over Europe:

It is quite obvious that, so far as taste and forms alone are concerned, the literature of England and that of America must be fashioned after the same models. The authors, previously to the revolution, are common property. . . . The only peculiarity that can, or ought to be expected in their [American] literature, is that which is connected with their distinctive political opinions. They have not been remiss in this duty. . . .[119]

and:

The literature of the United States is a subject of the highest interest to the civilized world; for when it does begin to be

[118] *England*, I, 208-209. See also I, 205; II, 154, 159, 193, 241, 242. The frequency of these allusions to the subject reveals Cooper's earnestness.

[119] *Notions of the Americans*, II, 131-132.

felt, it will be with a force, a directness, and a common sense in its application, that has never yet been known. If there were no other points of difference between this country and other nations, those of its political and religious freedom, alone, would give a colour of the highest importance to the writings of a people so thoroughly imbued with their distinctive principles, and so keenly alive to their advantages.[120]

He went on after the passage just quoted, to say that for half a century America had been operating silently upon Europe by force of example, but that the time had now come for people familiar with America's "doctrines and its experience" to press these upon the world's attention with articulate expression.

Cooper not only defined thus clearly the importance of American principles, but he explained the method by which such subjects can be presented in a novel. He said that any "chronicle of manners has . . . value," but that when the customs described "are connected with principles, in their origin, development, or end," then such a book is doubly important.[121] Customs, then, which grow out of, develop from or end in our American principles are concrete studies suited to fiction, and they take on universality or importance from their connection with the world issue of democracy.

There were, of course, a host of American reviewers who were pleading for an American literature between 1820 and 1840. For instance, the truculent American from Down East, John Neal, went to England and there wrote sensationally for Englishmen such wonderful ejaculations as that Irving, Brown, and Cooper had nothing national in them because "we require of the American people, great power; stout, original power. . . . Come forth naked . . . though your muscles *be* rather too large . . . do not come forth in a court equi-

[120] *Ibid.*, II, 160-161.
[121] *Satanstoe*, New York, 1855, Preface of 1845, vii.

page, with fine lace over your broad knuckles, and your strong rough hair powdered." He thought the writer who would be truly American must "go among the polite in his true shape—a rude, coarse man."[122] It certainly would have been difficult for Irving, Brown, and Cooper to go among the public as rude, coarse men, and yet stay in their true shapes. But there was an armed camp of reviewers who, though they were not so extreme as Neal, made it their war-cry that we must develop an American literature by differing from Europe according to our own genius. They favored an American academy, not to keep our speech nearer to the parent English, but to encourage Americanisms! They recommended more enthusiastic support of American authors as of America, claiming that lack of support would surely discourage American creation.[123] They had nothing of Cooper's definiteness in describing American literature as one based on American principles.

The critics who encamped over against these maintained that it was better for American literature to be literature than to be American. Fearful of provincialism, they insisted that nationality in literature is undesirable and even incompatible with greatness. They complained, of course, that American literature was being ruined by indiscriminate praise, and so they gave as little praise, themselves, as they could.[124]

Cooper was frequently introduced in these arguments, and by both sides. He was often named as the recipient of mis-

[122] *Blackwood's Magazine*, XVIII (September, 1825), 317.

[123] *E.g., Literary and Scientific Repository and Critical Review*, II (January, 1821), 69ff.; *New York Mirror*, X (July 21, 1832), 21; XI (August 3, 1833), 40.

[124] *E.g., American Monthly Magazine* (Willis's), I (August, 1829), 379ff.; *Southern Literary Messenger*, II (June, 1836), 312-315; II (July, 1836), 392-404; *Morning Courier and New York Enquirer*, July 10, 1833 (a debate with the *Knickerbocker Magazine*); *Atlantic Magazine*, I (May, 1824), 18-23; I (June, 1824), 130-139.

placed enthusiasm among critics, and often as an object of the grossest neglect.[125]

Now, when we examine what principles they were that Cooper called American, we discover that if he belonged to any party that supported him it would have had to be a political rather than a literary division.[126] It turns out that by 1830 and 1832, when Cooper was making his allegations of non-support, he had come to identify American principles with Democratic.

Cooper was incensed at American acceptance of the dangerous Toryism lurking in Sir Walter Scott's novels, which rendered helpless an American author who might attempt to combat his enormously successful aristocracy with Ameri-

[125] Edward S. Gould, widely quoted by journals, *e.g., New York Mirror*, XIII (April 16, 1836), 330; and *New Yorker*, I (April 23, 1836), 65-66; *Southern Literary Journal*, II (July, 1836), 394.

[126] Frank Luther Mott, writing an impartial *History of American Magazines* (New York, 1930), even goes so far as to see characteristics of the political parties in these literary parties themselves. He quotes (p. 391) from the *United States Magazine and Democratic Review*: "Our literature!—oh, when will it breathe the spirit of our republican institutions? . . . Why cannot our literati comprehend the matchless sublimity of our position amongst the nations of the world—our high destiny—and cease bending the knee to foreign idolatry, false tastes, false doctrines, false principles?" But Mr. Mott comments: "One smells something of Jacksonian politics in this . . ." By way of contrast, he cites the *North American's* presentation of the other view (in Lowell's words): " 'we must have a literature—as if we did not have Shakespeare and Milton!' " He does not say of the latter remark, as he does of the former, that it is consistent with the magazine's politics, though he implies it by comparison. He is conscious of the *North American Review's* politics, asserting in his book that "The *Democratic* and the *North American* may be taken as representative of the two sides of a very general debate [on the United States Bank]. The bank controversy is referred to in the *Democratic* as late as 1839 as 'the great question which has now, like the rod of Aaron, swallowed up every minor one.' " (p. 454). Probably it would be truthful to say that it was typical but not universal for a Democratic review to take the former position on literature, and a Whig periodical to take the latter.

canism, or "to compete with even a diminished Scott, on American principles." Such an author met the double handicap of finding his readers "already possessed by the hostile nations," so that an American novelist was put on the offensive even at home; and of finding his booksellers obliged to charge higher prices for American books than for foreign novels, because, in the absence of copyright exclusions, English publishers conducted a sort of literary "dumping" in the sense in which economists use the term. In the face of such a situation, the republican Ship of State being boarded by Tory literary pirates, Cooper stated vigorously that it is "one of the first duties of a political scheme to protect itself," and he proceeded to the corollary that it is the first duty of an author who believes in a country's political scheme to offer it his protection.[127]

It was this opposition in principle which constituted Cooper's difference from Scott, and caused his pride in the difference. This too little understood fact is, I believe, the secret of Cooper's annoyance at the phrase, "The American Scott." Critics have thought his annoyance to be a sign of conceit, jealousy, or ingratitude. As a matter of fact, Cooper was ready enough to refer to Scott as his "master," and to assist Scott's sales in America by an attempt to get his novels published cheaply here; these acts have been narrated many times. But he warned us in his famous review of Lockhart's *Life of Scott* that Sir Walter's Toryism was dangerous. Once he made a bitter statement to his closest friend that he had done his best to write from distinctive American principles as a direct counterblast to Scott's Toryism, and that the effort had gone unappreciated by his countrymen, even unnoticed; people were saying *Heidenmauer* was like Scott's books, but had not seen that the novel "was intended to be like, in order to show how differently a democrat and

[127] *England*, I, 207.

an aristocrat saw the same thing." (The "same thing" in this case was the break-up of the Middle Ages.) But Cooper, while indignant, was used to the treatment: "They may say it is like his if they please; they have said so of every book I have written, even *The Pilot*!"[128] *The Pilot* had been written deliberately as an answer to *The Pirate*, and yet it had saddled its author with the epithet, "American Scott." Under the circumstances, this nickname could not have been anything but an exasperating evidence to Cooper that Americans were not seeing his principles.

Cooper thought he saw the same American willingness to support Toryism in his country's loyalty to Washington Irving. American papers proudly reported Irving's social success in English Tory circles,[129] a success which Cooper sacrificed to his antipathy to that party. We need not fear to use the phrase "Tory party" in this connection, nor ask whether it was England or a political party in England that was unfriendly to him. Cooper once asked that question himself, and he got his answer. Saying that in London no Tory except Sir Walter Scott ever paid any attention to him, he asked, "Is this accident, or is it really the result of feeling?" When Lockhart replied, it was not to say that Cooper imagined things in suspecting party feeling. Quite the contrary. The Tory circles, Lockhart snorted,

> never so much as heard of this western luminary. For our humble selves, we were not aware that he had honoured us with a visit till long after his departure, when we heard a Whig—who had happened to meet him—amuse a dinner-table with instances of his vulgarity and impertinence. But if the Tories had heard of him, he would not have been a step nearer their dinner or drawing-rooms. *They* do not condescend to hunt for popularity with a strange pack; and they have their reward: while the unhappy Whigs, who pursue so low an object, have also their reward in finding themselves gibbeted,

[128] *Correspondence of James Fenimore-Cooper*, I, 283.
[129] *E.g.*, *Knickerbocker Magazine*, IV (July, 1834), 15.

either by absurd flattery or unmannerly censure, in the patibulary pages of such executioners as Puckler, Raumer, and Cooper.[130]

Irving knew how to make himself agreeable. When he was assisting Bryant to publish his poems in England, he changed the verses a little to suit the English ear by deleting from the "Song of Marion's Men" all mention of trembling British foemen.[131] This act was so unpopular in America that Irving was forced to write a long explanation to the press. His excuses, the pleas of courtesy to "our old home" and of financial expediency for Bryant, appeased the nation. One cannot imagine Cooper in such an act, sound as Irving's judgment may have been.

At any rate, we know that in 1832 Cooper expressed indignation because Irving had used his pen to write for a Tory journal, and because this behavior, which Cooper considered un-American, had not prevented a burst of enthusiasm over Irving in the American Whig press. He himself was actually suffering attack in the same papers for having published, in foreign liberal magazines, articles in defense of America. Morse and Dunlap agreed that a frightful outburst on the subject from Cooper was an expression of his injured sense of an American writer's duty: "C——— feels sore on account of attacks on him. He reprobates . . . Irving's writings for the English Aristocratical Quarterly when he was there as the representative of the government of America in character of Chargé des Affaires.[132] But, really, those defenses of America that Cooper had written were defenses of Jackson's policies. The attacks here referred to were consequently all Whig attacks, and indeed the Whig press con-

[130] Review of *England*, *Quarterly Review*, LIX (October, 1837), 327-361.

[131] Pierre M. Irving, *Life and Letters of Washington Irving*, New York, 1883, II, 202ff.

[132] *Diary of William Dunlap*, New York, 1930. December 6, 1832, III, 635.

stantly delighted, after this period, in drawing unfavorable comparisons between Irving and Cooper in this particular matter of their writing while abroad.[133] I do not wish, however, to stop to prove this here, or to launch now into Cooper's political troubles of 1832. I wish to illustrate the fact that Cooper saw Scott and Irving as men who did not use their talents in promoting what he thought were American principles, and to point out that his reason lay in the facts that Scott was a Tory and that Irving by being obliging to Tories was making himself pleasing to the American Whigs.

[133] Irving always avoided risking anything for party's sake at home, or else he was simply not a consistent party man. He was nominally a Jacksonian at first, but supported the Bank, and he was such a poor Democrat by 1831 that in that year a magazine reported that he had inquired in London about American "Federal" newspapers, was "lost" as to party differences of the day, and had expressed regret that such a man as Bryant should be connected with a journal and should be "poisoned with politics." (*New York Mirror*, VII, March 12, 1831.) Bryant's work with the *Evening Post* consisted in running the best Jacksonian newspaper in the United States and the only strong Democratic paper in New York. In contrast to Irving, Cooper thought Bryant's labors were noble; and Bryant's paper was the only one in the city which was strong enough in Democracy consistently to oppose the Whig avalanche when it roared down upon Cooper. In the next years, Irving carefully avoided connections with Tammany and yet kept up enough profession of Democracy to cause Van Buren to complain of his irregularity as a party member. (Pierre M. Irving, *op. cit.*, II, 213-217.) In 1842, he applied to Daniel Webster for a good appointment, of course from the other party, and there appears to have been some practice of petty deceit involved. Cooper remarked to his wife, apparently in connection with a political by-play, that "There has been more humbug practiced concerning this man than concerning any other now living." (*Ibid.*, II, 240-241; Cooper to Mrs. Cooper, New York, March 22, 1842, *Correspondence of James Fenimore Cooper*, II, 469.) To Rufus Griswold, Cooper once wrote that he thought Irving was guilty of meannesses, and that "His course in politics is of a piece with all the rest." (*Passages from the Correspondence and Other Papers of Rufus Griswold*, edited by W. M. Griswold, Cambridge, Massachusetts, 1898, pp. 114-115.) For an interpretation of Irving's attitude see S. T. Williams, *The Life of Washington Irving*, New York, 1935, II, 56-58.

As for so-called American Whigs, Cooper could see nothing American about them. None of their principles, as he saw it, could be called American. As a party, they had no excuse for being.[134] Like Washington Irving, he thought, they merely truckled to foreign opinion, foreign culture, and—foreign monarchy. In such frightening years as the era of revolutions around 1830, he thought they represented a threat to restore monarchy itself. This was not a party of Americanism; it was something extra- and even anti-American. Near the close of *A Letter to His Countrymen*, Cooper said epigrammatically that in America the conservative party were the liberals, and he prayed it might always be so. He did not mean by this that Whigs were liberal. He meant that in our republic it was the Democrats who were conserving the *status quo*, and the monarchists who were the revolutionists. A passage in *The Monikins* (Chapter XVII) ridicules America, through the satirical disguise of Leaplow, for adopting two parties simply because England had two; though there is no place for an aristocratic party in a government which is already established as a republic, yet, because England had a Tory party, America had imagined that she must invent the anomalous Whig opposition. He punished with his scorn the crafty or ignorant party-bolters who are found now in one party and now in another; and yet he took pains to show that such shiftiness of allegiance was a different thing entirely from recognition of the great party changes. There is always one party in America, he said, which might be called the horizontal, because it lies parallel to the principles on which our government is founded. The other party, which might be called the perpendicular, opposes it. This great crux of parties, however, moves in a rotary fashion so that now one line and now another may be the true horizontal.

[134] A common idea of his party. *E.g., United States Magazine and Democratic Review,* I (October, 1837), 10-11; VIII (November, 1840), 390-398. A democracy should be Democratic.

That is, party names change deceptively, but always one party, whatever it be called, is the soundly horizontal. People who are absorbed in toeing their party line according to its name rather than principles do not perceive when a change of position has been completed, but simply hold to the same line, wherever it lies. I think Cooper was referring here to the many resemblances between the original Federalists and the Jacksonian Democrats, and summoning those whose beliefs he thought were truly parallel to Americanism to join the truly horizontal party. So Cooper identified Americanism with Jacksonian Democracy as positively as his father's generation before him had identified it with Federalism.

If zeal for such "American principles" as this constituted the Americanism which Cooper was claiming for himself in *A Letter to His Countrymen*, we need not wonder that his countrymen did not unanimously support him in it. Especially would he fail of support in a nation in which after 1830 the press was notoriously under the control of the Whig party. The most outspoken Democratic magazine lamented in 1837, one of Cooper's hardest years, that "the anti-democratic cause possesses at least two-thirds of the press of the country."[135] In Cooper's own state, this domination was more complete than in the nation.

It is well known that political affiliations biased the reviewers of novels. "The political journals—indeed, most of the secular quarterlies—," says Mr. F. L. Mott, the historian of American magazines, "allow politics to affect their literary judgments. . . . German literature suffers at the hands of the *Select Journal* because it is connected with German 'free-thinking'; the French romantics cannot be considered by the *American Quarterly* or the *North American* apart from the Revolution of 1830."[136] Perhaps the French Romantics do

[135] *United States Magazine and Democratic Review*, I (October, 1837), 13.

[136] Frank Luther Mott, *op. cit.*, p. 407. Mr. Mott is here speaking of the 1830's and 1840's.

not deserve to be treated as non-partisan, if they did indeed comprise a part of that "*élite sociale*" which withdrew itself in disappointment from the party which that revolution had established; Cooper drew hostilities from these same *American Quarterly* and *North American Review's* when he began to attack the doctrinaire party, and is this surprising?

To be sure, the reviewers were always less enthusiastic about Cooper's work than were the public. At first, they seemed timid about praising an American. After *The Pioneers,* they were disgruntled because Cooper had made fun of them in his preface. And after *Notions of the Americans* there was a gathering of the cloud of political suspicion which broke over *The Bravo.* The critics themselves seemed to think they had been extraordinarily generous during these first years, and they were always emitting mumbles or grumbles to this effect, saying that Cooper's prefaces showed he did not appreciate their charity.[137] Other people did not think the reviews had done so well as they claimed for themselves. R. W. Griswold remembered for years that the *North American Review's* account of *The Spy* had been "very ill-natured" and that the magazine was "ever unwilling to do justice to Mr. Cooper." Even the editor of that very journal, Charles Henry Dana, thought Willard Phillips had written such a poor review of *The Pilot* that he regretted it for Phillips's own sake. It was, in fact, a review that was fearful of praising, and Dana's explanation was that Phillips "meant to steer a middle course between Cooper's petty enemies and those who have the good sense and the fairness to relish him and speak well of him."[138] The nation, in a way, repudiated the reviews; the reading public discovered *The Spy,* for instance, before the critics did; *The Last of the*

[137] *E.g., United States Literary Gazette,* IV (May, 1826), 87-94; *New York Review and Atheneum,* II (March, 1826), 285-292; *Morning Courier and New York Enquirer,* November 27, 1843.

[138] R. W. Griswold, *Prose Writers of America,* p. 264; Parke Godwin, *Biography of William Cullen Bryant,* New York, 1883, I, 194.

Mohicans had the most unfavorable notices and the largest sales.[139] And yet the tone of the reviews was far less hostile

[139] A record of the demonstrations of popularity among readers other than critics may be useful. Sales of *The Last of the Mohicans* have been said by Lounsbury (*op. cit.*, p. 52), Mrs. Cooper (*Correspondence of James Fenimore-Cooper*, I, 128), and Cooper (*ibid.*, I, 96) to have been the highest (but see the report of the publisher, *ibid.*, I, 129-131). *The Spy* went into a second edition within a month of publication (*Literary and Scientific Repository*, IV (January, 1822), 254), had other editions in 1824 and 1831, was pirated in England before Wiley and Irving could bring it out there (*Correspondence of James Fenimore-Cooper*, I, 89), was translated into French and "all the cultivated tongues of Europe" before long (T. R. Lounsbury, *op. cit.*, p. 36), and eventually was done into Persian, a volume of which exotic translation was the only piece of his own work that Cooper kept in his library (Susan F. Cooper, "A Glance Backward," *Atlantic Monthly*, LIX (February, 1887), 206). *The Pioneers* had an enormous first sale, assisted by its being announced at the height of *The Spy's* success, when that novel was in the third edition. On February 1, 1823, seven separate bookselling firms were advertising *The Pioneers*, and the papers announced that thirty-five hundred copies were sold before noon (*New York Spectator*, February 4, 1823). *The Pilot* had what was considered a wildfire sale, three thousand copies in a few days (*Niles' Weekly Register*, XXV (February 7, 1824), 357), with a third edition heralded in a month (February 11, 1824). John Miller was "truly happy" to reprint it in England (*Correspondence of James Fenimore-Cooper*, I, 95) but there was an English piracy in 1826 (*ibid.*, I, 96). A Philadelphia edition came out in 1833, and it was with the *Standard Novels* in 1835. *The Prairie* was in press for five editions in four countries at the same time (*New York American*, April 24, 1827), but the sales were smaller than the publishers had expected (Carey, Lea and Carey to Cooper, Philadelphia, July 14 and November, 1827. Unpublished. Cooper collection, Yale). John Neal declared that the price paid to Charles Wiley by Carey and Lea for *Lionel Lincoln* was a forecast of a literary revolution in the New World; he thought the payment was five thousand dollars and a bonus of two or three hundred dollars for only two years' publication of the single book (*Blackwood's Magazine*, XVIII (September, 1825), 317). Dramatizations of Cooper's novels were popular. The play of *The Spy* is famous for Enoch Crosby's insisting that he was the original Birch, and attending the 1826 production in a box (George C. D. Odell, *Annals of the New York Stage*, New

York, 1928, II, 446). But the story was dramatized long before that, with one version immediately in Philadelphia, and in 1822 a second version. This play of 1822 filled The Circus even during the epidemic of yellow fever. It was one of Maywood's most popular plays, and was chosen for a benefit night as late as 1827 (*ibid.*, II, 22-23; III, 47; theatre notices of the *New York American,* 1822 to 1827). Fitz-Greene Halleck assisted the play's success with his song, "The Harp of Love," sung by Frances Wharton. *The Pioneers* furnished a drama with that title which ran only three nights, in 1823, but another version, called *The Wigwam* was more successful (George C. D. Odell, *op. cit.*, II, 64; III, 465, 492, 494). The first had been enthusiastically expected (*Albion,* April 19, 1823), and in disappointing the nation's high hopes it was like the novel. In 1824 a dramatic form of *The Pilot* appeared, and in 1827 another version acted by Maywood met with great success and remained popular for twenty years after the novel's appearance (G. C. D. Odell, *op. cit.*, II, 141-524 *passim*; IV, 25-630 *passim*). *The Prairie* received spectacular dramatization (*New York Mirror,* V (May 10, 1828), 351; V (May 31, 1828), 375; G. C. D. Odell *op. cit.*, III, 319, 352, 422). Two of America's most noted artists painted scenes from Cooper, William Dunlap doing a scene from the drama of *The Spy* (*ibid.*, II, 23), and Thomas Cole, a large scene from *The Last of the Mohicans* which he exhibited at the National Academy of Design (*New York American,* May 15, 1827). Scenes from the novels were popular as frontispieces in magazines. Especially was this true of *The Spy* (*e.g., Port Folio,* XIV (August, 1822), 136; XVII (March, 1824), 253; *Casket,* XII (September, 1837), 385; XII (November, 1837), 481). There are many other indications that Cooper's novels were a part of the national life. People so completely forgot that *The Spy* was a work of fiction that not only did Enoch Crosby make himself famous as late as 1830 (*New York American,* November 27, 1830), but Connecticut people showed Susan Cooper a house at Fishkill from which Wharton and Birch escaped, with the room in which Frances was married and the clock that she watched for the stroke of nine. ("A Glance Backward," *Atlantic Monthly,* LIX (February, 1887), p. 205.) Though *The Last of the Mohicans* had been reviewed so unfavorably, a list in a newspaper of the fads and fashions of 1826 named this novel among the other popular crazes, saying that "without the slightest violation of *costume* or probability," Cooper had made Uncas "the fashionable Hero de Roman," and adding that it was "very interesting to compare this genuine young savage with the sentimental hero of M. Chateaubriand's Atala." (*New York American,* March 17, 1827; but this was quoted from the London *New Monthly Magazine,* and before Cooper's Jacksonian Americanism had shown itself definitely in his writings than it was in the 1830's.

Cooper had reason, on this very account, for thinking that his principles were unsupported in these first years. Reviewers really did not notice them until he published *Notions of the Americans* in 1828, and if I am going to show in my next chapters that after 1830 his principles became so definitely Jacksonian that they set the Whig tornado in action against the novelist, perhaps I ought to demonstrate that, correspondingly, before Cooper became so positive about his principles there was no trace of Whig opposition.

The criticism of the novels which appeared before 1828 (the year of *Notions of the Americans*) was blurred by confusions concerning realism and Gothic romance with which critics just then were befogging themselves. The dominant opinion in the country even through the next decade seems to have been that American novels must stand or fall on their romantic elements, and the question was whether the American scene could be made to furnish anything romantic.[140] If America could furnish romantic material, good; if she could not furnish it, let novelists turn to Europe, where it hung free for the plucking on every bush. Cooper was not uninterested in this same problem. It was a theory, along with the current objections to "lowness," which he questioned in his preface to *The Pioneers*; if only his critics had read

therefore may be invalid). There are casual references to Cooper's novels here and there which indicate national familiarity (*American Monthly Magazine*, I (November, 1829), 538; *New York Mirror*, X (July 28, 1832), 28) and the poets dealt in him ("Otsego Lake," anonymous, *New York Commercial Advertiser*, October 4, 1822; J. C. Brainard, "Leather Stocking" and "Mr. Merry's Lament for 'Long Tom,'" *Poems*, Hartford, 1847, pp. 94-96, 112-113). Edgar Allan Poe liked one of these poems (E. A. Poe, "J. G. C. Brainard," *Minor Contemporaries*).

[140] *E.g., American Monthly Magazine* (New York and Boston), VI (November, 1835), 23.

the preface thoughtfully, I think they could not have helped seeing that it was written to express a good deal of diffidence about his new project and a good deal of interest in the experiment. I wish this humorous preface were occasionally reprinted for present-day readers as an essay on these questions, so that it could be judged on its own merits instead of by the pique of contemporary journalists who did not like it and by fragmentary quotations from modern writers who have more appreciation of it. Well, some of his contemporaries were interested in Cooper's statements on romance instead of devoting themselves to pique, and it is significant of the opinion in those times that one of them could quote[141] his remarks on the dearth of romantic material in America, not to support the conclusion that a novelist might be permitted, as Cooper had said, to take "the earth for the scene of his story," but to claim that he must place his stories abroad. We can not trace in the criticisms any constant progression towards realism. What we find, before 1828, is a series of contradictory demands.

For instance, *The Spy* was written when the author was himself most nearly in accord with the romantic point of view, and he struck just the right note for the popular ear. Yet *The Spy* made its reputation almost unassisted by the critics. Cooper always remembered with gratitude his one cordial reviewer, Mrs. Sarah Hale, of the *Port Folio*, who rebuked American coldness. The bold Mrs. Hale, though a female, refuted indignantly charges of unreality and vulgarity which had been brought against the new-born work.[142] Forced to observe the enormous sales, which could not be hid, and the praise in foreign magazines, which they could not deny, the American critics at length gave up their luke-

[141] *American Monthly Magazine* (Willis's), I (September, 1829), 385.

[142] William Cullen Bryant, "Discourse on the Life, Character, and Genius of James Fenimore Cooper," *Memorial of James Fenimore Cooper*, p. 45. *Port Folio*, XIII (February, 1822), 90-101.

warm, cautious notices[143] to admit (occasionally even to boast) that *The Spy's* success was meteoric.[144] Some of them accepted vigor, patriotism, and well drawn characters of low life as compensations for defects of style, plot, and characterization of people in high life; but there was no complete acceptance. It was judged entirely by the canons of romance; the grudging Bostonian in the *North American Review* said the book had settled the argument as to whether the American Revolution could provide romantic material, but declared that though many of the scenes and most of the characters had been drawn to life, justice was not done to either. "We hope to hear from him again—not too soon. . . ."

This demand for romance injured the reputation of *The Pioneers*, and in the most curious way.

Critic after critic wrote of *The Pioneers* with "the warmth of honest pleasure," as one of them said. They delighted in the vivid recollections that it brought. No one even hinted that the book was untrue in its local color. The *New York Spectator's* reviewer confessed to being an Otsego man[145] and he found *The Pioneers* to be marvelously faithful, both in characters and scenes.[146] The *New York American* praised its descriptions of nature in all seasons and its true characters, and declared that the novel was being received with especial cordiality in the West, where its truth could best be appreciated.[147] A writer for the *New York Mirror* who had spent several years in Cooperstown said it was hard for him not to

[143] *E.g., New York American*, January 3, 1822; *New England Galaxy*, January 11 and 25, 1822; *New York Spectator*, January 1, 1822; *New York Commercial Advertiser*, December 28, 1821; *New York Mirror*, XI (March 29, 1834), 311.

[144] *E.g., New York Spectator*, January 29, 1822; *New England Palladium and Commercial Advertiser*, January 29, 1822; *Connecticut Mirror*, February 4, 1822, quoting the New York *Commercial Advertiser*; Niles' Weekly Register, XXII (May 25, 1822), 193.

[145] *New York Spectator*, January 17, 1823.

[146] *Ibid.*, February 4, 1823.

[147] January 13, 1824.

believe that Cooper was reproducing some of his own acquaintances in the town. He confessed to unremitting interest in the novel, and longed to quote from it indefinitely.[148] Joseph Denny, as Oliver Oldschool in the *Port Folio*, declared himself a competent judge of Cooper's accuracy: "We have been on the very spot . . . we have bathed in the same water where Mohegan paddled . . . we have witnessed the wilderness in flames, and contended successfully on the lake with the pride of the forest." Denny selected as especially effective passages the fishing scene, the forest fire, Natty's trial, and that rescue from the panther which recent sceptics who perhaps never saw a panther have been willing to ridicule. Denny admired Natty, also, whom he thought to resemble Boone. In fine, Denney believed that:

> In Europe the scenes of this tale may be received as the wild creations of fancy, and the actors as the phantoms of an ingenious imagination; but the American, who has ample evidence of their truth, will recur to them with deep interest and pride, unmingled with a tinge of incredulity. . . .These individuals will all be found in good keeping; not deformed by caricature nor frittered away by extravagance. . . . and they are, as we can testify . . . the very kind of persons who may be expected to be found in such situations.[149]

And yet all these reviewers exhibited a consciousness that the new book was less popular than *The Spy* had been, and all of them except the *New York Mirror* conceded that *The Spy* was a more interesting novel because it was more romantic. Evidently, they considered their pleasure in realism something illicit.[150] The disappointed public thought

[148] I (August 2, 1823), 4-5; I (August 16, 1823), 20.

[149] *Port Folio*, XV (March, 1823), 230.

[150] For other reviews of *The Pioneers* see *Niles' Weekly Register*, XXIII (June 8, 1822), 225; XXIV (March 22, 1823), 34; XXIV (April 12, 1823), 91; XXIV (May 24, 1823), 178; *Columbian Centinel*, May 14, 1823; *New York American*, January 13, 1824; *Port Folio*, XV (March, 1823), 230-231; *New York Spectator*, February 4, 1823.

the novel was a proof that the new author was already written out, a swift meteor indeed.[151]

The behavior of the *North American Review* in this connection was thoroughly exasperating. It did not notice *The Pioneers* in 1823, perhaps because Cooper did not aim at the mark of gothic romance which the journal had set up the year before in its review of *The Spy.* At that time, the *North American* had pleaded for an Indian novel which should substitute new but thrilling settings for the old backgrounds of the Castles of Udolpho and Otranto. It had noted that Indian mounds were our only available ruins, and Indian superstitions might be made "to supersede the worn out fables of Runic mythology, and light up a new train of glowing visions." The reviewer had grown positively rhapsodical over the possibilities:

At any rate we are confident that the savage warrior, who was not less beautiful and bold in his figurative diction, than in his attitude of death, the same who 'suffered not the grass to grow upon the warpath,' and hastened 'to extinguish the fire of his enemy with blood,' tracking his foe through the pathless forest, with instinctive sagacity, by the fallen leaf, the crushed moss, or the bent blade, patiently enduring cold, hunger, and watchfulness, while he crouched in the night-grass like the tiger expecting his prey, and finally springing on the unsuspicious victim with that war-whoop, which struck terror to the heart of the boldest planter in New England . . . is no mean instrument of the sublime and terrible of human agency.

To cap his own climax, he actually had added that the Indians' "best historian, the indefatigable Heckewelder" leads us to think that the red man's domestic life offers the novelist "not a little of softer interest." Now in 1823, Cooper did not follow this prospectus and set down Otranto at Otsego, and so the *North American Review* had for *The Pioneers* no

[151] R. W. Griswold, *Prose Writers of America,* Philadelphia, 1847, p. 264.

word of cheer. But in 1826, when Cooper came out with just the Indian tale it had been asking for, the Boston journal discovered realism. In order to say that *The Last of the Mohicans* was poor, it was willing now to pronounce *The Pioneers* a more important book because of its true detail and character. *The Last of the Mohicans*, the *North American* conceded, had really performed a difficult feat in throwing Scott's, Radcliffe's, Walpole's, and Brown's romantic glamor over places which are so familiar to us that they are "thronged with the vulgar associations of real life"; but Gothic success, the journal maintained, was a low success. Realism was superior, and Cooper had lost that by cutting his Indians after Heckewelder, whose pattern the *North American* now declared incredible.[152]

The rest of the journals had by this time discovered realism, too. One of them denounced the novelist for deserting the realistic;[153] one of them praised *The Last of the Mohicans* for masterly Indian portraits, surpassing Chateaubriand's, but thought the book inferior to *The Pioneers*, which bore in Natty Bumppo the indefinable stamp of reality found only in a master's work;[154] another loyally praised it for its fidelity to fact and its immortal truth.[155] One objected that the book was almost too realistic, destroying the romantic appeal,[156] but for the most part the novel was held to the test of realism and accepted or rejected according as the reviewer thought it measured up.

None of this indicates a steady tendency of the reviewers. *The Pilot*, which had come out on January 7, 1824, had been praised at first for its return, after *The Pioneers*, to romantic

[152] *North American Review*, XXIII (July, 1826), 150-197.

[153] John Neal in *London Magazine*, n. s. V (May, 1826), 27; *Museum of Foreign Literature and Science*, IX (July, 1826), 57-59.

[154] *New York Mirror*, V (August 4, 1827), 31.

[155] *New York Review and Atheneum*, II (March, 1826), 285-292.

[156] *United States Literary Gazette*, IV (May, 1826), 87-94.

feeling mingled with accurate observation.[157] Little can be learned, however, about literary trends from the reviews of *The Pilot.* Most of the reviewers, after giving some praise to the sea, Tom Coffin, and Boltrope, were disparaging, evidently because they[158] were offended at Cooper's having written in the Preface that the book was composed for his sea-going friend, W. B. Shubrick, and not for land-lubbers. Addressing this sea-going friend, in order to distinguish the latter from book reviewers, he used the phrase, "lubberly critics," and the critics were apparently ignorant of what the phrase meant; for they were piqued, and yet surely they could not have claimed really to have been seamen. With inconsistent revenge, they acted as land-lubberly as possible by writing that *they* did not like the sea in novels, anyway.[159] They had to admit that the book was very popular; and *The Pilot* was another book which was well received abroad.[160]

Then *Lionel Lincoln*, which author and public condemned, received the heartiest praise that Cooper had won since Mrs. Hale's welcome to *The Spy.* Boston actually showed its first enthusiasm—the Battle of Bunker Hill was the novel's prominent feature. The novel was actually praised not only for its patriotism[161] but for its realism, which was a trait more satisfying, one reviewer declared, than "delicate distresses"

[157] *New York Spectator*, October 7, 1823; January 23, 1824; *New York American*, January 13, 1824; April 12, 1825; *New York Mirror*, I (April 17, 1824), 301; *North American Review*, XVIII (April, 1824), 314-329.

[158] *New York Mirror*, I (April 17, 1824), 301; *North American Review*, XVIII (April, 1824), 314-329; *New York American*, July 15, 1824 (review of *Redwood* quoted from *Boston Daily Advertiser*); *Christian Spectator*, VII (February, 1824), 37-38.

[159] *Port Folio*, XVII (February, 1824), 132-146.

[160] R. W. Griswold, *op. cit.*, p. 264; *New York American*, May 3, 1824; *Museum of Foreign Literature and Science*, V (July, 1824), 87-106.

[161] *New York Review and Atheneum*, I (June, 1825), 39-50; Philadelphia *National Gazette*, quoted in *New York Spectator*, February 17, 1825.

and trap doors, and which was exactly the talent, he thought, in which Cooper excelled.[162] John Neal's contemptuous article in *Blackwood's* got a round answer this time:

> The contribution to the journal must have sadly fallen off when a man who could not find a reader in America, goes to England, and ranks first quill among the journal writers. Neal swears that there are only three original American writers, and these are Neal, Brown and Paulding![163]

Of course, all the American critics were constantly raising superior eyebrows at Cooper's faults of style. Those faults, indeed, are glaring, and Cooper's helplessness to meet his problem is revealed by his painstaking and inadequate revision of *The Spy*. Yet in reading the objections of the critics, one often finds the latter so absurdly finical that one sympathizes somewhat with the Cooper who thought his critics should have noticed his mistake about nautical customs rather than counting "commas with broken tails." For instance, the *North American Review's* critic of *The Spy* seems to press his own literary discrimination too far when he applies nothing less than ridicule to Cooper for giving so much personification to a turnpike that it climbs a mountain boldly and directly, flourishes at the top in triumph, and descends on the other side into slow meanderings. Persons who have ridden or driven horses for long distances over roads like that one know very well how constant, during such travel, is their feeling of the road's movement. Often, too, the reviewer's purism concerning some point of grammar is more mistaken than was the idiom criticized.

Cooper's reception by the American critics, then, before 1828, was timid and yet, on the whole, favorable. As compared with criticisms of other Americans, exclusive of Irving,

[162] *United States Literary Gazette*, I (March 1, 1825), 337-340. For an opinion quoted from *Blackwood's Magazine*, see *ibid.*, III (September 15, 1825), 467.

[163] *Atlantic Magazine*, I (May, 1824), 2-3.

it was enthusiastic. When the press gave or withheld praise it did so on some literary ground, such as theories of realism and of romance, or criticism of careless grammar and monotonous style. There was strong interest in the question whether Cooper was doing America credit or not. But there was no complaint that he had disgraced us, and there was no sign of political antagonism.

Notions of the Americans was differently reviewed. From this book Cooper had expected too much. His publisher told him so. To understand this, one must read the letters in the Yale library from Carey, Lea, and Carey about *Notions of the Americans* and its reception by the people of the United States.

You are, we think, in error as to the extent of interest the book will excite here. To produce much interest severity is required, and however we may grumble at it, we are more disposed to read a book in which we receive castigation than one in which we have praise. The fact, too, of its being the production of an American, & not the view of a foreigner . . . will be against it. We shall hope, however, that your view may be correct and that it may have as great a sale as a novel—We have read it with much pleasure, & cannot doubt it will have a good effect in Europe. It is necessary to have some such feeling produced there before Capt. Hall comes out with his book, in which he will denounce us in every possible way.[164]

The book has not met with so much favour as you anticipated —the natives find fault with it because it praises them, & we are strongly inclined to believe that if it had been a severe attack upon them it would have been almost as well received. They hardly deserve to be defended.[165]

Yet Cooper had written his book just to defend us. He wished, as Carey said, to prepare a sympathetic feeling in

[164] Carey, Lea and Carey to Cooper, Philadelphia, July 17, 1828. Unpublished. Cooper collection, Yale University Library.

[165] Carey, Lea and Carey to Cooper, Philadelphia, September 8, 1828. Unpublished. Cooper collection, Yale University Library.

Europe against the time when Basil Hall's almost scandalous account of us would be published; and he deliberately made his book a partial view, a view of the good America only, because he wished to counterbalance foreign books about us which he thought had also been partial but had presented the bad. He worked very hard over the *Notions* and he expected to get loud attack for it abroad but loyal defense of it at home. Said Mrs. Cooper: "your Father writes very hard, he gets up early, and sometimes writes until he is so nervous, and agitated that he can hardly keep his hand still."[166] She thought this book did her husband more credit than any other book he had written; and she had some hopeful auguries of its success: "Colbourn gives him 200£ for it, and he gets $600 dollars for the translation in France. This is doing pretty well."[167] Cooper had written to an agent of Colburn: "I have a new work a good deal advanced, and one that I think will attract attention in England. . . . The subject is of much interest for your country, and though it is one of fact, will be sufficiently embellished by adventure and fiction to give it interest to general readers."[168] To the home publisher he wrote, "I think this work will pay you a handsome profit, for several Americans who have read it think it will do better at home than abroad."[169] Perhaps Cooper was a little pleased at the prospect of foreign displeasure. He had mentioned in some earlier letter the possibility of offending Europe, for Carey had already written: "we shall be much pleased if it shall meet with the success you anticipate, even if you should receive castigation, as you think you will,

[166] Letter to Susan Fenimore Cooper, London, May 15, 1828. Unpublished. Cooper collection, Yale. See also letter to the same, London, May 19, 1828.

[167] Letter, Mrs. Cooper to Miss De Lancey, London, May 1 [1828]. Unpublished. Cooper collection, Yale.

[168] *Correspondence of James Fenimore-Cooper*, I, 136.

[169] Letter, Cooper to Carey, Lea, and Carey, London, May 6, 1828. Unpublished. Aldis collection, Yale.

from our friends across the Millpond."[170] But what Cooper did count on was that his labor of love would "do better at home."

But American journals were disappointing. They printed little about *Notions* except excerpts from British reviews,[171] and in copying these British opinions they actually seemed to agree with the foreigners in preferring Basil Hall's interpretations of America to Cooper's; evidently, Carey had been right about them. Certainly, the *Philadelphia Album*[172] was careful to commend John Bull for having "wrapped him pretty severely over the knuckles"; and the *North American Review* made Cooper's *Red Rover,* which had just come out, an excuse for assuring the world that America admired Irving's kind of Americanism, and for dropping remarks probably considered tactful about Geoffrey Crayon and our kinship with England.[173] A much quoted Scotch detraction of Cooper was one which was printed in the Tory *Edinburgh Review,* the first review which this journal had condescended to bestow upon any of Cooper's works. It was cutting in its style, and it said really untruthfully that Cooper had written the *Notions* "in the spirit of a man who should strut down the street, treading upon the toes, and putting his fist into the face, of every gentleman he met."[174]

The *Philadelphia Album* declared that *Notions* showed "a

[170] Letter, Carey, Lea, and Carey to Cooper, Philadelphia, April 28, 1828. Unpublished. Cooper collection, Yale.

[171] *E.g., Museum of Foreign Literature, Science and Art,* VIII. O. S. (December, 1829), 510-532; XIII (November, 1828), 668, (December, 1828), 739; XVI (March, 1830), 233-248. The *New York American* made a favorable independent statement, very brief, on September 5, 1828. *Ladies' Magazine,* I (September, 1828), p. 431, made an independent review, not very favorable, saying that Cooper was fairly good.

[172] III (October 29, 1828), 173.

[173] XXVII (July, 1828), 139-154.

[174] This review was copied, *ibid.,* VIII (December, 1829), 510-532; *New York American,* November 4 and 5, 1829. It was originally printed in June, 1829.

general deficiency of taste" and that the facts arrayed in it reminded a reader too much of "Miss Wright's rhodomontade" and were too highly colored.[175] Cooper himself had disapproved of the same Miss Wright in his time. His friend Wilkes now reminded him of that:

> I have smiled now and then when I recollected how indignant you was sometimes with my poor Miss Wright for her nauseous flattery, as I believe you called it—if her's was a picture all of lights and with no shadows, you will hardly escape the same charge.[176]

But since the days when he had complained of Miss Wright, Cooper had lived abroad and had learned how heavily the shadows would be rubbed in by his readers. In leaving out his shadows he gave some people the impression that his colors were too high; and yet even Wilkes had to admit that the colors were really true—that if there were errors in his deductions there were none in his facts. Whether *Notions* would add to his own fame or not, he had designed it to add to America's.

Now, there is reason for suspecting that American coolness towards *Notions of the Americans* was not caused solely by literary and factual deficiencies. There are several straws which indicate a flurry of wind from the Whig quarter. The two Democrats Willis and Bryant warned Americans to be independent of British jealousies and unfair antagonisms to Cooper;[177] and a belief in the existence of English hostility combined with an effort to combat it rather than truckle to it was more characteristic of Democrats than of Whigs. As Charles Wilkes pointed out to Cooper in connection with the

[175] III (September 24, 1828), 134-135.

[176] *Correspondence of James Fenimore-Cooper*, I, 151-152.

[177] *New York Mirror*, VI (August 23, 1828), 55; *Evening Post*, August 13, 1828. Other sympathetic statements occurred in the *New York Mirror*, VI (September 6, 1828), 67; (September 13, 1828), 77; (November 29, 1828), 167; VII (November 7, 1829), 139.

very book we are discussing, such an attitude towards England was too much like that which was "sedulously kept up by one of the political parties of the country"; Wilkes saw this attitude within the book and thought it gave to *Notions* a general political coloring.[178] The book had other vague suggestions of Democracy about it. A friend in Paris told Cooper that it was the "only pure—unsophisticated—uncompromising *vindication* since the 'notes' of Jefferson"[179] and the publisher, an impatient Whig, wrote: "we presume Jackson will be elected, and we should say, if we had not so recently read the *Travelling Bachelor*, that it was because he had all the vagabonds on his side— Since reading the book we are inclined to doubt if there are any vagabonds in the country."[180] The comparisons made with Fanny Wright remind us that in time "Fanny Wrightism[181] became a Whig epithet for Democratic radicalism.

But there were far more definite connections than this between the book and Jacksonian Democracy. Even William Dunlap, a Democrat, expressed the opinion that the book was too strongly Jacksonian, and in my second chapter I have shown how much space Cooper had given to Jackson in his discussion of the campaign of 1824. I have already pointed out, in the same chapter, that *Notions of the Americans* had defended the doctrine of strict construction and of Democratic tariff. All this would necessarily be noticed in 1828, an election year. Some passages on the comparative economy of our government and of foreign governments suggest the finance controversy and would call more attention a little

[178] *Correspondence of James Fenimore-Cooper*, I, 151-152.

[179] Letter, G. E. Erving to Cooper, Paris, n. d. Unpublished. Cooper collection, Yale.

[180] Letter, Carey, Lea, and Carey to Cooper, Philadelphia, December [?], 1828. Unpublished. Cooper collection, Yale.

[181] *United States Magazine and Democratic Review*, III (October, 1838), 97, complains of this.

later. But there was certainly a strongly and quite definitely Democratic coloring in the *Notions*.[182]

The fact of this Democratic coloring is mentioned here only as a reminder of my former discussion of it. At the present moment we are considering Cooper's critics and whether *Notions* affected their reviews after 1828. Now, I am unwilling to press a causal relationship which I cannot demonstrate, but it is a fact that *The Red Rover*, *The Wept of Wish-ton-Wish*, and *The Water Witch* were condemned, ignored, or very weakly praised. Only the Democratic *Evening Post* kept up its loyalty.[183] These novels are probably inferior to the earlier ones, and the coolness was perhaps merely a reflection of this inferiority. If so, the events of the next few years destroyed this ability to make balanced literary judgments, for when Cooper produced *Deerslayer* and *Pathfinder* a decade later, the reviewers did not respond to the higher quality of these novels. The coolness which appeared in 1828 continued.

[182] For illustrative passages, see II, 227-232; 242-243; II, 199-204; II, 434-439; I, 127; II, 264-282.

[183] On *The Red Rover*, see *Western Monthly Review*, I (February, 1828), 603-608; *North American Review*, XXVII (July, 1828), 139-154; *Philadelphia Album*, II (January 9, 1828), 252-253; *New York Spectator*, January 18, 1828; *Evening Post*, January 25, 1828. Foreign reviews, most of them favorable, were quoted in *American Monthly Magazine*, I (November, 1829), 560-565; *Philadelphia Monthly*, I (March, 1828), 294; *Museum of Foreign Literature and Science*, XII (February, 1828), 362-369; *ibid.*, XIII (May, 1828), 91-92; *ibid.*, XIII (June, 1828), 187-188. On *The Wept of Wish-ton-Wish*, *Philadelphia National Gazette*, cited in *Commercial Advertiser*, December 9, 1829; *Philadelphia Album*, IV (January 16, 1830), 21; *Southern Review*, V (February, 1830), 207-226; for defense about this time against William Hazlitt's essay on American literature, see *North American Review*, XXXI (July, 1830), 26-66. On *The Water Witch*, Philadelphia *National Gazette*, cited in *Correspondence of James Fenimore-Cooper*, I, 195; *New York American*, November 10, 29, 1830; *Evening Post*, December 14, 30, 1830; *New York Mirror*, VIII (December 18, 1830), 190; *Ladies' Magazine*, IV (January, 1831), 44-47; *North American Review*, XXXII (April, 1831), 508-523.

Now, before the *Notions*, Cooper's American principles had been neglected for the discussions of romance, and yet even with *The Spy* Cooper might have begun his anxiety to have his principles noticed. This book is not really partisan in its principles. It is obviously a glorification of patriotism and in that aspect alone would present something of what Cooper included in "American principles," but there was another characteristic more deeply American; namely, a democratic treatment in which a peddler is portrayed with all his imperfections on his head and yet glorified by his single virtue of patriotism. George Washington Greene perceived that this was the point of the novel (perhaps instructed by conversations with Cooper).[184] Birch was not low merely in station, a peddler-philosopher-gentleman. He was a peddler of a mean nature, of what Greene called "acquisitive instincts," and to make such a man into a hero by the stroke of patriotism alone was a principle of strong democracy, of something more American than writing of a war in which Redcoats were defeated. No reviewers discovered even this fact. They were too much occupied with the possibilities in American things. Several of them missed the whole point. Maria Edgeworth, though she admired some of the novel's realism, found that she could not admire any spy, peddler or not. As for Harvey's death, a hanging "goes against all heroic stomachs . . . would even Shakespeare venture the gibbet?" American journals, instead of explaining things, just reprinted Miss Edgeworth.[185] The *North American Review* insisted that Harvey's "voluntary descent to a degrading occupation" was inconsistent with "the lofty tone of moral feeling" which a patriot must have.[186] This is very like the talk of the American business man who complained, much to Cooper's disgust, that the author had not given Birch

[184] *Homes of American Authors*, New York, 1853, pp. 190-194.
[185] *Port Folio*, XVI (July, 1823), 85-86.
[186] XXXII (April, 1831), 508-523.

any motive for his heroism.[187] Cooper certainly must have thought he had American principles in *The Spy*. He even considered that his Indian novels showed a certain amount of republicanism in the red man.[188] But his reviewers praised anything but this. The *North American Review* once printed two sentences that are a complete example of the attitude Cooper found objectionable:

> We have a commonplace, hackneyed sort of enthusiasm, on the subject of liberty, republican principles, etc.; but this is so common a theme of declamation in all assemblies, from Congress to the bar room, that it is ordinary and tame, except now and then, when raised for the moment by some fortunate effort, or remarkable brilliancy. But on the subject of our naval skill and prowess, although we are not willing to confess it, we are, yet, real enthusiasts.[189]

Whether these are wise statements or not, they would convince Cooper that American principles were not valued here so much as things; and if enthusiasm for republican principles were hackneyed in Congress and the bar room, Cooper had not seen it overworked in the home reviews of his novels.

For instance, no American journal did for any of Cooper's fiction what the *Gazette de France* did in 1827 for *The Prairie*. The *Gazette* pointed out that Cooper's originality was his republicanism, and that in this principle lay Cooper's difference from Scott and the cause of Cooper's increasing vogue in France while Scott's popularity declined there. Not a single American reviewer could say this for Cooper. The *New York American* did translate and reprint the *Gazette's* review, and in this act only was American encouragement represented.[190] That the *Gazette* spoke of evidences in Cooper's books of his nobility as a man I will not stress, nor

[187] *The Monikins*, p. 368.
[188] Preface to *The Wept of Wish-ton-Wish.*
[189] XVIII (April, 1824), 314-329.
[190] *New York American*, September 18 and 20, 1827.

the fact that the *Philadelphia Album* said of the trapper's famous death, which both Thackeray and the *Gazette* admired as a brilliant piece of art: "the Trapper dies, but we think he dies rather heavily.[191] I will not stress these comparisons of American with foreign opinion because it was not on matters of this sort that Cooper asked for support; whereas the fact that it took a French journal to praise Cooper's republicanism would have been a bitterer mortification. Cooper did not realize that such a subject might really be more hackneyed on our continent than on the one he was inhabiting at the time.

And so, after the disappointments of the 1820's, the American Scott set about the work of making it plainer to his readers that he was an anti-Scott. He determined to make his American principles stand out in bold relief. For the first time, he cut out American things altogether and began to write novels with European settings on purpose to demonstrate his American principles alone. Just as he began making these principles bolder and balder, events took a turn which made them more definitely Jacksonian than they had ever been before. After *The Bravo* his American democracy was Democracy indeed, and from then on he had the embattled Whigs to face. The condition was incipient in his first desire to propagate American principles, in his tendency, even in 1828, to conceive of these principles in Jacksonian terms, and in American coolness during the years that followed the *Notions*. But the thickening of the plot with *The Bravo* and what resulted from it require new chapters for the telling.

[191] I (May 23, 1827), 7.

CHAPTER IV

Founding of the Cooper Myth

WILLIAM WORDSWORTH in his high room under a Paris roof listened for the return of revolution down the streets through which it had lately rolled; but Cooper a generation later heard the rising of a tide which seemed more ominous by far than revolution—counter-revolution. Monarchy had been only scotched, and Cooper's close friend Lafayette was continually in sight, working with his last strength to finish the serpent.

In 1830 on the twenty-seventh of July Paris had torn up its paving stones for barricades and had seized the capital of Charles X while he played his evening whist at St. Cloud; and on July 29 of that year the republicans were in control of the city, having placed their venerable Lafayette at the head of a provisional government in the City Hall. The great patriot and friend of moderation was then won over by Louis Philippe's promises of republican sympathy. He consented to appear with Louis Philippe upon a balcony, to embrace him there in public view; and only by this embrace did Louis Philippe achieve the throne of France. Following this, of course Louis Philippe steadily separated himself from republican sympathies; so that in 1832 Cooper himself witnessed a street rebellion against him and the party of the "juste milieu," a rebellion apparently instigated by a republican party which was uncertain in its mind as to whether it was for or against Lafayette and peaceful reform. Cooper witnessed this affair, heard the shots ring out, and saw Parisians fortify their shops by putting up their metal blinds against the bullets. He knew how the weary Lafayette was drawn about the town by revolutionists, partly in honor and partly in wrathful disaffection. He has told his own story of the events, and also of his conversation with Lafayette, when the veteran of many revolutions told him that it was not really the republicans who had arranged the fighting, but the government itself, to discredit the republicans. Between the liberals and their former ally, Louis Philippe, there could be no reconciliation now, said Lafayette, for they were separated by a "river of blood."[192]

This, then, was what Cooper was seeing of the world in 1832. On June 7 he was talking with a broken Lafayette whom he loved about the high hopes they had had in 1830, about the uselessness of expecting republican sentiments under a monarchical government, and about the unhappy prospects for French liberty. The date of this era of republican dejection should be remembered, for in June of 1832 Cooper was having his own troubles.

The French Doctrinaires and royalists alike had been issuing deliberate propaganda against America, endeavoring to give the impression abroad that the American experiment had failed. Some of this propaganda was utterly laughable. For instance, according to Cooper's story, the *Revue Britannique* on one occasion declared that Americans were already so far gone in luxury as to support a splendid country house for the President, besides a city mansion; and when Lafayette, for the sake of democracy everywhere, denied this, one misguided Leavitt Harris, an American, put him in the wrong by printing a letter in defense of the *Revue*, actually saying that it was all one, since the city mansion was so placed as to command the pleasures of both town and country. Cooper tells this as a merely amusing anecdote. But it was more serious that this Harris jumbled the causes of the American Revolution ludicrously; and that Saulnier, a leader of the opposition party, after much talk about procuring the real facts from Americans who were liberal enough to distinguish between national honor and national expenditure, published

[192] A large part of *Sketches of Switzerland*, Part Second, v. I is devoted to the narration of these events.

statistics about us which turned out to have come from Basil Hall's *Travels in America,* that piece of prejudiced abuse which Cooper hated.

Really, the attacks of the *Revue Britannique* had all been serious, and Cooper had been replying to these attacks since the preceding fall. Lafayette had requested his assistance in the controversy, and Cooper's letters on American expenditures ran in the *National* from November 25, 1831, into March of 1832, with another on May 3, 1832, to put down Leavitt Harris.[193]

The effect of these events upon his philosophy was, as I have said in an earlier chapter, to convince him that the real threat to democracy on both continents came no longer from tyrannical monarchs, but from powerful oligarchies which would work through legislative bodies and direct governments from behind figurehead kings. The Romantic Movement in literature had followed a sentimental return to the past which in the historical novel had fostered an attachment to monarchy. While the greatest romantic poets had served the cause of liberty, the chief romantic novelist had taken the opposite course. Cooper saw that Scott's way of looking at the past did not tell the whole truth; and as a sincere man and a progressive thinker, he wrote *Heidenmauer* "to show how differently a democrat and an aristocrat saw the same thing," namely, the mediæval structure of society, and human resistance to reform. Cooper was too thoughtful a man to be interested in pointing an old moral on monarchy which the world had already learned. He was interested, rather, in viewing the past to see what example it might yield of oligarchic government, the real contemporary problem. Venice interested him in this connection; and so *Heidenmauer* was preceded by *The Bravo,* in which Venice is represented as an oligarchy continually paying lip service to democracy.[194] It

[193] For Cooper's narrative of the finance controversy see *Sketches of Switzerland,* Part Second, I, 54 ff., and *A Letter to His Countrymen.*

[194] *The Bravo,* pp. 107, 390, and *passim.*

is a favorite topic of this novel that degrading servility and enforced ignorance among the lower classes are inseparable from aristocratic rule.[195] A very significant point, also, is that the power of the people is stolen by an oligarchy,[196] and this is a doctrine which Cooper applied, in later books, to the limited monarchy of England. Tyranny hiding under the title of republicanism is exemplified in the character of Signor Gradenigo. Both direct and indirect exposition are used to reveal the contradictions in the signor's conduct,[197] and there are numerous passages of direct didacticism, besides the manipulation of the whole plot, to point the general observations on oligarchy.[198] The final words of the book comprise its thesis: "the state of Venice held its vicious sway, corrupting alike the ruler and the ruled, by its mockery of those sacred principles which are alone founded in truth and natural justice." And the Preface declares the purpose; to

> lay bare the wrongs that are endured by the weak, when power is the exclusive property of the strong; the tendency of all exclusion to heartlessness; the irresponsible and ruthless movement of an aristocracy; the manner in which even the good become the passive instruments of its soulless power. In short, I had undertaken to give the reader some idea of the action of a government, which to use the language of the book itself, had neither 'the high personal responsibility that sometimes tempers despotism by the qualities of the chief, nor the human impulses of a popular rule.'

Naturally, such an effort would challenge agreement or opposition from readers of different political faiths. Cooper could not and did not expect anything else. He was, indeed, pleased to find that with *The Bravo* and *Heidenmauer* he had

[195] *Ibid.*, pp. 120, 345. Antonio is represented as the lowly man who knows his own dignity, and the struggle for self-respect in an oligarchy is important in the book; pp. 130, 160-161, and *passim.*

[196] *Ibid.*, pp. 394-395.

[197] *Ibid.*, pp. 82, 85-86.

[198] *Ibid.*, pp. 143-148, 288-289, 361-364, 384.

at last produced novels which were seen to present American principles. He declared[199] that he had no reason to be dissatisfied with *The Bravo's* reception, since with the mass of readers it became popular for its story, and among a few "who were accustomed to separate principles from facts" the political intention was perceived. He seemed ingenuously proud that his Italian novel was attacked in France by the Doctrinaires and welcomed by their opponents: "Figaro, without exception the wittiest journal in France, and one that was especially devoted to attacks on the *juste milieu*, contrary to its usual course, gave an especial article to the book, laying considerable stress on its political tendency. Praise from Figaro, on such a topic, almost inevitably drew censure from the other party. . ." But after *Figaro* was purchased by the government, Cooper said, the journal assailed Cooper openly by name. In the controversy which Cooper thought was thus inevitable, there was only one painful surprise; the reviews in the United States, a country that was committed by its Constitution to opposing the monarchist doctrine of the *juste milieu*, did not give him even such support as he drew from a French journal of wit.

To be sure, the first reviews of *The Bravo* were more favorable than the notices he had been getting just before, and they actually praised his American principles. They bolstered themselves with quotations from Colburn's English *New Monthly Magazine*, and said the book actually compared favorably with Monk Lewis's *The Bravo of Venice*. When they blamed it they did so on literary grounds, one magazine complaining that the title was unsuitable, the style faulty, and the language of the humbler Venetians strangely similar to the language of Cooper's Pawnees and Delawares.[200]

[199] *A Letter to His Countrymen*, pp. 16-19.

[200] *Philadelphia Album*, V (November 12, 1831), 365-366; (December 10, 1831), 396; (December 24, 1831), 411; *Ladies' Magazine*, V (January, 1832), 42-46; *Southern Review*, VIII (February, 1832), 382-399; *American Monthly Review*, I (February, 1832), 147-153.

The *Southern Review* approved of Cooper's comparison of the Venetian public with ours. It must be admitted that there was a conspicuous absence of any notice of the novel during these early months in many of the major magazines.

The first newspaper reports of *The Bravo* were, like the magazine reviews, superficially friendly but quite conscious of foreign opinion. *The Morning Courier and New York Enquirer* praised the exciting action, the exquisite description, and the republican moral. It declared that the book's republicanism was well planned to "catch the popular feeling at present existing in England" and that it would be "very popular across the water." This journal, be it noted, was Democratic at this date.[201] The *New York American's* review[202] is especially interesting because of the events which soon followed it. This reviewer made the comment—trite in reviews of Cooper, now—that the book was hasty, but he granted that it was a masterly work nevertheless. He said it had in it too much politics. The inevitable comparison with Scott was drawn in, but it was a favorable one this time. The descriptions of Venice were praised. Most important of all, the *American* declared that Cooper's alacrity in seizing all opportunities to make this country understood abroad ought to add to his popularity at home. The New York *Atlas* quoted a favorable review from the London *Spectator*,[203] and the *New York Spectator* copied the praise of the *New Monthly Magazine*, adding its own introductory note: "We take the liberty of criticizing him as freely as we please, but should feel as much vexed as he could feel himself, by ungenerous or unfair remarks on his productions, in any foreign journal. He is reaping, however, nothing but laurels."[204] These reviews seem to establish that *The Bravo*

[201] November 30, 1831.
[202] December 3, 1831.
[203] *Atlas*, December 10, 1831.
[204] December 30, 1831.

was accepted as a good piece of fiction and as an obviously republican work. But *The Bravo* had appeared in November, 1831, and on April 5, 1832, the *New York American* contained a dispatch from Europe which referred to "A curious discussion" by Cooper and General Bernard with M. Saulnier at Lafayette's request. Soon after this, everything changed. Cooper was forced to discover that it was not the United States but only the Democrats who supported his foreign contest against the aristocrats for our republican institutions.

The *New York American* in this dispatch was doubtless referring to Lafayette's introduction of a letter from Cooper on American finances, together with one from General Bernard, into the Chamber of Deputies on January 6, in the midst of discussion of the French budget bill.[205] Controversy had followed, and on March 16 Cooper had written a long and triumphant letter home. "The design of the Ministary," he said, "was to bring America into discredit all over Europe, and to crush La Fayette. . . . I stepped in promptly and in a few letters demolished all their hopes and cries of victory." Evidently Cooper enjoyed the fight. The French, Cooper said, had been shameless in their subterfuge and lies, but Bernard and the American minister and consul had stood by him well.

This was all exhilarating, but there was a painful, an extremely painful aspect. For there were Americans in France "who not only aid the Ministers but effect to add weight to their testimony by saying that they have held *Office* at home! I am afraid that some who hold office now are not quite innocent of encouraging the enemy in order to encrease [*sic*] their own importance in the French Salons. Never was a people more hum-bugg'd than the American people in this particular. One half of our Agents abroad

[205] R. E. Spiller, *Fenimore Cooper, Critic of His Times*, p. 170.

are scarcely American in feeling." Still more disappointing was what he heard from home:

> Well, now I have driven this M. Saulnier into a corner, his American supporters say it is beneath the dignity of a man like me to appear in a Navy paper! My answer to them is contempt, and to all others, that it is below the character of no man to advance the cause of truth.

There was a certain kind of recognition for which Cooper longed. He said he had not had "one frank manly gentlemanly allusion to myself as a writer in a single American publication in five years." This would be since he published *Notions of the Americans*, we may note. He did not ask for literary praise so much as respect as a man: "There may be better writers than I in the country, but there is certainly no one treated with so little deference." "I ask no puffs," he said, "—they disgust me, but for God's sake let me have not deprecatory praise and pealing censure." It was true that American scribblers for any journal from the *North American Review* down had treated Cooper with just such a combination of timidity and license as he describes. Doubtless he wished to tell them, as a man and a sailor, what he thought of them. He was sick of the sniggering comma-counters: "It is no crime not to be the best, in or out of the country, and as I commonly support sound political doctrines and always good I can claim to be alluded to as not disgracing the attic excellence of American Literature."

Let them recognize his sound politics, since he deserved that at least—this was his cry. But "One fact is beyond dispute—I am not with my own country—the void between us is immense—which is in advance time will show."[206] Alas for James Cooper, American!

Almost on the very day when Cooper poured out these

[206] Letter to William Dunlap, Paris, March 16, 1832, *Diary of William Dunlap*, 606-609.

feelings to Dunlap, the *New York American* had gone out of its way to make an unfriendly remark about Cooper in a paragraph ostensibly on American poets.[207] On June 7 that paper came out with a new review of *The Bravo*, very different from the last December's. This review was a letter signed Cassio, and Cassio was certainly wide of the mark. He shot, in fact, so very wide that his bad aim seemed to need an explanation. The theory of several friends of Cooper was that Cassio was a Doctrinaire, or at least an enemy of the French republic.

The letter made no reference to politics. There was one unfair allusion to greed for money. But the real purpose of the review must have been to miss the purpose of the book. This Cassio, without deigning to see that the point of the book was republicanism, asked, "what is it all about?" and found for himself no answer. To him the book was simply sans plot, sans incident, sans coherence, sans poetic justice, sans originality. Summing up, he said: "we are satisfied that every reader of the book will concur in the assertion, that, as a story, the Bravo is destitute of merit."

Of course, the readers of *The Bravo*, in the six months since its publication, had been expressing the contrary opinion. Aside from this, the review is simply two columns of nonsense. For instance, to prove that Cooper wrote obscurely, it asserts that he neither affirmed or denied in the course of the book that the Bravo really was an assassin. This is flatly a false statement; Cooper could not have revealed more openly than he did that Jacopo had never taken any man's life, but had merely borne the reputation of a bravo. Then, to show that Cooper had "very ill defined notions of poetical justice," the review complains that Jacopo, who is supposed to be a hero, is put to death, while "the wretches in power, who have done nothing but deeds of darkness" go scot free. To say this is, of course, stupidly or maliciously or politically

[207] March 14, 1832.

to miss the point of the book; for the ending is intended to be a tragic one, and the moral of the novel is that oligarchic rule produces injustice and cruelty.

Anyone who had read *The Bravo* with half a wit could have refuted Cassio, and an anonymous champion did so with a short and adequate reply in the *New York American* itself on June 9.

Now, Cooper's friends urged him to reply to Cassio, and for a special reason. They thought they saw the hand of French government agents in that letter on *The Bravo*. The idea was not impossible. He had had more than one evidence that this party was capable of attacking him without regard for the truth,[208] and W. C. Rives, our Minister, had told him only recently that the government party would not soon forget nor forgive his part in the finance controversy.[209]

But Cooper did not care to answer Cassio. As he said, he had known all the time that there were Whigs in America who dreaded Agrarian reforms (just then an issue) and dreamed golden dreams of an aristocracy that they really knew nothing about.

I confess I see nothing in its [*The Bravo's*] design of which an American need be ashamed. I had not been cooped up in a ward of New-York, regarding things only on one side, and working myself into a fever on the subject of the imminent danger that impended over this great republic, by the machinations of a few 'working-men,' dreaming of Agrarian laws, and meditating on the neglected excellencies of my own character on the one hand, and on the unmerited promotion of some neighbor, who spelt constitution with a *k* on the other: but it had been my employment for years to visit nations, and to endeavor to glean some general inferences from the comparisons that naturally suggested themselves. I knew there existed at home a large party of *doctrinaires*, composed of men of very fair intentions, but of very limited

[208] *A Letter to His Countrymen*, pp. 16-19; *France*, II, 82-83.

[209] *A Letter to His Countrymen*, *loc. cit.*; letter, W. C. Rives to Cooper, Paris, March 12, 1832. Unpublished. Cooper collection, Yale.

means of observation, who fancied excellencies under other systems, much as the ultra-liberals of Europe, fancy perfection under our own; and, while I knew what I was doing was no more than one nail driven into an edifice that required a million, I thought it might be well enough to show the world that there was a writer among ourselves of some vogue in Europe, who believed that the American system was founded on just and durable principles.[210]

It was S. F. B. Morse who grew warm over Cassio. Morse and Cooper were two devoted friends who had misadventures in their attempts to assist each other. At a slightly later day than this, between 1834 and 1837, Cooper's zeal for Morse lost the commission for mural paintings in the Capitol which Cooper had been trying to get him. John Quincy Adams was a member of the committee of the House of Representatives who were to commission an American artist for painting the panels in the rotunda of the Capitol. Adams, true to the prejudices of his party, submitted a resolution that no American artist was good enough. Cooper printed "a severe and masterly reply" in the *Evening Post* which was attributed to Morse and lost him the commission.[211] Morse's heat in defending Cooper's cause was ascribed to the novelist himself and injured him. Morse was the luckier in these events, for when he lost the commission as artist he turned to an old idea of his and invented the telegraph. Cooper gained nothing but the country's ingratitude.

A copy of the paper containing Cassio's article had been sent to Cooper and was opened in the presence of Morse and Lieutenant Paine of the Navy.[212] Paine was reminded of a similar review in the *Journal des Debats*. This journal long sought to convey the idea of American liberty's dissolution and eventually made the very name of Cooper's party

[210] *A Letter to His Countrymen*, pp. 14-15.
[211] S. I. Prime, *op. cit.*, p. 290.
[212] *Diary of William Dunlap*, III, 635.

a bug-a-boo to frighten European liberals.[213] He asked for the *American* and later reported to Cooper that he had found the French article and believed it to be by the same hand as Cassio's letter. Cooper, however, did not see the article; evidently, he had too little curiosity to ask for it.

Morse returned to America about this time. As an artist he found the America of 1832 highly unsatisfactory after Paris; as a Democrat, he found himself almost ostracized in New York; and as a warm, even an adoring friend of Cooper, he could not endure America's neglect of the author of *The Bravo.* He interested himself in discovering the identity of Cassio, and at length decided that he had found the man in "an obscure clerk in a counting house." This person had been in Paris at the time when the Cassio letter had been written, and Morse convinced himself that there was Doctrinaire influence at work. He confided in William Dunlap, another good Democrat, who was interested and thought the matter worth sifting.[214] Morse, indeed, was something of a spy-hunter by nature, and it is impossible to tell how much nervousness he communicated to Cooper. He wrote a pamphlet on "Foreign conspiracy" which was reprinted after its first appearance in the New York *Observer,* and which maintained that Austria and the Holy Alliance had adequate motive and ample means to conspire against the United States; the motive was simply self-preservation, since a successful democracy endangered them, and the means were being "actually employed." It cannot be questioned, in the light of recent events, that nations do feel strongly such impulses of self-preservation as this. How right Morse was about European activity I am not prepared to discuss. It is clear that he was inclined to suspect subterranean foreign activity against our institutions, and that he now wrote so urgently to Cooper as to convince his friend that Cassio's

[213] *United States Magazine and Democratic Review,* VII (May, 1840), 435.

[214] *Diary of William Dunlap, loc. cit.*

letter was connected with the French party. He did not succeed, however, with his recommendations that Cooper do something to show how our press was dominated. What could Cooper say which would not be interpreted as complaint about a literary review of himself? "The criticism on the Bravo, as a criticism, never excited any feeling in me," he once wrote, "nor did I ever express any in reference to it. . . . Its importance was derived from its supposed origin."[215] Cooper therefore kept silent.

Morse took some trouble to learn the identity of this Cassio, and upon learning it felt more hurt than ever, for he turned out to be a man to whom Cooper had shown some kindness when he was abroad.[216] He was E. S. Gould, who

[215] *A Letter to His Countrymen*, pp. 32, 39-40.

[216] Morse to Cooper, New York, February 21, 1833, unpublished passage in a typewritten copy, Library of Congress. (Letter published, with omissions, in Edward Lind Morse, *Samuel F. B. Morse, His Letters and Journals* (New York, 1914), II, 21ff.): "By the way, I have something to tell you in relation to the Review in the American about which we had so much conversation; I gave you the name of the writer in Paris, on the authority of Lieutenant Payne; since I have been at home, it has been declared to me that the Review was written here by an obscure clerk in a counting house and Verplanck was cited to me as having assured my informant of the fact. Now notwithstanding the authority cited, I think the document itself is proof against such an origin. My informers were silenced by my exposé of the matter, and I have heard nothing of the subject for a long time. There has been some trickery in this business you may depend upon it.—This clerk whoever he is, is made to father it, and he might have been the translator. If you can ferret the truth out, and expose this contemptible meannes by ascertaining, as I think you can, whether Nizard actually wrote it, I should delight to see the authors arraigned at the bar of public opinion for their tricks." Morse to Cooper, New York, July 25, 1833. Unpublished. Cooper collection, Yale University Library: "I send you the Evening Post of the 20th inst. being the last shot, and which I fear has sunk the enemy; everyone I meet says so at least. Here are 5 days passed and no answer; I have sincerely been hoping for one, for I am now confident that the more the subject is agitated, the more you will be appreciated

wrote under the same pseudonym for the *American Monthly*, the *New World*, the *New York Mirror*, and other journals. But another signature of Gould's was "the Man in the Claret-colored Coat"[217] and doubtless Cassio was identical with that

and your opposers humbled. If the controversy has done no other good it has at least shown you who they are, that have been endeavoring to influence the public mind against you. One is E. S. G. the cidevant Secy. of our Polish comtee, who has proved himself as complete a blackguard, and as impertinent as a billingsgate fish woman; in proof of which besides the evidence you have in the American and in the Traveller I have two impudent letters that the fellow has written me signed with his own proper name, and which I keep to show occasionally to my friends to make them acquainted with the kind and quality of Mr. King's foreign correspondents. This fellow threatens in his last letter to me to send you all that is published against you, and seems to chuckle mightily that he has wounded you and your family; you were little aware what a viper you were cherishing, I mean in temper, not that he has any power, he is too contemptible to notice in any way.—The coadjutor of the Commercial is a different person altogether, one whom you would as little suspect as your own brother, it is *William Kent*; I have learned this since my last piece was written. He is the *Paris correspondent* of the Commercial! Is it not a pretty piece of business altogether? A young aristocrat, for I learn that his feelings are aristocratic, who has scarcely been out of New York gives to the world his sage opinions on foreign politics and to give them weight commits the pious fraud of dating them from Paris! I want to state this before the public, and hope I shall have the chance yet. But I fear the Commercial & Co. are too-well aware of the ticklish ground on which they stand, and that they will be mum.—Gould by the by says he has sent to Paris for the Journal de Debats containing the critique and when he gets it intends translating it for the American to show how true you are in calling his a translation of that article. Now as this fellow will not stick at anything and as he is mad after *fame* he will probably make a noise again as soon as he gets it. I apprize you of [this] that you may put me in possession of any thing you can collect that may [be of] service in exposing him. [L]eave him to me, I will serve him up, and exhibit him in his true colors if he or his protector of the American open their mouths again [on] the subject."

[217] *National Encyclopaedia of American Biography*, New York, 1897, IV, 527.

Man in the Claret-coloured Coat who wrote an article for the *Mirror* mocking *A Letter to His Countrymen.* Now, Cassio's other literary effusions do indicate that Cooper and Morse were not overimaginative in believing Gould to be one of those Americans who, when abroad, behaved themselves as monarchists. Two selections from Cassio's "Extracts from a Manuscript Journal of a trip to Paris, in 1831," will be definite enough in their indications.[218] In one, he reproaches Louis-Philippe for having expunged the fleur-de-lis from national monuments. Cooper's friend and the republic's, Lafayette, had remarked that the king had been slow to do this, signifying that he himself would have done it earlier. But Cassio, Cooper's enemy and the republic's, was disgusted, and after protesting the act, he wrote: "He even carried his liberalism and condescension so far, that a certain shield (on which one of his insignificant grandfathers, some centuries gone by, had blazoned this token of his dignity and his power), was submitted to the discussion of the dishcloth—and these proud insignia of the greatest monarchs that have swayed an earthly sceptre, at the bidding of the vile rabble, were blotted from his escutcheon forever!" Without choosing between Lafayette's point of view and Gould's, a modern American can simply note that there was a political difference, here, and one of some violence; especially when he finds Gould going on to ask whether Americans, imitating Louis-Philippe, would change their flag "at the demand of scurril jacobins." In another passage, Cassio strained arguments very hard in order to discredit Lafayette's national guard; he objected to the praise for moderation that had been accorded to the revolutionists of July, 1830, and spoke with contempt of the whole affair. The facts were repressed, he declared, and if there actually was moderation on the first

[218] Appearing in the *New York Mirror*, X (November 17, 1832), p. 157; (October 6, 1832), 109.

day, that was because the weather was hot, and during battle men "are not wont to commit excesses"! After the battle, according to Gould, the national guard did commit them.

Meanwhile, American journals had grown increasingly unfriendly to the novelist rather than friendly, and in that exasperating saucy way which Cooper detested, professing all the time not enmity but kindness. Their deprecatory praise and pealing censure were not invented for use on James Fenimore Cooper. It was an old trick of the journalists to finish off a savage or ironic attack with a bit of affectionate protestation. Thus, James Gordon Bennet asseverated in the *Herald* one day (September 20, 1836) that he had always had a lingering kindness for James Watson Webb and hoped the latter would make money on his last venture—but the wish is the climax of an accusation that Webb was now puffing the National Theatre in his paper instead of the Bowery Theatre because he was printing the National's playbills; and two weeks later Bennet was saying Webb deserved a term at Blackwell's Island (October 4). *Heidenmauer* came out in Philadelphia on September 25, 1832, and here was a new opportunity for reviewers to make cutting remarks and praise their own gentleness.

Friends and Democrats liked the new novel. Dunlap thought it had too little excitement for common readers, but wrote encouragingly, "The grand view you take of the effect of Luther's reformation on Society generally and on individuals of various classes and different educations is great and worthy of yourself."[219] Dunlap contributed a very short review to the Democratic *Evening Post*, introduced by an editorial paragraph approving of Cooper's recent efforts in defense of his country and of Lafayette.[220] This little article

[219] *Correspondence of James Fenimore-Cooper*, I, 299.
[220] October 4, 1832.

is the only good word spoken for the novel by an American reviewer.[221] Cooper did not see this review, as it happened.[222]

The Whig papers had a different tale to tell. Cooper had "become a politician," complained the *New York American*,[223] and wrote to reform abuses in Europe's political systems, not to amuse his readers; the plot of the new novel was simply a drinking bout. Scott had done the Reformation better, much better than Cooper should have expected to do it, said the *Boston Daily Advertiser*, a powerful paper which kept the old party title of National Republican but was embracing Whiggery.[224] The *American Monthly Review* professed itself bored at the obviousness of Cooper's moral and said Cooper ought not to arouse European jealousy by unfavorable comparisons.[225] Boredom also was the complaint of the *New York Mirror*[226] (still freed from Willis), which called the book Cooper's poorest since *Precaution* and complained that *Heidenmauer* obviously imitated Scott's last two tales without securing their interest. So spoke the *New England Magazine* also.[227] They made no attempt to point out Cooper's difference from Scott on the point of principle. I am not

[221] Non-committal advance notices which were conventionally polite had been printed, but these are negligible. See *Evening Post*, February 28, 1832; *Morning Courier and New York Enquirer*, September 26, 1832; *Ladies' Magazine*, V (September, 1832), 428, quoting London *Literary Gazette*.

[222] Letter to William Dunlap, Paris, November 14, 1832. *Diary of William Dunlap*, III, 646.

[223] September 29, 1832.

[224] October 16, 1832.

[225] II (November, 1832), 411-415.

[226] X (October 6, 1832), 107.

[227] III (November, 1832), 423-424. The *New England Magazine* must be remembered as a Whig journal conducted by Park Benjamin; see the *National Cyclopaedia of American Biography*, New York, 1897, VII, 166.

anxious to press a case here, but must record the simple fact that Whig journals differed from the *Evening Post*.[228]

Editors now seemed to take delight in casting reflections upon Cooper in their reviews of other American authors; whereas, in Cooper's more fortunate years, the highest praise to an American fiction writer had been that he approached "the American novelist," the reviewers began to hail new talents as finer than his.[229]

Cooper was not unaware of this treatment nor unsuspicious of a political cause. His editor, Carey, had enforced both points by informing him that the *Journal des Débats* had been influential against him at home. Cooper sent Carey's message on to Dunlap for his friend Morse, simply adding: "He will understand me."

The American Scott was suffering serious losses, though he could report them with a pleasantry: "'faling [*sic*] houses' as you would say in your book, is a symptom not to be mistaken. My booksellers have been cutting me down gradually these four years, and they have lately written me such a letter, as they would not have written to a man, who had a cordial, or even a respectable support from the public." The Cooper household were to return in a year, and the family income was not sufficient to support so many people of their habits in New York. Mrs. Cooper's fortune yielded little, and Cooper's would be "sadly reduced by this abandonment of public favour." Cooper felt that he was being forced into retirement. "Europe, I think would sustain me a while longer but I can not forget that I was born an American gentleman. The idea of becoming a hack writer in a foreign land is not to my humour." He would not feel

[228] There was a moderately favorable review in the *Ladies' Magazine*, V (October, 1832), 475-477.

[229] *New England Magazine*, III (November, 1832), 424; *New York American*, November 10, 1832; *Morning Courier and New York Enquirer*, April 17, 1832. All were Whig.

entirely bitter in this discouragement, for some of his friends had told him that "the mass of the nation" would still support him. He could admit that America had a set of "quasi litterateurs" who did not really reflect national opinion; "but then," he said, "these men are in possession of all the reviews, do all the talking, and give the ostensible tone to all things, and it is too much for me to put these men down." What he really suspected was that Carey and Morse were right about foreign influence, for he said sadly, "I think there has been foul play and that the truth will one day be known."[230]

Cooper wrote to another friend of his during this summer, telling him of these suspicions of foul play. The friend was Peter Augustus Jay, one of that family of staunch Federalists who had turned Whig when Cooper turned Democrat. Jay was always free to differ from Cooper's political opinions, and he wrote on everything as a liberal Whig would write. When Cooper told him his anxiety over the Cassio affair, Jay answered like a true friend and a Whig: "You hate aristocrats and therefore should not complain that they hate you. Your publications are intended to do them harm, and their writers attempt to injure you." Apparently Cooper was not accustomed to excitement over reviews, for Jay said in surprise, "I did not think you were so thin skinned."[231] Being in America instead of France, perhaps Jay did not understand the intensity of Cooper's fears. Cooper's countrymen honored him, he said.

"You hate aristocrats and . . . they hate you." This Whig preachment could have been no solace to a Democrat who thought there should be no aristocrats—that is, of the political kind—in America.

In this discontented autumn of 1832, Morse wrote Cooper a letter in which he followed a course of inconsistency com-

[230] Letter to William Dunlap, Paris, November 14, 1832, *Diary of William Dunlap*, III, 646.

[231] *Correspondence of James Fenimore-Cooper*, I, 295.

mon among friends; he told Cooper to look at a newspaper article called "Something Strange" because he himself had just thrown the paper down in disgust.[232] "Something Strange" is in the *Commercial Advertiser* of September 8. Livingston had begun to collect statistics on American taxation, to assist Cooper's side of the finance controversy. But as the *Commercial Advertiser* was accustomed to screaming its Whig animosities at every activity of Jackson's government, it denounced this procedure as an imposition on the voters calculated to make them suppose that "measures were in train greatly to alleviate their imaginary burthens, and perhaps to put money in their pockets." As a little gratuitous fine writing, there was added this Whig compliment: "A firm belief in the thorough corruptibility and want of intelligence in the mass of the people . . . is entertained and acted upon by Mr. Van Buren and his kindred spirits." After this came a series of flourishes as to whether Whigs or Democrats were the upholders of tyranny, with a typical Whig sneer at King Andrew's meddling in local affairs:

> The Editor of the Portland Daily Courier, as a sort of Jackson paper, says: 'We guess the Yankees will hardly take a King yet, let them come ever so cheap.' . . . But if the 'request' comes from the President . . . we should suppose that the Legislature and people of Maine would think it an impertinence; and would rap their governor over the knuckles, for prosecuting inquiries with which the National Executive as such, has no business.

And what has all this to do with Cooper, except that it concerns the finance controversy? Why, it is an article about Cooper himself; at least, it opens with the statement that "It is well known that a controversy had been carried on, in which our countryman, Cooper, has borne a conspicuous part, as to the relative amount of taxation in France and in the United

[232] *Ibid.*, I, 298. The paper is referred to as *Commercial Advocate*, but the article was printed in the *Commercial Advertiser*.

States." Between this opening and the abuse which follows there is no protecting barrier for Cooper; if the novelist was not directly called a mean politician, he was certainly associated, in "Something Strange," with mean politics.

Most men are shocked at having their best motives and their deepest trusts maligned. If they are shocked, they may speak or keep silent. The only steps Cooper took were to urge that Livingston discontinue his efforts, because he saw that they would do more harm than good; the French figures did not include local expenditures, and to offer in comparison the total of American expenses would be unfair and misleading. He explained this in an American journal.[233]

The editor of the *Commercial Advertiser* was William L. Stone, an old acquaintance of Cooper's, now a political enemy. An article in his paper on May 9, 1836, praising Louis Philippe for having done all in his power to bring about indemnity payments, is a key to his attitude towards that matter. Had he centered his ambition upon stinging Cooper until he drew a retort? On February 1, 1833, he achieved this end. Here he set forth two foreign comments on Cooper's republicanism. To both excerpts he added his own comment, endorsing the unfavorable one and denying the favorable. The first was a review of *Heidenmauer* which complained that Cooper had "constituted himself . . . the literary antagonist of the monarchy, aristocracy, and feudality of all Europe, and particularly of England." Of this the editor said that the treatment of Cooper was severe but probably pleasing to the novelist, since he had announced in his preface that he preferred the censure of the newspaper press to its praise. (The last statement is a malicious misreading of Cooper, in particular of Cooper's use of the word "vulgar" as meaning common.)[234] The second excerpt was

[233] Philadelphia *National Gazette*, December 5, 1832, cited by R. E. Spiller, *James Fenimore Cooper, Critic of His Times*, p. 172.

[234] *A Letter to His Countrymen*, pp. 48-49.

an article lamenting the attacks which English Tories and French *juste milieu* had been directing at all things American merely from detestation of the word "Republic." Referring to the failure of these parties "to deny that the Americans are well and cheaply governed," it gives Cooper commendation for his recent victory. To this French praise the American editor answered: "even the government-party in France would have no inclination to attack us, if Americans abroad had pursued the same reserve in politics which we enforce upon Europeans here."

At last Cooper was stirred to fight; and be it noted that he was stirred by editorial remarks which contained no aspersions upon his literary abilities. He simply would not allow what he considered real national treachery to go unrebuked. It must be remembered that the finance controversy was by no means closed, and such behavior as the *Commercial Advertiser's* was damaging to our interests in the indemnity claims. Early in the year, too, Leavitt Harris of obnoxious conduct had actually been appointed our representative in France to succeed W. C. Rives. Morse wrote on February 28 to break the news. "Now Mr. Cooper don't swear," he said, "nor breathe hard words, at what I am going to tell you"; Harris's appointment was then before the Senate, Morse could not believe that it would be confirmed if the Senate knew the facts, he had written to his Senator, Rives was in the Senate, and Morse had heard him speak contemptuously of Harris and warmly of Cooper—but Morse was miserable:

Come home in the Spring, do. You shall not stay in Paris, if Harris is the representative of our country; if you do, I shall despair of ever seeing a smile on your face again; I would not answer for myself in such circumstances, I assure you. My dear Sir, you are wanted at home; I want you, to encourage me by your presence. I find the Pioneer business has less of romance in the reality than in the description, and I find some tough stumps to pry up, and heavy stones to roll out of the way, and I get exhausted and desponding, and I should like a little of your sinew to come to my aid at such times, as it was wont to come at the Louvre.[235]

Morse wanted Cooper's encouragement, failing America's. But so did Lafayette. He wrote to Cooper mournfully in April about Harris's arrival in France, and about the attempts of the government to blame him for the failure of the very treaty on indemnity that he had been working for.[236] The old warrior-statesman was too loyal to America, however, to discontinue his efforts on behalf of the indemnity treaty, for which he was even then endeavoring to procure a favorable hearing in the Chamber. Nor was he deserted by his friend Cooper, however annoyed the latter might have been over the Harris episode. Cooper was concerned for his country, and Morse and Lafayette looked to him for steadying support.[237]

A part of this support was his acceding to Morse's pleas, at last, and rebuking the American papers for the trouble they were making. Morse had reported more detective work on Cassio,[238] and he was determined to get some statement from Cooper. But the letter which Cooper now sent to him for publication said comparatively little about the *Bravo* affair. It was not a letter of personal defense. Cassio's old letter was referred to as an example of foreign influence upon our press, with a summary of the evidence. But the single important argument of the letter was that the nation did not understand the conduct of its own agents in the finance dis-

[235] *Correspondence of James Fenimore-Cooper*, I, 310-311.

[236] *Ibid.*, I, 315.

[237] Letter, Mrs. Cooper to her sister Martha, Paris, April 20. Unpublished. Cooper collection, Yale.

[238] Letter to Cooper, New York, February 21, 1833, Passage unpublished by Edward L. Morse, *Samuel F. B. Morse, His Letters and Journals*, New York, 1914, II, 21 ff., but present in typewritten copy of the original, Library of Congress.

pute, and it centered in what Cooper called the Jesuitism of Stone's attaching the note that he did to the congratulatory French article on that debate. With a pitiful kind of dogged loyalty, Cooper insisted that "Nothing but publicity is needed to extort the corrective" from America. He closed with a paragraph pleading with Americans not to tolerate longer a slavish dependence on foreign opinion.

Lounsbury wrote of this letter that it was the commencement of a line of conduct "which it is charity to call blundering." Let us say, rather, that Cooper's honest letter drew a line of retorts which it would be blundering to call charitable. In itself, his unfortunate writing was an ordinary act enough.

Morse now had his opportunity to show what he could do in the way of friendship. He not only sent Cooper's letter to the Albany *Daily Advertiser*, but he wrote a long and wonderful introduction to it, reviewing Cooper's connections with the finance controversy, explaining why the Doctrinaires hated him and Lafayette loved him, and complaining of the politics and spleen of the *New York American* and the *Commercial Advertiser*. He said that to undermine Cooper's reputation at home, by concealing "malignancy under the cover of ordinary literary criticism," would be the Doctrinaires' best triumph. The New York *Evening Post* copied all this in two columns on June 28, 1833.

The Whig papers gathered their forces, and even before Cooper's letter was printed in New York City they attacked it. James Watson Webb's *Morning Courier and New York Enquirer* led off on June 15. This newspaper was a leopard with frequently changing spots. On January 17, 1832, the editor had advertised: "In its politics, the Courier and Enquirer is purely Democratic—adhering to the principles and usages of the Republican Party, and advocating the reelection of General Jackson to the Presidency." The paper had earlier been strongly opposed to the Bank, but about this time began to favor it. This was inconsistent with Democracy, but it seems Noah and Webb had borrowed heavily of the Bank.[239] On August 23, 1832, the paper gave up its equivocal position by printing a long letter to the public renouncing Jackson and cleaving to the Bank. By 1834, the paper was thoroughly and avowedly Whig. Now, on August 31, 1832, this paper had complimented Cooper in its condescending way, lauding him for having, like Irving, advanced our position abroad, and crediting him with a novel which was one of the "*avant couriers* of liberty and political revolution." Moreover, it prophesied an attack upon *The Bravo* from "a literary party in Europe entirely connected with the old principles of despotism." Probably Cooper never saw this Democratic mention of him. He did see the article of June 15, 1833, written after the paper had turned Whig, and he later took the trouble to show that it was not "written with sufficient attention to the facts of the case."

Nor was it so written. It whined that Cooper had publicly reproached the press of America for not having sustained him against the Doctrinaires, when he had set the press at defiance (a silly statement referring to Cooper's remark that fame conferred by the press is uncertain). It insinuated that he had been most hurt by Cassio's letter (a patent untruth), and asserted that this letter had really been published before Cooper's foreign controversy had occurred (a flat falsehood). It said that Cooper had done his duty in that controversy, and no one disputed the fact (a piece of smug ingratitude). Its finale was an insult:

> Assuredly Mr. Cooper has nothing to complain of . . . . Let him compare his situation with that of Homer, Milton, Dryden, Otway, Fielding, Le Sage, Cervantes—the inimitable Cervantes!—the immortal labours of whose whole lives were insufficient to keep the wolf from the door. Let him remember the fate of these illustrious writers, and thank God for all his mercies.

[239] Notice the issue of May 3, 1832. An account of the loans is given by James Melvin Lee, *op. cit.*, pp. 157-159.

Magnificent effrontery, coming from one who had it in his power to alleviate an author's troubles. So a man ought to thank God that people who enjoyed his books paid for them! And how much the more insulting that this should have been said to a man who had lost severely and yet had not complained publicly concerning his losses either in profits or in popularity. Cooper had made a political point, and James Watson Webb had managed to evade it completely. A politician is, indeed, a quilted anvil. This article, rather than Cooper's letter, gives the impression that Cooper was a hypersensitive fool.

Of course, the *New York American* enjoyed the fun, and let Cassio return to make a sarcastic defense of himself. He said that in reading *The Bravo* he had "never for one moment *suspected* his [Cooper's] heroic purpose, nor his ability to accomplish it." With italics he begged Cooper not to subvert all the kingdoms of Europe too suddenly with his goose quill: "the overthrow . . . had better happen 'by degrees.'" To this voluntary disclaimer by Cassio of all intelligence as a reader, the editor added an accusation that Cooper had seen fit "to flout his Americanism in the face of foreigners . . . whose hospitalities . . . he may be partaking," and offered Cassio's exemplary conduct abroad as an admirable contrast; we may note that a sentence from Morse is quoted and ridiculed as if it had been Cooper's. With no particular connection, unless it might be the hidden political one, he added that he would never think of putting Cooper's novels on a level with Scott's.[240]

Morse returned to the fray with passionate gallantry, approved by William Cullen Bryant's statement that after the *American's* "gratuitous and ill-natured personal allusions, this warmth will be no cause of surprise."[241]

I have also known Mr. Cooper in his social and domestic character for more than a year in Paris. Is it necessary for

[240] June 24, 1833.
[241] *Evening Post*, June 28, 1833.

me to repeat to Americans what hundreds and thousands of his countrymen will attest, that no citizen of the United States more nobly sustains the character of his country, by hospitality and benevolence, and liberality. Need I say that no American name whatever, is more universally known and respected. Need I inform my countrymen that Mr. Cooper maintains too, among the highest aristocratic classes, who seek his acquaintance, the distinctive principles of his country unflinchingly, or, as the editor prettily expresses it, 'he flounts his *Americanism*;' that is, he is not ashamed of his *Americanism*, unless it may be the *New York Americanism*, 'in the faces of foreigners in whose land he may be sojourning, and of whose hospitalities and kindnesses he partakes;' aye, and whose kindnesses and hospitalities he repays too in kind and with interest, and in whose respect he holds a higher place for this very independence than is held, or can be held, by any doughface of the school of the American that ever crossed the water. Hence the supercilious flings at Cooper's *Americanism*; hence the taunt, '*tant pis*, for Europe.'

Morse attributed the attacks on Cooper to a combination of politics and jealousy, and in his conclusion, reminding his readers that the subject of the whole quarrel was political, not personal, he besought the editor of the *New York American* "for his own sake, if he cannot for his country's sake, to forbear expressing a maudlin opinion upon Cooper or Scott; the great moral and political bearing of their writings is infinitely beyond the grasp of his mind." Some of Morse's phrases had been quoted by the *New York American's* last article, and in this second defense Morse furnished others which were now bandied about among the Whig columns; it was his outpourings, rather than Cooper's statement, which invited this sort of thing.

The *Morning Courier and New York Enquirer* now advanced, preening itself.[242] It urged the point that Cooper had shown "a degree of morbid sensibility in making such ado about a criticism, which, severe and well written as it

[242] July 4, 1833.

was, could have done him little injury, had it not combined a good deal of justice with its severity." Cooper's case was now hopeless, and remained hopeless for a century. He had done nothing that indicates he was morbidly sensitive, he had never complained of Cassio's criticism as severe, and yet from now on who would believe it? As for Cassio's article having been severe, well-written, or dignified by the least shred of truth, that statement is malicious though absurd.

Stone spoke next for the *Commercial Advertiser*.[243] He assumed the tone of lofty nobility that men adopt when, having committed an injury and having been roundly answered for it, they draw themselves up and say, "What! Can you not rise above quarreling?" The most astonishing thing about the editorial is that Stone could admit his motive in attacking Cooper to be "squaring accounts, in behalf of the corps editorial" for Cooper's remark in the preface of *Heidenmauer* that newspaper glory was transitory, and yet could give the impression that it was Cooper that was "much too sensitive to criticism." He said Americans regretted, and he with them, that Cooper had left the American scene which had been the best inspiration of his work, and that our American author had mingled "in the strife of politics—volunteering his services as a sort of Republican Propagandist in Europe, when no possible good was to result from such a course either to himself or others." He sent his final shafts home by pulling the old bow of preferring Toryism and the amiable, never controversial Walter Scott its prophet; the papers seemed to have learned that this manner of ignoring Cooper's republicanism was the most painful one to him.

Cooper sent not a word from France to all this talk of his sensitiveness, but poor loyal Morse nearly went frantic in a third letter which was printed in the *Evening Post* on July 20 with another word of sympathy from Bryant. He had just written Cooper on July 16 that he had seen Stone, who was

[243] July 17, 1833.

really better disposed than the "*hollow hearted*" King and who was going to explain in his paper that day. Morse had just spent the Fourth of July "at Mr. Jay's at Rye in the old mansion," and that good friend and Whig had advised him to use silent contempt.[244] But now the promised well-disposed explanation had become Stone's article of July 17. Morse felt called upon to answer Stone on July 20 by briefly reviewing the *Commercial Advertiser's* self-defense point by point, hinting that the paper aimed at persuading Cooper not to meddle in political strife or, like Scott, to take the Tory side. He showed that nothing the editor had said could "avail one jot in freeing him from the charge of *having ungenerously wounded the feelings of an absent countryman, by circulating the prejudiced statements of foreign enemies against him, at the very moment, too, when that countryman was sacrificing much in* defence of his country's Institutions." At the same time, he aimed at combatting the false allegation of Cooper's sensitiveness. Perhaps it is only Cooper's due that we read Morse on that subject.

That Mr. Cooper's feelings have been wounded, is admitted: but what feeling? It is that which none but the noblest natures possess or can duly appreciate. It is that strong love of country . . . which a residence abroad usually increases, and especially in a heart like his—a love which prompts a man, in defiance of all selfish considerations, to step forward to the defense of that country. . . . That men . . . should be desirous of diverting from themselves the frown of a generous indignation is not surprising; nor is it to be wondered at that having goaded Mr. Cooper to complain . . . they should wish to make it believed that his *feeling* was the wounded pride of authorship. But is this right? Will there not be some in the community who will detect their artifice. . . .?

Can not we detect it?

[244] Letter, S. F. B. Morse to Cooper, New York, July 16, 1833. Unpublished. Typewritten copy. Library of Congress.

Few shots were fired after this. The *New York American* printed something on December 3 which purported to be a translation of Cassio's alleged source in the *Journal des Débats*. There is no verbal resemblance, but both articles found fault with the same weaknesses in *The Bravo*. One can see how Americans who had suffered much injustice in France might have supposed that Cassio had learned to think in Paris.[245] On July 25, Morse wrote Cooper that his last letter in the *Evening Post* had sunk the enemy, or at least everyone said so. But he was buzzing with excitement about various aristocrats he had discovered.[246] On August 9, he considered that the controversy was at an end and that "The attempt to make the impression . . . that you were mortified at the literary criticism of your works has entirely failed."[247]

Would that this attempt had really failed.

Meanwhile, the exchange of hostilities had naturally influenced other periodicals, and unfavorable reviews increased. The *New York Mirror* found itself in a peculiar position. One editor, N. P. Willis, was in France sending home praise for the lively interest of *The Bravo* and encomiums on Cooper's republicanism:[248]

And speaking of Mr. Cooper, no one who loves or owns a pride in his native land, can live abroad without feeling every day what we owe to the patriotism, as well as the genius of this gifted man. If there is an individual who loves the soil that gave him birth, and so shows it that we are more respected for it, it is he. Mr. Cooper's position is a high one; he has great advantages, and he improves them to the uttermost. His benevolence and activity in all enterprises for the relief of suffering, give him influence, and he employs it

[245] Cooper sent a short paragraph to the Philadelphia *National Gazette* saying he would soon clear up the whole controversy, and the *New York American* copied this with a retort, December 7.

[246] Letter to Cooper, New York, July 25, 1833. Unpublished. Cooper collection, Yale.

[247] *Correspondence of James Fenimore-Cooper*, I, 319-320.

[248] X (February 2, 1833), 244.

like a true philanthropist and a real lover of his country. I say this particularly . . . because Americans abroad, are *not* always *national*. I am often mortified by reproaches from foreigners, quoting admissions made by my countrymen, which should be the last on their lips. A very distinguished person told me a day or two since, that 'The Americans abroad were the worst enemies we had in Europe.' It is difficult to conceive at home how such a remark stings. Proportionately, one takes a true patriot to his heart, and I feel it right to say here, that the love of country and active benevolence of Mr. Cooper, distinguish him abroad, even more than his genius. His house is one of the most hospitable and agreeable in Paris; and with Morse and the circle of artists and men of distinction and worth about him, he is an acquaintance sincerely to regret leaving.[249]

Then the other editor, G. P. Morris, would contradict all this by saying the paper begged to be excused from commending "the poor 'Bravo,'" or belligerently asserting that he did not admit Cooper had suffered unjust strictures of the press, as a correspondent had said, and that he "marveled at their moderation and infrequency."[250]

In such a year Cooper took it into his head to return home.

Two months before he was set ashore in New York, the newspapers announced that he had engaged passage. The announcement was a bare statement of the fact,[251] meagre indeed in contrast to the outbreak of elaborate journalism which had heralded Irving's return. On November 7, the Whig papers which had given full page accounts to Irving's arrival simply printed notices that Cooper had landed. The *Morning Courier and New York Enquirer* had more to say: a statement that the event should not pass unnoticed, and a reference to the late unpleasantness by which it put Cooper in the wrong while pretending a noble tolerance and loyalty on its own part.

[249] N. P. Willis, "Letters from Paris," Number 21, *New York Mirror*, X (July 7, 1832), 4.

[250] X (February 16, 1833), 262.

[251] *E.g., Morning Courier and New York Enquirer*, September 2, 1833.

Cooper has not recorded his thoughts upon this. It is certain that when he left France he loved America. But Mrs. Cooper had misgivings on one point. She feared her husband might be treated with injustice. What this injustice would consist of is not perfectly clear, and it may be that she had in mind accusations of weakened patriotism.

> If you knew how I felt, when the moment is before me, in idea, when I shall again put my foot on our own Shores—you would smile with contempt on all the Stories you hear of our remaining abroad—be assured my dear Sisters, that nothing could induce us to remain—I am indifferent as to what others say or think on this subject; but I *will not* have *you* distrust us—or do us this vile injustice—and do not be uneasy lest we should be disgusted on our return. I know what my Country is, and I know what we are, and trust me when I say we shall be happier there than in any other on earth—there is but one point on which I have misgivings—You have seen enough of this world, to have percieved [*sic*] —there is a spirit among men that makes them misinterpret, misrepresent, quick to blame, and slow to do justice. Mr. Cooper you well know feels deeply and speaks promptly—and should he meet with injustice from his Countrymen—whom he has supported with so much ardour and so much ability abroad—his feelings will I know burst forth.[252]

His feelings did not burst forth on November 7, at any rate. When a number of his old friends invited him to a public dinner in his honor, he replied graciously thanking them for their kind feelings which prompted the invitation, and expressing "particular satisfaction in learning that so respectable a portion of my fellow-citizens approve of my course, in reference to our common character and national institutions. . . ." Regret was expressed, at the time, that Cooper had not accepted,[253] and there has been a tendency,

[252] Letter to Martha [de Lancey], Paris, August 29, 1831. Unpublished. Cooper collection, Yale.

[253] For both invitation and reply, see *New York Mirror,* XI (November 30, 1833), 175. For expression of regret, see *ibid.*, XI (December 7, 1833), 183.

since then, to make a mystery of Cooper's action. I see no reason why we should not take the plausible excuse of illness, especially since we know Cooper suffered from a fever which beset him in crowded gatherings and made him so ill for twenty-four hours afterwards that in Paris he had had to forego attendance at large functions.[254] Mrs. Cooper wrote that an illness prevented his going as soon as he wished to Cooperstown. Cooper gave a "short but severe indisposition" as the cause of his declining, and Cooper was not the person to hide some matter of principle under a social fib.

There seems to have been no bitterness in the Cooper household. Mrs. Cooper wrote about the family's happy feelings upon their return, and of the kindness they had received from many friends, in spite of some individuals who regarded them as "some sort of foreign wild beasts."[255] The country struck Cooper pleasantly, and he was firm in his belief that "the heart of the nation" was sound, though he had been criticized on his first appearance in society by a young nobody.[256]

Poverty enforced Cooper's retirement to Cooperstown[257] and in the following years kept the family there. "The girls can not go to New York to visit you because their father can not afford to outfit them. Do not think hard thoughts of him. He has many people to assist and would find the money if he could." Thus Mrs. Cooper was to write one day.[258]

But perhaps if the Coopers had remained in New York

[254] Mrs. Cooper to Mrs. Pomeroy, New York, December 27, [1833]; Mrs. Cooper to Martha and Caroline De Lancey, Paris, November 29, 1830. Unpublished. Cooper collection, Yale.

[255] Letter to Mrs. Pomeroy quoted above.

[256] *Correspondence of James Fenimore-Cooper*, I, 329; 342-343; 328.

[257] *Correspondence of James Fenimore-Cooper*, *passim*, and letter, Mrs. Cooper to Mrs. Pomeroy, New York, December 27, 1833. Unpublished. Cooper collection, Yale.

[258] Mrs. Cooper to her sister, Cooperstown, March 13 [n.d.]. Unpublished. Cooper collection, Yale.

they would have found life even more difficult. No Americans seem to have been pleased with their native country in those days after sojourning abroad. Cooper had been warned not only by Carey but by Morse, who said, "The only way I can keep up my spirits is by resolutely resisting all disposition to repine, and by fighting perseveringly against all the obstacles that hinder the progress of art. . . . You will certainly have the blues when you first arrive, but the longer you stay abroad the more severe will be the disease. Excuse my predictions. . . ."[259] Carey had described to Cooper Irving's disgust,[260] and Bryant had been ostracized. Indeed, life in New York was especially disagreeable for Democrats; for, as Bryant's son-in-law said, "The more opulent and cultivated classes of the city were 'Whigs,' who detested Democrats as agrarians and levellers. Even the most charitable among them found it difficult to understand how a gentleman of education and refinement, impelled by no craving for office or leadership, would take the side of an unkempt and unwashed multitude. . . ."[261]

On the whole, Cooper seems, in comparison with his peers, to have been quite amiably inclined towards his fatherland.

The heart of the nation was sound. Who cared for a few erratic pulse beats from some Whig journals and flippant society men? Cooper felt himself at home in his own country, and he liked it. Irving did not like America. But Cooper liked it and basked in it. Meanwhile, with complete irrelevance to the facts, America began to weave about this man the myth of the self-centered, hypersensitive pretender to Scott's laurels.

[259] S. F. B. Morse to Cooper, New York, February 21, 1833, E. L. Morse, *op. cit.*, II, 23.

[260] *Correspondence of James Fenimore-Cooper*, I, 263.

[261] Parke Godwin, *op. cit.*, I, 336.

CHAPTER V

Who Mr. Effingham Really Was

"IF Cooper had gone to that welcoming dinner," his biographers are wont to say—and then we are all tempted to pursue this subjunctive with conjectures of the better life that might have followed. If Cooper had gone to the welcoming dinner, I prefer to ask, and if we had been there, too, what manner of man should we have seen as the guest of honor?

One thing is certain; his appearance would have been distinguished, his manner and expression spirited, and his gray eyes very clear and very bright. All the accounts concur in this description. Even in 1838, when the myth has it that Cooper's disposition had been ruined, it was said that "His manners are perhaps somewhat reserved, but his address is courteous and pleasing."[262] One twentieth century critic of the American novelists has declared that Cooper's familiar portrait is in accord with the "written description" of the man: "his eye was deep, slow in moving and not very bright, and his heavy features, in repose almost stolid, suggested a peasant ancestry." I have found no such "written description." I have, however, seen the vast difference between the genial and interested face shown in the original of the Brady portrait and the lifeless reproduction of it which Lounsbury's biography has unfortunately made the familiar picture. Now that Mr. Boynton has given better circulation to the fine study by Jarvis, an American can have a spirited painting in his mind's eye which really does accord with the descriptions. The *New York Mirror* said of Jarvis's paint-

[262] *E.g.*, Isaac N. Arnold, *A Centennial Offering*, p. 205; Elihu Phinney, *op. cit.*, pp. 22-23; J. W. Francis, "Reminiscences of Cooper," *Memorial of James Fenimore Cooper*, p. 102; S. T. Livermore, *op. cit.*, pp. 218-219; *Southern Literary Messenger*, IV (June, 1838), 378.

ing when it was exhibited at the American Academy of Fine Arts in 1828 that it was "a faithful likeness and an excellent painting."[263] And the descriptions show that the pleasing fire was still in Cooper's face years later at Cooperstown.

If Cooper had revealed at that dinner the characteristic best known to his friends, it would have been his humor. A really dominating trait in him was a "relish of the comical and ludicrous." He laughed hard, and when he read something that amused him, the tears rolled. He boasted, "I very well know what fun is."[264]

The youth who is said to have touched off gunpowder in the lock of a schoolmate's room for a practical joke grew up into a church warden who enjoyed passing the collection plate to friends who happened not to have brought any money. That is a story of the days at Cooperstown, after he had returned from Europe. Spying in his Episcopal church two luckless Presbyterians, he marched to their pew door, "straightened himself to his full height and stood motionless awaiting contributions—which did not come." Then he stooped and whispered close "with a mischievous smile: 'Can't you give us a *little*?' "[265] A carpenter who had worked for Cooper in those years at the Hall narrated expressly for an example of his kindliness the tale that once when the author had been vainly endeavoring to compose in the midst of terrific hammerings, he threw his spoiled manuscript into the fire and remarked, "It is a pretty place to write a novel in a carpenter's shop, and if you don't look sharp I shall have *you* in one."[266] This sort of humor, to be felt as kindly, has to be accompanied by an infectious geniality in the speaker, and Cooper's evidently was.

[263] V (May 31, 1828), 374.

[264] Susan F. Cooper, *Pages and Pictures*, p. 274; *Correspondence of James Fenimore-Cooper*, I, 304.

[265] Elihu Phinney, *Reminiscences of the Village of Cooperstown*, Cooperstown, 1891, p. 24.

[266] S. T. Livermore, *op. cit.*, p. 206.

Cooper always wrote well when he was describing a comic physical predicament like an unskilled épicier attempting to propel a punt or an old woman in a chapel taking him for a ghost. No mixture of malice added to his pleasure; the frightened old woman had her nerves quieted by a piece of money. He relished the tale of his own father's having carried off a remonstrating Frenchman to a frontier merry-making, only to discover at the party that the enforced guest had no shirt under his coat.[267]

Cooper's friends paid him the compliment of repeating his stories, and all that they borrowed were pieces of broad humor.[268]

Since Cooper's humor was of this practical and ironic nature, it is not surprising that when he wrote an article as he said to give a little fun, it turned out to be a satire.[269] We need not wonder that touchy journalists could not fathom his laughing prefaces; and of course the book which was intended to be his chief humorous work, *The Monikins*,[270] was supposed by the unimaginative to be ill-natured. But it is strange that Lounsbury, at least, did not know Cooper better than to say his humor was grim and of the kind "that gleams in fitful flashes from the men of earnest purposes and serious lives, and gives a momentary relief to the stern-

[267] *France*, II, 94-96; *Correspondence of James Fenimore-Cooper*, I, 280; Journal, August 15, 1832. Unpublished. Cooper collection, Yale; G. P. Keese, "James Fenimore Cooper," *Harper's Weekly*, XV (July 29, 1871, Supplement), 707.

[268] Charles Mathews, letter to Mrs. Mathews, New York, April 30, 1823, in Anne Mathews, *Memoirs of Charles Mathews, Comedian*, London, 1839, III, 405, tells a story in connection with a trip he took with Cooper (p. 403). For other stories see William Dunlap, *History of the Rise and Progress of the Arts of Design in the United States*, Boston, 1918, I, 349; J. G. Wilson, *Bryant and His Friends*, p. 240; Elihu Phinney, *op. cit.*, pp. 23-24.

[269] *Correspondence of James Fenimore-Cooper*, I, 304. The article was evidently "*Point de Bateaux a Vapeur. Une Vision.*"

[270] Susan F. Cooper, *Pages and Pictures*, pp. 27 ff.

ness and melancholy of their natures."[271] How unfounded a remark that was! Cooper's letters, even in 1832, certainly reveal anything but a stern and melancholy nature; an active and cheerful nature, rather (with many courageous references to his own illness, too, which have been deleted for some unaccountable reason from the published correspondence). It was doubtless the success of the press in its campaign against Cooper's dignity which affected Lounsbury's backward-looking judgment in 1883.

For the writings of people who were actually acquainted with Cooper are full of anecdotes of his geniality. People now are beginning to admit that he must have been a pleasant companion before he left New York. The gentleman who was reputed to be the city's most noted conversationalist[272] admired his talents in conversation, especially his power of "accommodating his conversation and manners with the most marvelous facility" to all sorts of people, high and low.[273] One of the severest tests of Cooper's gaiety must have been his trip up the Hudson with Charles Mathews, the English actor. Mathews so loathed the United States that he "actually came to rehearsal with his nose stopped with cotton, to prevent his smelling 'the d—— American mutton chops!' "[274] The optimistic Cooper prescribed an excursion up the Hudson to convert him. Mathews accepted, but he was offended "by both the matter and manner" of the only meal, and when night revealed that all the men passengers must sleep in one cabin, his "feelings revolted, and he protested against taking rest on such terms." Cooper saved the night. He roused Dunlap from his mattress on the floor; he hunted up the agreeable Dr. Francis; he got permission

[271] *Op. cit.*, pp. 119, 239.

[272] *National Cyclopaedia of American Biography*, New York, 1898, I, 393.

[273] J. W. Francis, "Reminiscences of Cooper," *Memorial of James Fenimore Cooper*, p. 95.

[274] Joe Cowell, *op. cit.*, Part II, 62.

to use the captain's cabin; he ordered the right kind of supper and enough whiskey punch to last to dawn. Mathews, conciliated, happily drank and exchanged stories and actually wrote home to his wife that he had taken the trip, even confessing, "most amply was I gratified."[275]

Cooper's spontaneous sympathy drew men out. S. G. Goodrich one time found the poet James Gates Percival stranded in New York penniless and bewildered. Goodrich at once thought of Cooper as the person who would give help, and he got the two together at dinner. The men were totally unlike. Beside the emaciated Percival, abashed and whispering, Cooper sat "in person solid, robust, athletic; in voice, manly; in manner, earnest, emphatic, almost dictatorial—with something of self-assertion, bordering on egotism. The first effect was unpleasant, indeed repulsive, but there shone through all this a heartiness, a frankness, which excited confidence, respect, and at last affection." Even Percival felt this goodness. While Cooper waited and "took his wine as if his lip appreciated it," Percival began to talk and at length poured out his mind "as from a cornucopia." Then did "Cooper's gray eye dilate with delight."[276] And Cooper got along just as well with the real notables of the Bread and Cheese Club, who appear to have had a true affection for him. Mr. H. W. Boynton has described these associations so well that the gaiety of those days needs no enforcing here.

But what was Cooper like after he sailed, and when he came home again in 1834? Such an active and cheerful man could hardly have changed to the grim home-comer we are told that he became. Even biliousness would scarcely work a complete transformation. The truth is that there is no historical basis for any belief that he changed greatly. If we make an album of the remarks descriptive of Cooper recorded

[275] J. W. Francis, *op. cit.*, pp. 100-101; William Dunlap, *History of the American Theatre*, New York, 1832, p. 384; Anne Mathews, *op. cit.*, III, 403.

[276] S. G. Goodrich, *Recollections of a Lifetime*, New York, 1857, II, 134-135. Goodrich, or "Peter Parley," was editor of the Boston *Token* from 1828 to 1843 and is noted for the encouragement he gave to Hawthorne.

during the early eighteen thirties, we can have something with which to test the truth of Editor Stone's, Editor Webb's sneers; and it will show us that the adverse criticisms made during this period come from people who did not know him. His friends admitted that people who were not acquainted with him supposed him to be cold and dogmatic; but they insisted that persons who were acquainted with him expressed loving admiration, even when they were persons who met Cooper for the first time during these years of his supposed morbidity. Moreover, they speak of the magnetism he exerted upon a first encounter.[277] The most naive of these tributes comes from Alvan Stewart, written while he was three years younger than Cooper's youngest daughter, before he became something of a figure in New York politics. Stewart was in Paris, making a youth's "regular attack upon the Magazine of all that is Splendid in Art." He met Cooper at a Fourth of July dinner where Cooper presided amidst toasting and cheering for the liberty of the Poles. Cooper invited the young man to breakfast, and next morning Stewart was impressed by the sumptuousness of the life he saw. After breakfast, in the garden, he "was made very happy by this most learned author and great traveller" until half past one. There was another breakfast on July 9, when Cooper invited him to drive to Versailles, "which I consider very kind in Mr. Cooper. As I was coming away I was most affectionately requested to come and Spend Monday Evening with them. This is the man whom the Americans in Paris call haughty distant, proud, and with whom they cannot get acquainted. . . . " On the twelfth, Cooper gave the young American "a most interesting day;" he got him into "a Superb carriage with elegant horses and a genteel driver,"

[277] George Washington Greene, "James Fenimore Cooper," *New York Quarterly*, I (June, 1852), 216-217; Alvan Stewart, diary, July 5, 9, 12, and 13. Unpublished. New York Historical Society; Southern Literary Messenger, IV (June, 1838), 378; S. M. Shaw, *op. cit.*, p. 206; H. T. Tuckerman, *North American Review*, LXXXIX (October, 1859), p. 304; W. C. Bryant, *op. cit.*, pp. 69-70; Lewis Gaylord Clark, "James Fenimore Cooper," *Lippincott's Magazine*, VIII (December, 1871), pp. 625-629.

and "hastened away . . . to the gorgeous Palaces of Versailles costing $200,000,000."

Perhaps Cooper was so charmingly hospitable in the hopes of making a disciple. But, as N. P. Willis put the case, "His private friends are singularly devoted to him, and there are few men of whom you may hear more excessive praise, or more extreme censure." The censure must have come from persons who were not "private friends." Willis's full description is as follows:

> Mr. Cooper is now, perhaps, forty-five or fifty. He is in the full vigor of his powers, and we may still expect from him many additions to our own pleasure, and his own fame. He is very striking in his personal appearance—of a cold, military address—a severe eye, of a peculiarly light grey—a commanding head, and an expression of decision about his mouth, amounting at times to austerity. It is this unconciliating, and easily-mistaken, manner and look, probably, which has prejudiced against him all who have not had the opportunity of knowing him more intimately.

This was printed in 1835,[278] when Cooper's enemies of the American press were stirring against him. How Willis sided in that struggle is clear enough; he said on the same page that although the press did not represent all American opinion, Americans did not deserve to have Cooper when they allowed him to be so mistreated. Willis had printed, in 1832, a statement explicitly approving of Cooper's conduct in the finance controversy and corroborating his opinion that Americans in Europe did not support their country as they ought:

> He [Lafayette] called upon me a day or two ago, to leave with me some copies of a translation of Mr. Cooper's letter on the finances of our government, to be sent to my friend Dr. Howe; but, to my regret, I did not see him. He neglects no American, and is ever busied about some project connected with their welfare. May God continue to bless him!
>
> And speaking of Mr. Cooper, no one who loves or owns a pride in his native land, can live abroad without feeling every day what we owe to the patriotism, as well as the genius of this gifted man.[279]

[278] *Athenaeum*, VIII (January 3, 1835), 11.

[279] "First Impressions of Europe," No. 21, *New York Mirror*, X (July 7, 1832), 4.

Willis, by the way, felt exactly as Cooper did about the American manner of offering sneering praise, and in 1832 he complained of the *New York American's* behavior in this regard.[280] But Willis not only approved of Cooper's conduct. He liked him and thought him attractive: "His house is one of the most hospitable and agreeable in Paris; and with Morse and the circle of artists and men of distinction and worth about him, he is an acquaintance sincerely to regret leaving."[281] These lines have become a classic quotation. If we are interested to know what Cooper was like in later years, we should read also Willis's description, in *Rural Letters*, of meeting the same man, evidently as well liked, in 1848. "Mr. Cooper . . . was as unpretending as any other man" when he walked with Willis in Cooperstown, "His peculiarly manly and rich voice certainly rings as clear as ever, and his pale grey eye . . . sits as bright and steady in its full socket. He walks with the forward-bent head of a thoughtful man, but his back is unbending."[282]

Those private friends of Cooper's who were so devoted to him were no small circle, and moreover they were friends who clung to him through all their lives.

One was William Dunlap, whose labors for American art Cooper assisted. Dunlap did not end his affection for Cooper when the Lunch Club died for want of Cooper's spirit. In 1831, Cooper was no unhappy misanthrope, but "my merry writer and critic," "as young and full of fun as ever."[283]

Horatio Greenough was a more interesting character than either Dunlap or Willis, an artist of finer intellect. Emerson said of him, "I told him I would fife in his regiment. The

[280] *Ibid.*, X (September 8, 1832), 79.

[281] *Ibid.*, X (July 7, 1832), 4.

[282] N. P. Willis, *Rural Letters*, New York, 1849, 321-322.

[283] *Correspondence of James Fenimore-Cooper*, I, 240, 242-243, and *passim.*

grandest of democrats." Emerson appreciated Greenough's difficulties as an American artist, and asked:

What interest has Greenough to make a good statue? Who cares whether it is good? A few prosperous gentlemen and ladies; but the universal Yankee nation roaring in the Capitol to approve or condemn would make his hand and heart go to a new tune. Well, what shall nourish the sense of beauty now?[284]

He penned this question about nourishing beauty in 1836, but for years before that, James Fenimore Cooper had been the principal nourisher of Horace Greenough. He had discovered Greenough as a talented young artist in Florence whose work was ignored by Americans because they preferred ordering statuary that was inferior so long as it was Italian.[285] As Cooper modestly tells the story, he engaged Greenough to make a portrait bust and then a group in marble, the first statuary group ever carved by an American artist.[286] Greenough, however, tells it differently: "Fenimore Cooper saved me from despair. . . ."[287]

When the marble group was finished, two chanting cherubs copied from Raphael, Cooper sent it home for public exhibition in order to assist the artist and at the same time cultivate American taste. With the sculpture he sent a letter urging that "In a country like ours, the acquisition of a good sculptor is no trifle." This letter is itself an event in American history and has been quoted as the first sign of American interest in sculpture.[288]

Dunlap made arrangements for the exhibition, and to the

[284] Ralph Waldo Emerson, *Journals*, New York, 1910, VIII, 318-319, entry for August 18, 1852; IV, 88, entry for September 20, 1836.

[285] William Dunlap, *History of the Arts of Design*, III, 222.

[286] *Correspondence of James Fenimore-Cooper*, I, 167.

[287] Letter to William Dunlap, Florence, December 1, 1833, in William Dunlap, *op. cit.*, III, 226.

[288] William Dunlap, *ibid.*, III, 223-224; John Durand, *The Life and Times of A. B. Durand*, New York, 1894, pp. 64-65.

three friends the event seemed a test for American judgment. Washington Allston and Bartolini praised the work; hopes were high.[289] But what a fiasco the exhibition proved to be! People came, but from what motives! In New York, as De Kay informed Cooper, the Cherubs failed because the people were disappointed that they did not really sing; "and when the man turned them round in order to exhibit them in a different position, they exclaimed, 'Ah, he is going to wind them up; we shall hear them now.' "[290] In Boston, the Cherubs were exhibited "with small pieces of muslin festooned round a part of the figures," and some exasperated person hoped that Boston's "pure spirit of delicacy may be extended over Boston common, until every cow shall wear panteletts."[291]

If Cooper had given up his hopes for American art after this, who could have blamed him? Professor De Kay wrote to him, "I wish the scene of this story lay anywhere but in New York, but it cannot be helped, and I must continue to consider my townsmen as a race of cheating, lying money getting blockheads." Peter Augustus Jay also wrote in gloom over the prospects for art here.[292] The artist felt himself to be "rebuked and mortified" by the "loud complaints of their nudity" in a country where a little later "all the harlot dancers who have found an El Dorado in these Atlantic cities" aroused no breath of censure.[293] In the December following the failure of the Cherubs Greenough wrote despondently to Cooper saying that he must borrow more money of the novelist instead of paying back a former loan.

[289] Letters, Greenough to Cooper, Florence, December 20, 1830, and June 21, 1831. Unpublished. Cooper collection, Yale.

[290] *Correspondence of James Fenimore-Cooper*, I, 264.

[291] *Niles' Weekly Register*, XL (June 18, 1831), 283.

[292] *Correspondence of James Fenimore-Cooper*, I, 262.

[293] Horatio Greenough, *The Travels, Observations, and Experiences of a Yankee Stonecutter*, New York, 1852, p. 19; Letter, Greenough to Cooper, Florence, December 17, 1831. Unpublished. Cooper collection, Yale.

But Cooper did not give up or grow despondent as he might have done. Instead, he kept on with his assistance (and this at a time when he was wondering how he should support his own family after he came home). Eventually he secured for Greenough his appointment for a statue of Washington to be placed in front of the Capitol.[294] He not only persuaded Lafayette to sit to Greenough for a bust, but, when Greenough could not get enough sittings, saved the sculpture by pinning "the old gentleman to his chair one morning for two whole hours with stories and *bon mots*." He simply continued the faithful, tactful, and, above all, cheerful friend, acting with a generosity "that would bind the coldest mortal." In the same miserable year, 1832, Greenough wrote, "How do you progress in the little room where we sat with Morse one night and had such a grand discussion of the means of renovating art? . . . I shan't forget the number as long as I live"; and in another letter, "I do not wish to bore you but believe me it will give me more pain than I would inflict on any body not to hear sometimes from you"; or in another, "I have not told you how happy I have been in seeing Cooper."[295] In 1843, Greenough was pleased that Cooper, having heard he was in this country, had invited him to visit and would not "take no for an answer."[296] Almost twenty years later, when Cooper died, he wrote to Susan Cooper, "your father was . . . my ideal of an American gentleman. . . . You know not how I have grieved that I was forced to live so separated from him, or what a blow I received in the news of his death." To Bryant he wrote of his disappointment at not having looked once more "into that blue eye where I

[294] William Dunlap, *op. cit.*, III, 224.

[295] *The Letters of Horatio Greenough to His Brother, Henry Greenough*, Boston, 1887, pp. 87-89, 47, 83, 152, 238; letter to Rembrandt Peale, Paris, November 8, 1831, *New York Mirror*, IX (March 3, 1832), 279; S. I. Prime, *The Life of Samuel F. B. Morse*, New York, 1875, pp. 212-219; Letter, Greenough to Cooper, December 18, 1832. Unpublished. Cooper collection, Yale.

[296] *Letters of Horatio Greenough to . . . Henry Greenough*, p. 152.

never saw noght less than goodness and nobleness." To his brother he wrote, "Glorious Cooper! Those who wrote and sold their spiteful attacks on him, now rave about his glory." To the public he pleaded for a monument to Cooper that would express the man in being "simple, fervid and true."[297] This does not sound as if Greenough had ever seen that mythical morose Cooper, whom he might better have symbolized by Impatience on a monument.

Cooper's letters reveal his relationship to S. F. B. Morse to have been full of humor, affection and understanding. Morse's biographer has commented that some of their correspondence shows "a humor peculiarly beautiful" in the two men.[298] To this artist, as to Greenough, he was a source of comfort, cheer, and courage. In that same hard year of 1832, Morse was ill,[299] and he evidently took pleasure in his friend's manly cheerfulness as he did later, when, beset by discouragement in New York, he longed for a little of Cooper's sinew. Cooper admired and respected the painter's talent, and when he made up a gift of pictures and books for Dunlap's Academy of Design, he asked Morse to make the selections for the purchase, since, as he said, "I am not yet thank Heaven, Ass enough to believe I have the best taste." Cooper and Greenough laughed together over what Cooper called Morse's monkishness,[300] and a rumor that Morse was in love with the novelist's daughter required some ridicule.[301]

[297] Letters, Greenough to Susan Cooper, Newport, August 11, 18[51]. Unpublished. Cooper collection, Yale; Greenough to William Cullen Bryant, Boston, November 4, 1851. Unpublished. Penniman collection, Yale; Letters of Horatio Greenough to . . . Henry Greenough, p. 237; Horatio Greenough, "The Cooper Monument," in *A Memorial of Horatio Greenough*, edited by H. T. Tuckerman, New York, 1853, pp. 184-187.

[298] S. T. Prime, *op. cit.*, p. 141.

[299] *Correspondence of James Fenimore-Cooper*, I, 292-293, 306.

[300] Cooper to Greenough, Cooperstown, June 14, 1836, *Correspondence of James Fenimore-Cooper*, I, 358.

[301] Cooper to Richard Cooper, Paris, March 12, 1833, *ibid.*, I, 314; Cooper to Mrs. Cooper, Philadelphia, July 10, 1836, *ibid.*, I, 365.

But in Rome the two friends visited the Coliseum by moonlight, and managed to press near to the Pope at a Holy Thursday service; in Paris they presided together at the Fourth of July banquet, shared enthusiastic labors for the Poles, loved Lafayette together, and together doted on the Louvre, which Cooper persuaded Morse to paint.[302] After Cooper's death, Morse wrote almost with heartbreak of their years of close intimacy "never for a moment clouded by the slightest coolness." He spoke of "daily, almost hourly, intercourse while in Paris during the eventful years of 1831, 1832," and followed this immediately by saying, "I never met with a more sincere, warm-hearted, constant friend. No man came nearer to the ideal I had formed of a truly high-minded man." He spoke, also, of Cooper's generosity to struggling men of talent, who would hear "of his decease with the most poignant sorrow."[303] To test whether Morse had a true impression of the happy days in 1832 we might read a letter about them by the novelist himself which exhibits his own boyish ingenuousness as well as Greenough or Morse could have described it:

> I get up at eight, read the papers, breakfast at ten. . .—work till one—throw off my morning gown, draw on my boots and gloves, take a cane that Horace Greenough gave me, and go to the Louvre, where I find Morse stuck up on a high working stand, perch myself astraddle of one of the seats, and bore him just as I used to bore you when you made the memorable likeness of St. Peter. 'Lay it on here, Samuel—more yellow—the nose is too short—the eye too small—damn it if I had been a painter what a picture I should have painted.'—and all this stuff over again and which Samuel takes just as goodnaturedly as good old William. Well there I sit and have sat so often and so long that my face is just as well known as any Vandyke on the walls. Crowds get round the picture, for Samuel has quite

[302] S. I. Prime, *op. cit.*, pp. 187, 199, 232, 228, 236, 239, 227. William Dunlap, *History of the Arts of Design*, III, 98.

[303] *Memorial of James Fenimore Cooper*, p. 36.

made a hit in the Louvre, and I believe that people think that half the merit is mine. So much for keeping company with ones betters. At six we are at home eating a good dinner, and I manage to get a good deal out of Morse in this way too—We had Greenough up here for three months in the Autumn and then we had a good time of it.[304]

George Washington Greene,[305] who also knew Cooper abroad, became somewhat of an idolator. Greene recognized faults in his friend, but called them "the failings of a strong, original, active mind, conscious of its powers, patient of observation and research, but accustomed, from early habit as well as natural tendencies, to self-reliance and independent judgment."[306] Cooper, he said, "would not give up an opinion without a reason," but on the other hand those who knew him were always confident that he would respectfully hear and consider any sensible objection. His generosity, Greene thought, was not only large but judicious and tactful. The young American delighted in seeing how much Cooper's companionship was esteemed by other men, and apparently thought all time spent in his company was pleasant. He said that while abroad Cooper showed "the face and manner of a man whose mind is ever busy with something that he loves, who comes to his task cheerfully, and still feels bright and cheerful when he lays it aside, because he knows that there are new pleasures in store for him, when he shall return to it again." Cooper seems to have preferred being a man to playing the author when he was among his friends: "When

[304] Letter to William Dunlap, Paris, March 16, 1832. *Diary of William Dunlap*, III, 606-609.

[305] George Washington Greene when he met Cooper was a young man traveling in Europe for his health. Later he was United States consul at Rome, Professor of Modern Languages at Brown University, member of the Rhode Island Legislature, and Professor of American History at Cornell.

[306] George Washington Greene, "J. Fenimore Cooper," *Homes of American Authors*, pp. 206-211.

he left his desk, he left his pen in it. He came out into the world to hear and see what other men were doing." If men wished to hear him speak of his work:

There he was, with no opinion that he was not perfectly ready to express, whether it concerned men or things, his own books or those of others. But he never seemed to feel that his authorship gave him a right to make himself the hero of the piece; and more than once I have been half-vexed with him for it, though it was impossible not to respect his motive.[307]

A recent writer regrets that we have no record of how James Cooper appeared to his Yale professors. Fortunately, this is not quite true. There is a fine letter on this subject in the Cooper collection, written by one of the greatest of James Cooper's Yale professors, Benjamin Silliman. "I always remembered you with kindness & now have your image distinctly before me as you appeared at Mr. Twinings a fine sparkling beautiful boy of alluring person & interesting manners. I felt a deep interest in you & never lost it & it was a grief to me to learn that you had been removed & cut of [*sic*] from the institution." But the bearing of Silliman's letter upon this chapter is that it was written in the notable year 1831, to tell Cooper of the pleasure he had drawn from the "enlarged views" of a recent letter from the novelist, and to express a desire to have the letter published.

The curious thing is that if we search every record, we do not find anyone who could quite dislike Cooper except the halfcrazed and jealous recipient of his kindness, James Gates Percival, who styled him by a lengthy euphemism for "literary louse."[308] Poor Percival on one occasion when he was "distracted" had been "finally rescued by James Fenimore Cooper, who took him to his house, where he spent several

[307] "James Fenimore Cooper," *New York Quarterly*, I (June, 1852), 217-219.

[308] Julius Ward, *Life and Letters of James Gates Percival*, Boston, 1866, pp. 158-159.

weeks, meeting Fitz Greene Halleck and other congenial people."[309] But the poet was suffering from jealousy. Percival differed sharply from Cooper in politics.[310] When I say that no one else would really dislike him, I am speaking of persons who were acquainted with Cooper, not of persons who knew him by hearsay, since we are seeking some first-hand estimate against which to test the hearsay. Philip Hone, for instance, expressed the idea that Cooper had more spleen, malice, and presumption than any other man living, disliking him even while he could not help admiring: "What a pity it is that so good a head should be joined to so bad a heart! He will not let people like him!"[311] But Hone knew Cooper very slightly; he was an absolute believer of what Webb wrote about the novelist,[312] and Mr. Allan Nevins has alluded to Cooper's having offended not only the Whigs but Hone in particular with *The American Democrat*.[313] People who could claim acquaintanceship did not speak of him in this way. There is evidence, to be sure, in the comments of four acquaintances, that Cooper never lost his earlier brusqueness, but in each case the comment is accompanied by amused affection. These four comments constitute the complete record of dislike for Cooper. We must bring them out of the closet, but as skeletons they make a very poor showing.

Henry Brevoort once wrote to Washington Irving that he had seen Cooper in Paris, the "Jupiter Tonnans" of the circle there, and laughed a little at the two Democrats Cooper and Paulding, saying Cooper was planning to strike a political blow through his next novel, and "He and Paulding will

[309] F. H. Cogswell, *James Gates Percival and His Friends*, New Haven, 1902, p. 19.

[310] J. H. Ward, *op. cit.*, pp. 171 ff.; G. W. Curtis, *The Life, Character, and Writings of William Cullen Bryant*, New York, 1879, pp. 15-16; New Haven *Daily Herald*, November 16, 1840.

[311] *The Diary of Philip Hone*, edited by Allan Nevins, New York, 1927, I, 346; II, 604.

[312] *Ibid.*, I, 360-361.

[313] *Ibid.*, I, 362.

never rest until they have laid that old sinner England upon her back. . . . It is an enterprise worthy of Don Quixote."[314] This is not very severe criticism, certainly, and it has never been taken as evidence that Paulding was bilious. It loses what severity it has when it is joined with Brevoort's tacit approval of a remark he quotes from his wife concerning Cooper's treatment of some friends in trouble: "Cooper is really a good man. He has been their consolation and friend and talked to me with tears in his eyes of the event."[315] After Cooper had returned to Cooperstown, during the years when his gloom is alleged to have fallen upon him, this same Brevoort "looked triumphant and sang out satisfied 'I thought so' " when a friend told him that the pleasantest part of a northern journey had been spent "with my dear Fenimore's." Very likely the most complete expression in brief space of the feeling of acquaintances is Brevoort's: "Mr. Spy Cooper is now in Paris . . . I hope you will see him—he has a rough and confident manner of expressing himself, but you will find him a right good fellow at bottom."[316]

Then another person who tried to dislike Cooper was the novelist Catharine Sedgwick, a charming woman who knew Cooper well and who was disgruntled enough when a novel of hers was taken for Cooper's to say that she hoped his "self-complacency" would not be wounded. But this was in 1825, before Cooper is reputed to have "soured." Perhaps the remark was affected by a quarrel which had occurred between Cooper and her brother Robert in 1824. After he returned from Europe he offended her by saying in her house in the presence of two saintly ladies that Americans were going down in "civilization . . . *morals* and manners." Yet

[314] *Letters of Henry Brevoort to Washington Irving*, New York, 1918, pp. 236-237. See also p. 301.

[315] *Ibid.*, pp. 268-269. See also p. 160.

[316] Letter, E. W. Laight to Charlotte Cooper, New York, August 30, n. d. Unpublished. Cooper collection, Yale; *Letters of Henry Brevoort to Washington Irving*, p. 160.

she could not help adding, "With all this, he was good-humored, and talked strongly and amusingly. He is a perfect John Bull in shape, dimensions, action, even to the growl."[317]

If Cooper was good-humored and amusing at Miss Sedgwick's, his fault must have lain in being too frank for the ears of two saintly ladies. In a publishing house they knew better how to take him, presumably; at least, an acquaintance who had seen him in such a place reported that when he stood there with his back to the fire, "his legs apart and his coat-tails under his arms, pouring out diatribes" about his country's institutions, he "did not seem half in earnest."[318] He poured out diatribes, then (and very probably quite in earnest), but something jovial about his presence seems to have affected his hearers.

This secret of some infectious geniality in Cooper must be the explanation for Parke Godwin's saying that the intercourse of Cooper and Bryant was "singularly courteous and agreeable" at the same time that he described the novelist as "burly, brusque, and boisterous, like a bluff sailor, always bringing a breeze of quarrel with him" to the newspaper office. The contradiction is explained in another statement by Godwin: "In spite of his positive and, at times, overbearing manner, the novelist was a fascinating companion." There was something engaging about the breezy sailor, for Godwin's characterization is clearly intended, throughout, to be the description of an attractive character, a man whom Bryant admired for "thorough-paced honesty and independence" and who was able, with all his brusqueness and vigor, to admire the delicacy of the shy poet. "We others get a little praise now and then, but Bryant is the author of America"—so Godwin quotes Cooper as speaking. In the first year of their acquaintance, Bryant declined to review a

[317] Mary E. Dewey, *op. cit.*, pp. 172, 441.

[318] Maunsell B. Field, *Memories of Many Men and of Some Women*, New York, 1874, p. 178.

book of Cooper's because Cooper was hard to please. Yet Cooper admired Bryant and treasured his praise. This shy Bryant in his youth when he had come to the city "from the seclusion of a country life" was startled by the novelist's "emphatic frankness," but afterwards, Bryant himself said, he came even "to like and to admire" this very thing. As for that first fear of Cooper's brusqueness, we might remember that, as Godwin says, Bryant was always "delicate as a woman."[319] We should be somewhat morbid ourselves if we harped upon that small reference to being startled and forgot Bryant's great tribute to Cooper's sweetness:

so independent and uncompromising, and with a sensitiveness far more acute than he was willing to acknowledge, it is not surprising that occasions frequently arose to bring him, sometimes into friendly collision, and sometimes into graver disagreements and misunderstandings. For his infirmities, his friends found an ample counterpoise in the generous sincerity of his nature. . . . A manly expression of opinion, however different from his own, commanded his respect. Of his own works, he spoke with the same freedom as of the works of others. . . yet he could bear with gentleness any dissent from the estimate he placed on his own writings. His character was like the bark of the cinnamon, a rough and astringent rind without, and an intense sweetness within. Those who penetrated below the surface found a genial temper, warm affections, and a heart with ample place for his friends, their pursuits, their good name, their welfare. They found him a philanthropist . . . a religious man. . . hospitable, and to the extent of his means, liberal-handed. . . .[320]

Bryant could say this after a life-time of friendship, and at a moment when important testimony declares that political feeling still ran high and it took some courage to say such words.[321]

This is the whole sum of adverse criticism of James Feni-

[319] Parke Godwin, *op. cit.*, I, 221, 196, 336, 363, 368.

[320] W. C. Bryant, *op. cit.*, pp. 69-70.

[321] G. W. Greene, *Homes of American Authors*, p. 79; Parke Godwin, *op. cit.*, II, 62.

more Cooper. It does a good deal to confirm one in liking James Cooper, after all. H. T. Tuckerman says that the first acquaintance of Cooper's whom he ever met and questioned about the novelist said he was "the most disagreeable man in the world." But Tuckerman soon discovered that the informant had not a single fact or illustration to adduce, and that he was the kind of person who would fill any great man with disgust. Tuckerman decided, after comparing this person with the noble men who loved Cooper, that the allegation he had heard was a "signal tribute" to Cooper's worth.[322]

George Hillard, who first became acquainted with Cooper when the novelist was at the height of his troubles, wrote that "Cooper's dauntless courage would have been less admirable, had he been hard, cold, stern, and impassive: but he was none of these. He was full of warm affections, cordial, sympathetic, and genial; he had a woman's tenderness of heart; he was the most faithful of friends; and in his own home no man was ever more gentle, gracious, and sweet. The blows he received fell upon a heart that felt them keenly; but he bared his breast none the less resolutely to the contest, because it was not protected by an armor of insensibility."[323]

[322] Two other references to Cooper should be mentioned here. J. C. Derby, *Fifty Years among Authors, Books, and Publishers*, New York, 1886, p. 295, said Cooper turned morose after his return from Europe. But Derby did not know Cooper, and he seems to have inserted this remark on his own authority into Charles Wiley's description of the Cooper of the 1820's, "full of life and spirit, of a very happy temperament and in every way an attractive man." Longfellow, who had not known Cooper well but had been in cordial correspondence with him in Europe (Samuel Longfellow, *op. cit.*, I, 98; *Correspondence of James Fenimore-Cooper*, I, 352-353; II, 438-439) said, when the novelist was involved in his libel suits, "Decidedly a disagreeable individual!" (Samuel Longfellow, *op. cit.*, I, 328.) But we can understand this easily when we see where he got his information on Cooper; Longfellow said Park Benjamin's *New World* was the best paper he saw (*ibid.*, I, 342). It was the worst paper for reporting of the libel suits.

[323] George S. Hillard, *Atlantic Monthly*, IX (January, 1862), 67-68.

Cooper may have shared some qualities with that horse of his which in his young and happy days he rode in parades—the steed which Susan Cooper says was named Bull Head. Perhaps not everyone could have had for Cooper the affection of his Bread and Cheese Club friends when they laughed at his lectures on orthoëpy for the French language. Yet the persons who actually listened to the lectures were not, in fact, bored.[324] His Quixotic devotion to principle and stubborn insistence upon property rights expressed themselves in actions which may have been variously agreeable. George Washington Greene admired Cooper because when he caught a man stealing fruit in his garden:

> instead of flying into a passion and sending for a constable, he reproved the culprit mildly, told him how great a wrong it was doing him to make his neighbors believe that there was no other way of getting at his fruit but by stealing it, and bidding him, the next time . . . come in at the gate and ask for it, helped him fill his basket and let him go.[325]

It was such action that Cooper must have seen himself as taking when he insisted that the populace recognize his title to the point of land on Otsego. If he was capable of explaining "minutely" to a foreigner the difference between the words "voyage" and "passage," he also was as eager to ask a foreigner the fine points of usage concerning "*signora*" and "*signorina.*" So Cooper "was earnest, and was therefore supposed to be bitter, and the sensitiveness which he was unwilling to acknowledge to himself or to others, often exposed him to ungrounded and even unwarranted suspicions."[326]

Dr. Francis wrote of the "severe firmness" with physical pain which Cooper maintained both in his last months and

[324] *Correspondence of James Fenimore-Cooper*, I, 108.
[325] *Homes of American Authors*, p. 208.
[326] *Ibid.*, 208, 209.

"in the meridian of his life."[327] This essential strength it may have been which made itself felt in those moments when he was too serious about "passage" or orthoëpy or apple stealing; or perhaps what saved him was his humor. At any rate, those who knew him loved him in spite of his peculiarities.

Greene, Hillard, and Bryant all wrote explicitly that in his love for argument Cooper was always ready to acknowledge himself wrong if met with the same frankness and fairness which he offered others; but H. T. Tuckerman has gone farther and given examples of this trait in operation. Tuckerman said a "certain prejudice" arose against Cooper which made him "a stranger to many estimable admirers" of his earlier works and "greatly interfered with the legitimate success" of his later ones. This prejudice against the man simply arose because "He was too proud and too sincere to conciliate, by any blandishments of speech or bearing, the antagonism which his defiance of the press had engendered." This operated upon "hundreds who never saw him, and many who knew him casually" to make them feel "repelled as by a cold and aggressive nature." But Tuckerman knew what he was doing when he wrote that such persons were not repelled by a cold and aggressive nature, only "as by" such a nature. For he goes on to state the truth about Cooper under a "whereas":

whereas it was needful but to approach him candidly, to meet him on his own ground of frank utterance, in order to find him at once a most interesting companion and a noble-hearted gentleman. For ourselves, we confess that effeminacy and sycophancy, verbiage and sensitive vanity, so often degrade the literary character, that such a strong, courageous, honorable, unpretending, and unaffected man as Cooper in the ranks of authorship was absolutely refreshing; we enjoyed his direct, free, uncompromising tone; we respected the

[327] Dr. J. W. Francis, *op. cit.*, in *Memorial of James Fenimore Cooper.*

thorough honesty of purpose and sentiment evident in his manners and speech; we rejoiced to find a writer whose vocation had not overlaid his manhood, and whom success had not weakened into an improvident parasite, but whose form, eye, voice, grasp, and talk were fresh and salient. . . .

But Tuckerman actually gives examples of Cooper's frank ability to retract statements:

Our first personal knowledge of Cooper confirmed the instinctive feeling that he was essentially what his writings attest. A meeting of gentlemen was held, at which he was to expose what he declared to be a piece of charlatanism. Upon examination the evidence of deception was not what had been confidently predicted, but the reverse. Cooper was the first to retract his hasty charges, and to acknowledge himself mistaken, even though he was prominent on the other side, while the rest of the party were non-committal.

Tuckerman's second encounter of this sort with Cooper was an occasion when he called the novelist's attention to "some omissions," in the *History of the Navy*, concerning a Revolutionary hero.

'You are right,' was his response. 'I will do him justice in the next edition. The fact is, he and my father were political rivals; he won the election, and I did not feel like hunting up, as I was bound to do, the materials of his renown. I was wrong, and I will repair the injustice.'

Cooper had been at fault, certainly, but as Tuckerman said, "How few authors would so ingenuously acknowledge a fault and its motive, and so heartily proffer amends!"[328]

So there is ample testimony that the Cooper who laughed hard, lectured, and thundered away at injustice was not to those who saw and knew him the same Cooper who has been manufactured and handed down by the press and by hearsay.

[328] H. T. Tuckerman, *North American Review*, CLXXXV (October, 1859), 303-305.

So, also, Carey's prophecy of Cooper's return was not realized. Carey had been in a wretched state of mind in July of 1832, and had written Cooper: "Heaven only knows, but I fear we are destined to see bad times in every way. Politically and morally they are all bad enough, notwithstanding your puffs, which do well enough for the people of Europe." The trouble all lay, he maintained, in Jackson and Van Buren, who would send the nation to the Devil, provided they could rule it there. He would stand the cursed cholera "If it could only carry off Jackson." Everything in the American system was being ruined "to gratify the cupidity and lust of power of a parcel of dxxxd scoundrels." He ended with hoping Cooper was in a better humor than he was himself, and saying they looked for nothing better at home than another Revolution. In the midst of this tirade he wrote his prophecy:

When you return here you will be almost as much shocked as Irving has been—not quite so much, as he was absent 18 years and you only 6. We have, however, made more progress downward in 6 years than we did in the previous 12.[329]

Cooper in his most despondent depth became restless and dissatisfied,[330] but never wrote like Carey; but, of course, he was not of the party that wanted Jackson carried off by the epidemic.

A month before the Cooper family reached New York, the novelist had presented his country with another foreign novel about American principles. It was called *The Headsman*, and it was better than *Heidenmauer*; almost as good as *The Bravo*, but more strained in its moral. The plot is more original than has been appreciated; it deals with a high-born heroine in love with an executioner's son, and its new and highly democratic variation of this theme was that Cooper granted his couple a wedding without causing the humble

[329] *Correspondence of James Fenimore-Cooper*, I, 267-269.

[330] Parke Godwin, *op. cit.*, I, 317, 355.

hero to be revealed as a noble in disguise. In *The Bravo,* he used a tragic ending, in *The Headsman* a happy, but in both novels he was true to the situation he was illustrating. In both, this originality made him trouble. The happy ending was called a truckling to worn-out and despicable tastes,[331] as the tragic one had been called a want of poetic justice.

But most of the criticism on this book was frankly political. There was only one important friendly review in New York, the *Evening Post's.*[332] Most reviewers compared the general merits of Toryism and republicanism, decrying republicanism, and wished Cooper would get back to the American scene—the old preference of American things to principles.[333] The *Morning Courier and New York Enquirer* did not hold out even this hope for resuscitation of Cooper's power; it complacently revealed to the world that Cooper had been flattered into a niche of fame too high for him and must now be established more appropriately on a lower level.[334]

Cooper now believed he must really perform that retirement he had long been considering, for the charge that he lacked patriotism hurt him.

> The *critiques* in news-papers never gave me any concern as critiques, indeed I rarely saw them; but when critical acumen degenerates into personal hostility, when parties are formed, and calumnies are resorted to as the agents of reviewers it is time for me to stop.[335]

[331] *Metropolitan Magazine,* [I] (October, 1833), 409-410.

[332] October 22, 1833; another friendly review was printed in the *Literary Journal and Weekly Register,* I (December 28, 1833), 237.

[333] *New York Mirror,* XI (December 7, 1833), 183; (November 2, 1833), 143; *North American Magazine,* III (November, 1833), 70-71; *New England Magazine,* VI (January, 1834), 88-89; *Commercial Advertiser,* October 21, 1833; *Ladies' Magazine,* VI (November, 1833), 520-524. All these magazines except the first and last were of decided Whig editorship.

[334] December 9, 1833.

[335] Letter to John Whipple, New York, January 14, 1834. Unpublished. Photostatic copy, Yale.

He still venerated the republican idea, but his interest in the country itself was fearfully undermined. He even forgot, as he wrote, how much he had longed for America when he had been abroad.[336] But he interrupted an unhappy sentence with "I dislike the ungrateful subject, and will say no more."

He had several works under way, and he decided to publish them before his retirement. The first to come out was *A Letter to His Countrymen,* about which no two critics since Lounsbury have ever said the same thing. It is, as Professor Spiller has at last pointed out, a logical piece of writing, not the hodge-podge Lounsbury thought it. I will add that it was not, as some have said, an outburst on his personal affairs, with politics drawn in; it was intended, on the contrary, as a piece of political criticism with some personal experience drawn in for illustration. The Democratic press unanimously received it as such.

William Gilmore Simms said, while Cooper was still living, that this pamphlet mixed up literary, personal, and literary grievances and was, as a whole, written in bad taste, with disagreeable egotism; but that it:

> brought into the field a new and more bitter host of enemies —unscrupulous . . . and with interests . . . actively involved in the pressing concerns of party,—such as never suffer any restraints of justice or veneration. . . ."[337]

These political reviewers were certainly self-declared. If the *Evening Post* simply printed an announcement that *A Letter to His Countrymen* was coming off the press, the Philadelphia *United States Gazette*, a Whig paper, retorted: "If Mr. Cooper has entered the troubled waters of politics, and performed to win the applause of the Post, then, we suspect, that we have seen the last of the 'Mohegans.'" Bryant must

[336] *Correspondence of James Fenimore-Cooper*, I, 232.

[337] "The Writings of James Fenimore Cooper," *Views and Reviews*, New York, 1845, First Series, pp. 229-230.

in return remonstrate against the *Gazette's* attempt to prejudice readers.[338] Then the *Morning Courier and New York Enquirer* would wonder how the Albany *Argus*, a Democratic sheet, could bring itself to quote an unfavorable review of *The Monikins*, and must explain it by hinting at a schism in the Democratic body; the *Argus* has lately quarreled with the *Evening Post*, and "The Post is a branch of the Monikin family."[339] On the other hand, a paper with Democratic sympathies like the Buffalo *Republican* would accuse "The worn out hacks of Blue light Federalism, and the abettors of Dartmoor massacres" of conspiring to prevent the sales of Cooper's works in order to blind democracy to "the merits of her best advocate," and to subsidize the press of a free people in the interests of the aristocracy. This drew a stately refutation from the Boston *Daily Advertiser*, a paper which was just becoming Whig.[340]

Bryant had a vigorous detestation of this conduct. A long editorial in his paper for August 14, 1838, denounced the Whig practice of condemning every piece of literary work a Democratic writer produced. He struck out hard against the Whig system of slandering in his personal character any author who began to show Democratic leanings, while every Whig pamphlet was "lauded and extolled as a miraculous production." As Democrats who had suffered he mentioned James K. Paulding, George Bancroft, and Alexander H. Everett, and he said that even Washington Irving had lately been suspected of Democracy, and was threatened with the loss of his reputation if he accepted the nomination for mayor. But Cooper, he said, had been the worst sufferer of all; the "universal whig press . . . resorted to every foul artifice to degrade his literary and personal character." The "garbage" of Tory periodicals "is always like cordial to the whig taste,"

[338] *Evening Post*, June 13, 1834.
[339] September 22, 1835.
[340] November 21, 1834.

Bryant said, and this had been "copied and hawked about" for the sake of its "despicable slanders."

This was the situation of Cooper in 1838; but the strongest impulse to the Whig slander had been given in 1834 by *A Letter to His Countrymen.* Bryant was quite right in saying: "Was Mr. Cooper an editor, or a candidate for office? Oh no,—a private citizen, who simply *dared,* in a free country, express his political sentiments! Fortunately, his firmness of character is too great to suffer any annoyance from the contemptible and fiendish spirit of partisanship."

The Democrats had entire good will towards Cooper, and a wish to defend him in his troubles over *A Letter to His Countrymen,* but their position just then was extremely difficult. Most of New York State's papers were at this time controlled by the Whig party, and this was just the era when Biddle was subsidizing a Bank press. Abuse was more spectacular than truth for selling papers at a time when New York had far too many papers to sell. The *Evening Post* was a more dignified journal with a vestige of tradition against scurrility, and this was a handicap. The real delicacy in the situation lay in the explosive powers, just then, of the word "aristocrat." The Whigs were at the climax of their campaign to turn this word of reproach against the party which had used it so successfully against them. They could (and in Cooper's case did) see an "aristocratic" tendency in any belief, act, or expression, from Jacksonism to beautifying the ground of one's home. One American—but perhaps he was not a Whig—saw "aristocracy" in keeping strangers from looking in one's wife's bedroom windows.[341] Of course, the Whigs were attacking the Jacksonian principle of a strong

[341] On this amazing incident and the complaint of "aristocracy" which it aroused, see the threatening letters to Cooper from an incredibly rude man from Honesdale, Pennsylvania, who signed himself "The Stranger," especially the letter of June 12, 1848. Unpublished. Cooper collection, Yale. Cooper has written his comments about the bedroom windows on one of these manuscripts.

executive. The Democrats were in the dilemma of supporting this principle and yet of evading the charges of tyranny. Cooper did not make their defense of him easy by publishing his A. B. C. letters in 1835, arguing against Daniel Webster for the constitutionality of strong executive power. And *A Letter to His Countrymen* presented the same problem in June, 1834.

Cooper kept to a rigidly logical outline in this pamphlet, making two principal points: first, that the nation was increasingly falling under the spell of foreign opinions, especially political opinions; and second, that this subservience not only was "degrading to the character" but might "become dangerous to the institutions of this country." After announcing these points, Cooper stopped to make an energetic disclaimer of all personal motives in his pamphlet, explaining that he was obliged to enforce his points by his own observations, a necessity which would be liable to misinterpretation. Perhaps this apologia was unfortunate; once he got into the body of the pamphlet's argument he did keep unwaveringly to the national and political issues, but his enemies could ignore that and treat his introductory protestations of disinterest as mere talk about himself.

However this may be, after this defense of his motives he proceeded to discuss his first point. He used Cassio's review as one illustration, and his love of logical gymnastics made him draw out this point to a boring length. Then he took up in turn the Whig articles which had followed Cassio's, and examined them coolly and inexorably, exposing the Whig evasions of his point about foreign influence. He returned dignified argument for their sneers and insults, and when he had completed his discussion of the first point he went in orderly progress to the second.

Now, this second part of the letter, which is the main part, called by Cooper himself the heart of the book, reads like a Democratic tract. It looks as if Lounsbury did not read this far, but the Whig editors did. They were clever enough to see that they could do their most annoying damage not by answering the arguments they found there, but by exaggerating, twisting, and ridiculing the personal statements in the unimportant introduction. Only one Whig writer took up Cooper's Democratic points and returned argument for argument in a tract which kept purely to politics. This was Caleb Cushing, who was a very orthodox Whig at the moment, having just been elected to Congress by that party. Later, he was to earn by his change of politics Lowell's lines in the "Biglow Papers":

> General C. is a dreffül smart man;
> He's ben on all sides that give places or pelf.[342]

The first of Cooper's pronouncements in this second section is that the American government is unique, far more different from the English system and other European systems than many citizens suppose. There are three ways, he said, in which our institutions differ from foreign ones. First, the United States is a union of separate commonwealths; in such a nation, dissolution would occur quickly if the activity of the government were not restricted purely to matters of common interest; the delimitation of federal and state powers thus necessitated is the only cause of American political parties. To this Cooper added the strict-constructionist Democratic opinion that upholding constitutional limitation is our only safeguard. Second, our government is the only one which allows the possibility of friction among the legislative, judicial, and executive branches; the nominal three estates of England do not interact as checks, for parliament rules the King and a moneyed aristocrary rules parliament, holding their ascendancy "under the cry of liberty." This statement is a reiteration of the thesis of *The Bravo.* Of course it was received as another thrust at Tories and American Whigs.

[342] Cushing wrote *A Reply to the Letter of J. Fenimore Cooper.* By One of His Countrymen, Boston, 1834.

Third, our government is peculiar in placing its highest authority in the constituency; in England liberty has long been spoken of in terms of limiting the king's power, and Americans have been deceived by this fact into a distrust of the American executive; but in America it is the legislative department, not the executive, which "is the branch of this government most likely to abuse its trust." Cooper thought we should sweep aside the foreign-made mystification and perceive that our President "is a creature of our own forming, and for our own good," not to be confused with princes. All we had to do, he said, was to construe the Constitution "on its own principles" and avoid drawing comparisons between our government and limited monarchies. Cooper followed these principles with illustrations of unconstitutional actions by both Jackson and the Senate, concluding that there was really no harm in Jackson's act, though it was technically illegal, but there was much danger in the Senate's act, for "If this Union shall ever be destroyed by any error or faults of an internal origin, it will not be by executive, but by legislative usurpation. . . . England has changed its form of government, from that of a monarchy to that of an exceedingly oppressive aristocracy, precisely in this manner." In the course of this discussion Cooper warmly and cogently rebuked the Senate for its opposition to Jackson on the Bank issue, a very touchy political subject at the moment.

Next, Cooper turned to the constituency itself, and to the dangerous susceptibility of our people to the influence of foreign precedents. Notable examples of this failing, he said, were the coercion of the ballot, traceable to the English representation of property; the "niggardly" treatment of the veterans of the War of 1812, our patriotism having been sapped by Doctrinaire influence; pusillanimous submission to foreign impressment of our seamen; and the un-American spirit and behavior of anti-republican Americans living abroad. On the last topic Cooper wrote with gentle though sad humanity; and if he is allowed by fair minded readers to reveal himself, nothing could do more to dispel the myth of the gloomy and irritable Cooper than the honest, hopeful, and loving words with which in his conclusion he exhorted his countrymen to be proud of their republic. And this is the work which his enemies represented to be a bitter diatribe against the nation!

At the end, Cooper announced his intention of retiring when the books then under way should have been published. He said he could not complain that America had failed to encourage his early work, for it had given him a generous welcome. But he charged the nation with having lost its patriotic enthusiasm as soon as he had attempted to be American not merely in "things" but in "principles." He spoke modestly of his proposed retirement, saying his disappointment was not in having missed immortality, which he had never expected to gain anyway, but in having failed to be useful in the support and propagation of American principles. Yet he did not couch this regret as a Jeremiad against the country; he concluded that, after all, America did not need him, because the nation was really sound, and:

> the democracy of this country is in every sense strong enough to protect itself. Here, the democrat is the conservative, and, thank God, he has something worth preserving. I believe he knows it, and that he will prove true to himself. I confess I have no great fears of our modern aristocracy, which is wanting in more of chivalry than the *accolade*.

These were strong and hopeful words for the future of America.

But these were strong and hopeful words for the Democratic party, also; and the ink in them was hardly dry before Bryant quoted them editorially against what he considered the arrogant property-aristocracy of the Bank party in such a way as to give Cooper's word "democrat" a partisan significance whether the novelist intended it or not.[343]

[343] *Evening Post*, June 18, 1834.

Perhaps Cooper had not consciously intended any part of his *Letter* to bear a partisan connotation. He actually sent a letter to the *Evening Post* on June 14, before the book's publication, saying that the forthcoming work contained the "unbiassed sentiments of a man who is perfectly free from all party connections, party feelings, or party designs." I must confess that this statement is surprising, when we know how strong were Cooper's party sympathies. But he wrote the note in reply to an accusation that his book had been written by arrangement with Van Buren as a step towards gaining office. This kind of party connection, feeling, or design was certainly foreign to Cooper; he was always unbiased in this sense. Caleb Cushing, when he returned Whig answers to Cooper's Democratic arguments, avowed that he himself was not writing in a partisan spirit. In the sense Congressman Cushing means, of course Cooper was not partisan. Another Democratic writer once said of Bryant that he had not "regarded politics . . . as a factious strife for party supremacy, . . . but as the solemn conflict of great principles."[344] Perhaps it was by some such reasoning that Cooper thought his booklet was unpartisan. But whatever Cooper meant by his statement, Bryant accompanied it with an editorial note which connected the book with the Democratic party completely enough; he said the Van Buren rumor had been circulated by the Bank press, and then quoted more than a column from *A Letter to His Countrymen*, all on the subject of the removal of deposits.[345]

But this was nothing to what was to come. Three days later, Bryant gave two columns to the *Letter*, writing half a column of strong and manly praise for Cooper's defense of national institutions against the "inroads of free construction" and "interpretations derived from European usages." He said more serious things were at stake than the mere literature

[344] *United States Magazine and Democratic Review*, X (March, 1842), 294.

[345] *Evening Post*, June 14, 1834.

of the country, and Cooper was fighting out a very large issue. This was followed by two columns of excerpts from the book on such subjects as "Danger to the Constitution from Legislative Usurpation," "The true character of the resolution of the Senate censuring the President," "Executive custody of the public money," "Proscription for political opinions," and "Habit of Americans of deferring to foreign opinion lessens them in the eyes of other nations."

Reading over these excerpts, one is struck by their cogency. Whatever undue imagination may have been expended on the Cassio affair, the problem of American independence and individuality was a real one, and Cooper wrote on it admirably. Congratulatory letters began to come in from those who had been regretting, as one man said, that Cooper, Irving, and Paulding "did not employ their pens upon something more useful than works of mere imagination and fiction."[346] Of course, from the Whig side came the too easy retort that a writer of fiction had no business getting beyond his depth in serious matters, and that Cooper had been unwisely "*romancing* on the first principles of free governments."[347]

One of the minor risible incidents of this journalistic excitement was the conversion of a reader of the *Evening Post* who thought Bryant must have been too severe on one of Cooper's critics. Bryant had done nothing but quote the writer's own sentences, but the subscriber could not believe anyone would write like that. He hunted up the original, and was so horrified at what he saw that he wrote the *Evening*

[346] *Evening Post,* June 20, 1834; June 24, 1834.

[347] Boston *Daily Advertiser and Patriot,* August 1, 1834; June 16, 1834; *Niles' Weekly Register,* XLVII (August 23, 1834), 428; XLVI (June 21, 1834), 292; *New England Magazine,* VII (October, 1834), 333; VII (August, 1834), 154-157. *The Southern Literary Messenger,* IV (August 20, 1834), 5-6 expressed, evidently sincerely, a wish that Cooper had not entered politics.

Post a letter of his own to tell the world how incensed he was at this "precious piece of billingsgate."[348]

Dominant over all the Whig press were the *Morning Courier and New York Enquirer*, the *Commercial Advertiser*, and the *New York American*. That village Weeklies should have followed in the train of the James Watson Webbs is only to be expected, but journals of greater dignity surrendered, apparently, to the mere loudness of this talk. The *New York Mirror* behaved badly,[349] and the *Knickerbocker*, though it kept a superficial dignity, accepted the dogma of Webb and King, saying that politics had been dragged into Cooper's pamphlet for no apparent reason, that Cooper was compact of defiance, egotism, and morbid sensibility, and that nine-tenths of Cassio's readers had thought the article on *The Bravo* just and fair.[350] The *Knickerbocker* might honestly have seen defiance and egotism in the pamphlet, but it is hard to believe anyone could have thought Cassio's article just and fair, provided he had read *The Bravo*. This would seem to be mere Whig infection; and there is reason to suspect that the *Knickerbocker* was predisposed to infection from that quarter.[351]

It is reassuring to know that Cooper took the criticism of the Whigs at the true valuation. To the one person who

[348] *Evening Post*, July 15, July 18, 1834.

[349] Compare the articles in XII (July 5, 1834), 7, and XII (July 19, 1834), 18-19. Willis was still abroad.

[350] *Knickerbocker Magazine*, IV (July, 1834), 75-76.

[351] Charles Fenno Hoffman, the journal's first editor, had previously been editing the *New York American* jointly with Charles King. He left the *Knickerbocker* in 1833, after three months with it, and took over the *American Monthly Magazine*, which he and Park Benjamin soon made into a Whig organ. S. D. Langtree, who was Hoffman's actual successor, Flint's editorship being nominal, was fresh from an editorship on Stone's *Commercial Advertiser*. He had left the magazine, two months before this review was published, to Clark and Edson. (F. L. Mott, *op. cit.*, pp. 606, 607.) But the *Knickerbocker* could not be called a really partisan periodical.

might have allowed him to pour out spleen if he had had any, he wrote calmly:

You say nothing of the letter, which has brought out Messrs. King and Webb. The latter is vulgar and abusive and contradictory. The former cuts the subject, avoiding all the points at issue, and affecting to laugh at that which he cannot refute. On my return, I shall probably make a short rejoinder and let the matter drop.

He really considered the book a success, for "The political part of the letter will stick."[352]

The battle was conducted by the bank press on these principles: the real political arguments were not to be met frankly and fairly, but only jeeringly and in asides or digressions or subordinate paragraphs, as if Cooper's opinions did not form the main issue and were at best only laughable puerilities; Cooper's early novels were to be consistently degraded from their former position in our literature, and the European novels were to be regularly denounced as un-American; Cooper himself was to be established as a cranky and irritable egotist, crazy for extravagant praise, very snobbish in social tastes, grasping in matters of property, and so unpatriotic that he sneered constantly at Americans and had taken on all sorts of absurd foreign airs.

An article in the *New England Magazine*[353] was the perfection of this kind of reviewing. The recognition of Cooper's real point in *A Letter to His Countrymen* is reduced to a mere half page of comment, and the political bias of the magazine is sufficiently clear:

The second part of the letter is a sort of political essay upon the powers of the various departments of the government, written apparently with the amiable purpose of enlightening the people of the United States, who have hitherto had no better teachers in constitutional law, than such shallow

[352] Letter to Mrs. Cooper, Cooperstown, June 26, 1834. Unpublished. Cooper collection, Yale.

[353] VII (August, 1834), 154-157.

tyros as John Marshall, Joseph Story, Daniel Webster, and others. It deserves very little notice of any kind. He has some very original notions, such, for instance, as that the Union is more in danger from legislative than executive usurpation. He gravely censures the Senate, for passing their late vote of disapprobation upon the President, and maintains that they thereby transcended their constitutional powers. How unlucky it is that Mr. Webster did not know Mr. Cooper's opinion upon this subject, before he printed his speech, as he probably would not, in that case, have so exposed his gross ignorance of the constitutional authority of the body to which he belongs.

It takes three full pages to contain the *New England Magazine's* sneers not only at the dullness and heaviness of Cooper's late novels, but at the flight of his common sense along with his genius; at his "soreness," "sensitiveness and conceit," "monomania," "self-love," "hallucination of his own importance," "undignified and unmanly" counseling of "his passion and not of his reason" and "false and morbid cast." The attack, indeed, is only an amplification of its thesis: "If the old saying be true—that whom God wishes to destroy, he first deprives of his wits—we advise Mr. Cooper to make his will and set his house in order, for his time is at hand."

Now let us see how far Webb advanced this program in The *Morning Courier and New York Enquirer* of June 20, 1834. His two columns of abuse opened with some remarks about us, if we constitute a part of posterity:

Mr. Cooper . . . has given us a work which we do not hesitate to pronounce *invaluable*—not to the public, but to the future historian upon whom may devolve the task of writing the biography of 'The Walter Scott of America,' as he assures us he has been called on the other side of the Atlantic. We say this work will prove invaluable to his biographer, because as everybody knows, to prepare a good biography, the writer should be familiarly acquainted with the prominent characteristics of his subject.

How valuable Webb's article is to the biographer may be tested by his gibe about Cooper's wishing to be called after Sir Walter. "If there is a term that gives me more disgust than any other, it is to be called, as some on the continent *advertise me*, the 'American Walter Scott.' It is offensive to a gentleman to be nicknamed at all, and there is a pretension in the title, which offends me more than all the abusive reviews that ever were written." This was true because, he said, the idea of rivalry with Scott never crossed his brain; he thought of Scott's writings as of Shakespeare's, as something he was not called upon to link with himself or his position.[354] This is what we know Cooper had really said on the nickname in 1831, to dissuade from its use an English editor whom, at the same time, he was thanking graciously but modestly for some recent encomiums. But it is too difficult for a nation to rise up and confront a Webb flatly with the proper refutation; and so the article's innuendoes lived on. Cooper had formerly been James F. Cooper, so Webb said, but since going abroad he had been J. Fenimore Cooper. (The reverse is true; Cooper had earlier hyphenated his mother's name with his—she had wanted a son to take her name—but had dropped the hyphen after going away.) Until Cooper had "expatriated himself both in person and feeling," according to Webb, literary critics had been very generous with him, having praised the beauties of his writing, applauded his patriotism, and "studiously concealed his manifold faults." But he had been so overwhelmed with egotism that lately he had deserted the American scene, where novelty had assisted him, and had boldly entered competition with Scott in Scott's field; the European novels had been criticized with freedom but with a "kindness and forbearance which Mr. Cooper has not properly appreciated." A "childish and characteristic *egotism*" had caused Cooper to blame the decline of his popularity on the jealousy of "*Louis Philippe* and the other Crowned Heads of Europe." He had taken offense at Cassio's article because he could not conceive that an "*American* could be guilty of so great a sacrilege as to question his superiority to all the Novelists of the age." The *Morning Courier and New York Enquirer* had "strenu-

[354] *Correspondence of James Fenimore-Cooper*, I, 227.

ously endeavored to defend him" by its editorial of June 15, in which editorial there was not a breath of offense. But the real cause of Cooper's pique, Webb asseverated, was the *Morning Courier and New York Enquirer's* unfavorable but highly just review of *The Headsman*; and he said the American press should be indignant at Cooper's attempt to "arrest the custom" of copying from English journals. As for Cooper's politics—the Constitution, the Senate, the President's protest, and removal of the deposits are all "drawn into this letter, without any apparent reason, other than to administer to the pride of Andrew Jackson, and to exhibit the immense superiority which a few years residence in Europe has given Mr. Cooper over his countrymen, in defining the character and principles of our government." But Cooper's childishness had produced a book which will call forth the ridicule of all readers who are not "biased by its party character" (or, as I take Webb's meaning, of all Whigs and Bank men).

The editorial closes with a paragraph saying that Cooper's fame:

> is not so perfectly overwhelming as to cause Americans to forget, that even if he should carry his *threat* into execution and write no more, they may still find some consolation in the reflection, that the beautiful Addisonian style and graphic sketches of Irving will remain to delight us, whilst the more vigorous and patriotic productions of Paulding, will continue to inculcate a deep love of country and keep it alive in the bosoms of future generations, when both Cooper and those he esteems the ephemeral conductors of our daily Press, shall have ceased to be remembered.

Webb added pointedly that he was in doubt whether Cooper thought the *Letter* would make him Secretary of the Navy by demonstrating that "Andrew Jackson is the solon of the age" and that Webster, Clay, and Calhoun were ignorant of law.

Charles King's editorial in the *New York American* of June 21 did, as Cooper said, avoid all the points at issue. It appears to be a really clever satire, and must have amused and convinced hundreds of readers who did not realize that it was a complete misrepresentation. It purports to be a review of two works: *A Letter to His Countrymen*, by J. Fenimore Cooper, and *A Letter to His Countrymen*, by C. Colored Coat. The first pretends to be a serious treatment. It states that Cooper had two objects in the pamphlet; first, to defend himself against certain attacks from American editors, and second, to oppose the practice of quoting foreign opinions in American journals. To the first object, King replies that the *American* has never done anything to warrant the charges. To the second, he makes this evasive but doubtless effective retort:

> we certainly could not keep our countenance if attempting to discuss the rest of the volume; unless indeed the mirth that was provoked by the unheard-of vanity and assumption it displays, should be checked by sorrow for such fatuity in a gifted mind; for such, all undisciplined as it is, do we regard that of Mr. Cooper.

The other review is a parody of Cooper's *Letter*. It mingles quotation and mimicry cleverly enough to make him appear absurd. It shows a high degree of the supposed egotism and sensitiveness; it amusingly touches off Cooper's actual tendency to explain the obvious; it ridicules his fears of Doctrinaires and mocks his ideas on the union, the Bank, Jackson's wisdom and the Senate's inadequacy. A footnote intimates that the Man in the Claret Colored Coat expects an appointment from Van Buren. The whole is funny without being good natured. It is just the kind of thing that is quotable in a gossiping corner of the club. It was written by "Cassio."

The *Commercial Advertiser* had enough to say for two days' printing.[355] Yet it did little except repeat all its old offenses; call the political arguments trivial without refuting them; add a ridiculous insult about how "aristocratic" Cooper had been in his youth when he wrote *Precaution*;

[355] June 20, 23, 1834.

and say it hoped it had now withdrawn its mischievous assertions (when in truth it had not even mentioned the crux of Cooper's objections).

So the author of *Precaution* had been an aristocrat in his youth, and it was only recently, when professions of democracy were a politic thing, that so much had been heard from him about the people! One would think absurdity could not go farther, but it could. The fictitious Aristocrat Cooper was only being sketched in. Before long the myth of his irascibility was to be so successfully circulated that a journalist of Plattsburg who did not know Cooper but battened on his party's editorials was to think, by an immemorial association of ideas, that Cooper was a bachelor, and was to write:

Mr. Cooper is, we believe, an old bachelor, and doubtless is becoming deeply tinctured with the misanthropy which peculiarly characterises the unhappy class of beings, to which he belongs. Get married, Mr. Cooper get married, and cultivate the domestic and social virtues and live in peace with your neighbors.[356]

Thus in Whig journalism lies the real origin of the Handsome Mr. Effingham of law-suit fame. During the next few years his imaginary personality grew more and more distinct upon the yellow sheets. With the publication of *Homeward Bound* he found his name; he stole it from the most interesting character in that novel. The Effinghams of *Homeward Bound* and *Home as Found* were created by Cooper to exemplify some admirable American characteristics and some which he did not approve. That fact was of no consequence to Webb and his ilk. Effingham had faults, and he resembled the fictitious character they had created. By certain tricks of interpretation, he might also be called an autobiographical portrait. Cooper was Effingham; Effingham was a disagreeable, sensitive, aristocratic snob. *Voila!*

Towards this vantage point in reviewing, the Whigs were already well advanced in 1834.

[356] *Plattsburg Whig*, October 14, 1837.

CHAPTER VI

The Building Up of Effingham

COOPER had other books already written, to be thrown out soon to this school of sharks. He did not write a new book for four years after his farewell, but a year after the publication of *A Letter to His Countrymen*, *The Monikins* came from the press,[357] and after this the books of European travel appeared with the old Cooperian frequency of one or two a year. In the spring of 1835[358] he printed the A. B. C. letters on the power of the executive, the noble stand of Jackson, and the contemptible stand of the Whigs regarding the indemnity payments.

The papers had not needed a new book as an excuse for attacks. When there was nothing to write about, they could at least punish him by omitting his name from places where it belonged.[359] When N. P. Willis said in his article on American literature in the British *Athenaeum* that the ungrateful American press did not deserve so fine a man as Cooper to write for their country, the Whig *Daily Advertiser* in Boston copied the rest of the essay but omitted all references to the author of *The Spy*.[360] When the depression, which Cooper's publisher and all other Whigs blamed upon the Democrats, brought down Cooper's sales along with other men's, the enemy took this as an opportunity to exult over a report that "a cannon of so large a *bore*" was having difficulties, and that publishers were refusing his "cumbrous manuscripts."[361]

[357] July 9, 1835.
[358] March 14, 21, 25, 28, 31; April 4.
[359] *E.g.*, article on American authors, *New York Mirror*, XII (April 4, 1835), 317.
[360] *Athenaeum* (British), VIII (January 3, 1835), 9-13.
[361] *New Yorker*, VI (December 15, 1838), 205.

But of course the A. B. C. letters did give opportunity for volleys of sarcasm about his "beauties" and his hacking away at Webster in a manner "too blood-thirsty, for so amiable a man."[362] Always, in one guise or another, this accusation of unamiable nature was the jewel the Whigs preserved.

Now, *The Monikins* was built upon a really clever satirical conception of the "stake in society" doctrine. The leading character is Sir John Goldencalf, a divertingly literal-minded young Englishman who is convinced that the more stakes a man holds, in the more societies, the more excellently he will govern. Impelled by this political idealism, he sets forth on a world journey, investing in social stakes as he goes. There are many good laughs in the book, and many shrewd comments to be enjoyed by anyone who has a knowledge of early nineteenth century political ideas. The Leap-lowers are ridiculously subservient to Leap-high opinion, and the satire against American Doctrinairism is made sufficiently plain by the use of the epithet "political indoctrinated." A highly amusing adventure symbolizes the futility of the monarch in the British government. The difference between the British constitution, which nominally recognizes three estates, and the American, which rests upon a threefold division of power, is shown in parable by the ingenious comparison of a tripod, composed of king, lords, and commons and held unsteadily by three unequal legs, and a single beam with three branches, planted sturdily in the people. The evil of American commercialism is represented by the allegory of a great moral eclipse which takes place in Leap-low; during the eclipse men think only of dollars and act not according to principle, but according to interest. The strongest satire in the book occurs here, and plain hints relate the eclipse to the American Whig party. Sir John Goldencalf, for instance, noticed that

[362] *Morning Courier and New York Enquirer*, March 26, 1835. See also *ibid.*, March 18, 1835; *Evening Post*, March 17, 1835, quoting *New York American.*

during this moral darkness "All the money-getting classes, without exception, showed a singular predilection in favor of what is commonly called a strong government." In some surprise, he asked a Leap-low friend the reason for this circumstance, saying, " 'I have always been led to think that trade is especially favorable to liberty; and here are all your commercial interests the loudest in their declamations against the institutions.' " The explanation of the Leap-lower, who must have been a Democrat, was as follows:

> 'Now, your merchants, dwelling in towns, and possessing concert means, and identity of interests, have been able to make themselves remarkable for contending with despotic power, a fact which has obtained for them a cheap reputation for liberality of opinion; but, so far as monikin experience goes, . . . no government that is essentially influenced by commerce has ever been otherwise than exclusive, or aristocratic.'

Upon receiving this reply, Sir John at once bethought him of the aristocracy of Venice; Cooper's reader, meanwhile, remembers *The Bravo* and its association of Venice with Doctrinairism and the Whig commercial aristocracy.[363]

The *Sketches of Switzerland* had a good deal of Democratic opinion, too. Morse at once recognized that it was a triumph over the *New York American*,[364] and Bryant pleased the author by saying the "extreme aristocrats" complained of its democracy.[365] Now, the democracy of *Switzerland* was in part simply Cooper's habitual defense of republicanism.[366] But it does not stop with antagonizing the Whig press by remarks of this vaguely Democratic nature; it boldly assumes a partisan position on more than one strictly political issue.

[363] *The Monikins*, p. 326; Chapters XVIII, XX; pp. 331-333, 356ff.

[364] *Correspondence of James Fenimore-Cooper*, I, 355-356.

[365] *Ibid.*, I, 361.

[366] *Sketches of Switzerland*, Part First, II, 145-147, 166, 179.

Cooper casts slurs at the Yankees;[367] he accuses the commercial class of imitating what he denominates a British habit of blackguarding;[368] he insists that American free trade would benefit England but not the United States;[369] he explains to foreigners that a state has a right to do anything which the constitution does not forbid, even to governing a colony;[370] he asserts that the Senate's vote of censure against Jackson during the session of 1833-1834 is the kind of thing which will ultimately destroy liberty;[371] he declares that the president's veto power is liberty's defense;[372] and he strikes a blow at the face of the whole Whig opposition to "King Andrew" when he says: "The school-boy use of the epithet tyranny can delude no honest and reflecting American, on these essential points."[373] The thesis of *The Bravo* is revived in a paragraph commenting on the apparent but unreal democracy which Cooper believes to have formerly existed in Schaffhausen.[374] But the most daring political comment in the book is a startling passage which declares that Cooper knew from his personal acquaintance with the old Federal party that many Federalists of the old school actually "meant revolution and a monarchy."[375] After such a statement, it is of small avail to Cooper that his preface protests his aloofness from both of "the two great parties that divide the country, and which, though so bitterly hostile and distrustful of each other, will admit of no neutrality."[376]

If the Whig critics were disgruntled at the first part of

[367] I, 145-146.
[368] II, 123.
[369] II, 126-129.
[370] I, 55.
[371] I, 210-211, note.
[372] I, 211, note.
[373] I, 212.
[374] I, 135-136.
[375] *Ibid.*, II, 156-158.
[376] *Ibid.*, I, 10-11.

Sketches of Switzerland, they found nothing to appease them in Part Second. These volumes were permeated by constant and openly expressed distrust of Louis Philippe and all his party. An author who writes that "The system of the *juste milieu* . . . is a stupendous fraud, and sooner or later will be so viewed and appropriately rewarded,"[377] and who reiterates this opinion with the enrichment of plentiful anecdote is certainly inviting Whig animosity. When such a man also asseverates that the true motto of the French government party is a cry raised by the merchants, "vive le commerce!"[378] and when he describes this mercantile governing class as one which practices "stupendous frauds,"[379] he is not endearing himself to the American commercial faction. Nor is he winning over the Whig party when he describes Louis Philippe's declaration of martial law in Paris in 1832 as an unconstitutional and needless act which had the single merit of "throwing aside the mask, and of showing the world in what manner the present authorities understand a government of the people."[380] But the frankness of such remarks in *Sketches of Switzerland* is not less remarkable than their frequency.

Besides the distrust of the Doctrinaires which runs through this book, Cooper interpolated in *Switzerland* miscellaneous allusions to American politics which could only irritate his Whig readers. He admitted,[381] for instance, that he had drawn his information on the old *regime* largely from Lafayette, a man identified with the revolutionists. Then, he wrote a passage[382] concerning Gouverneur Morris which was enough to arouse the old party antagonisms of the 1790's, days when Federalists supported England and the English monarchy, and Republicans cheered on France and the French

[377] *Sketches of Switzerland,* Part Second (Philadelphia, 1836), 1, 73.
[378] *Ibid.,* I, 80.
[379] *Ibid.,* I, 90.
[380] *Ibid.,* I, 111.
[381] *Ibid.,* I, 8.
[382] *Ibid.,* I, 12.

republic. President Adams had found it a nice problem to choose a minister to France, with England taking offense at the appointment of Monroe, who was too much inclined to liberty and equality, and the Republic herself refusing to receive the monarchical Morris. This old quarrel had been smouldering since Cooper's boyhood.[383] Now he stirred the fire by reporting Lafayette's opinion that Gouverneur Morris had contributed to the downfall of Louis XVI by consistently giving opinions "against democracy, advising resistance, when resistance was not only too late, but dangerous." He added to Lafayette's statement an expression of his own disapproval of Morris's conduct; and by this criticism of a Federalist hero he strengthened all the political implication of his frequent and impassioned complaints of the un-American behavior of American representatives abroad.[384] It was *Sketches of Switzerland,* Part Second, which furnished Cooper's definition of the French Doctrinaires, the definition which asserted that there existed in America a party similar to this but more extreme in its eagerness for retrogression. Certainly the four volumes on Switzerland, when all is considered, bore heavily upon the entire Whig faction.

Then there were two other real dangers to Cooper in the *Sketches.* One was a severe criticism of newspapers, though not especially of American ones.[385] The other was the very just judgment, repeated many times, that Americans are not superior to the rest of the world in scenery nor in taste, but in republican institutions.[386] The latter judgment gave a rich opportunity to the papers to slander Cooper in revenge for the former criticism; it became, in their misquotation, an intentional insult to American scenery and taste.

Gleanings in Europe; *France* contained less political matter,

[383] For an echo of it in 1832, see *Niles' Weekly Register,* XLIII (October 13, 1832), 99.

[384] *Sketches of Switzerland,* Part Second, I, 71.

[385] Part First, II, 122-125.

[386] *Ibid.,* I, 72, 176, 188; II, 115, 166, 237-238.

though it was shot through with fears of Doctrinairism and distrust of the English.[387]

But *Gleanings in Europe*: *England* was different from the other books of travel. It was not really a book of travel at all, but a comparison of the social and political institutions of the two nations, with the conscious aim of showing Americans the evils of imitation.

In pursuing the comparison between English and American institutions, Cooper found that the fundamental difference is one which he had already described in *A Letter to His Countrymen* and in *The Monikins*; "The government of the United States has no pretension to a trinity in its elements, though it maintains one in its action; and that of Great Britain pretends to one on its elements while it has a unity in its action." This statement of difference may be taken as the thesis of *England*; all of Cooper's remarks lead back to it. The single power which rules from above the tripod of English government is an aristocracy of property; the single class which supports America's triple-branched column is a superior mediocrity.[388]

In this difference, Cooper believed America to have the advantage of England. But it was an advantage which might be lost by persistent neglect of the American superiority and by subservience to domination from the foreign system. Americans who continually repaired to outworn English standards were holding back American principles until they lagged behind the country's actual progress in facts; in matters of taste as well as in matters of principle, America was sure to be retarded by a course of perpetual imitation. In his attempt to warn the younger nation of her danger, Cooper collected illustrations of England's domination of American thought and of American slavery to English prejudice. To

[387] I, 53, 257, 265; II, 163-164, 189.

[388] *England*, I, 233-234; II, 247; I, 237; II, 140; I, 85ff.; II, 96; II, 115-116.

make the picture the more instructive, he described in detail the contempt with which he believed the English repaid their American idolators.[389] He insisted that he did not feel towards England either personal dislike or a sense of injury; but he took pains to describe certain slights which he believed that he was offered because he was an American. Though the narration of these incidents was interpreted as being an evidence of peevishness by readers who would not or could not understand Cooper, yet Cooper certainly intended his painful anecdotes to be contributors to his thesis.[390] They are a part of his plea to the United States to recognize its own character and live up to that character with dignity. What Whig could have enjoyed this book?

The book on Italy was the least political of all the travel volumes. There are a few political references. There were the remarks that commercial interests in America lost our country the respect of Europe because they led foreigners to think we would not fight; that commercial powers overawe the press, and "will ever be found in opposition to any administration that loyally carries out the intention of the government"; that Jackson had made an attempt to preserve government and principles in his dealings with France, but Congress had blocked his action; that politicians are afraid of commercial men and their press. There were frequent attacks on Congress in the second volume.[391] But in the main it is a pleasant, desultory collection of impressions.

The American Democrat followed *Italy* in 1838. Here is a book in which Cooper disclaimed not only partisan aims but all party connections. He said he stood between the two extreme parties; the one, which had fantastic conceptions of democracy's power to correct every ill, and the other, which desired a return to aristocracy, hoping to get it by

[389] *Ibid.*, II, 136, 134-135, 221, 112ff.; I, 116-117; II, 130, 156-158, 246.
[390] *Ibid.*, I, 24.
[391] *Italy*, II, 27, 30.

allowing democracy to run a course of excesses. Of course he was sincere in his statement. Nevertheless, *The American Democrat* was undeniably a Democrat with a Jacksonian eye. He professed a wish to do away with parties altogether, but we can see that the one American party which would result would have more resemblance to the Democratic than the Whig. He repeated just the opinions which had already offended the Whigs and pleased the Democrats over and over.[392] Not only did he interpret the constitution in a Democratic way, but he lamented the existence of an opposing party. Writing on legislative and executive usurpation, upholding the necessity of the President's veto power, he said: "Such is the intention of the constitution, though the tactics of party, and the bitterness of opposition, have endeavored to interpret the instrument differently, by appealing to the ancient prejudices derived from England." This is the same disagreement with the Whigs which had broken out in *A Letter to His Countrymen.*

All these books were reviewed as *A Letter to His Countrymen* had been. There were a few incidental words of praise from the West and South,[393] but in the papers I have read there was only one real review of Cooper that was friendly in 1835, and this came from a Jacksonian section. The *Baltimore American* published it, and the *Evening Post* loyally brought it into Whig territory.[394] It spoke well of the dispassionate and tranquil observations Cooper had been

[392] See the sections "An Aristocrat and a Democrat," "On Commerce." Note the preference for the evils of democracy to the evils of aristocracy in "On the Disadvantages of Aristocracy" and "On the Disadvantages of Democracy." Note pp. 9-11, 14-15, 16-17, 27-28, 33-34, 56, 66-68, 105, 160-162.

[393] *Southern Literary Messenger,* I (February, 1835), 315; (May, 1835), 478, 482-483; *Western Monthly Magazine and Literary Journal,* IV (January, 1835), 24. Both of these journals were inclined towards Jacksonism or to sectional distrust of Whigs.

[394] July 15, 1835.

making, of his wide and keen vision, and of his unenfeebled sympathies for American republicanism. The *Knickerbocker Magazine* said the opposite about the novelist's character, and seemed to think *The Monikins,* which it called "a mass of husks and garbage," had disgraced the country.[395] Both this magazine and the *Journal of Belles Lettres* objected to the introduction of the finance debate. So it went with journal after journal.[396] The *Morning Courier and New York Enquirer* would not review the book, but it commented freely on other reviews. Park Benjamin's Whig *New England Magazine* printed a savage review of *The Monikins,* and then[397] in an article called "Literary Humbug" complained that Cooper's mere name could still sell copies of his last work, though it was "as bad a book of its kind, as can well be written." The political color of this article consisted in some ridicule of Cooper's opposing the Holy Alliance. Webb facetiously took up this article as being "a blot and a disgrace," surely printed by an oversight of the editors, for in America "Whose books sell worse than his?" Then when the Albany *Argus* quoted an adverse review, Webb expressed surprise, but took it as another sign of a recent tendency for the *Argus* to "cut the *Evening Post* and all its adjuncts."[398]

The year 1836 and *Sketches of Switzerland* produced no change of heart. Webb plucked the old Whig string of

[395] *Knickerbocker Magazine,* VI (August, 1835), 152-153. But the magazine had condemned the book even before publication: V (April, 1835), 362. *Journal of Belles Lettres, Waldie's Select Circulating Library,* VI (July 14, 1835), Number 2; *ibid.,* VI (July 21, 1835), Number 3.

[396] *Portland Magazine,* I (August 1, 1835), 352; *American Quarterly Review,* XVIII (December, 1835), 444; *Museum of Foreign Literature, Science and Art,* XXVII (October, 1835), 343; *Journal of Belles Lettres, Waldie's Select Circulating Library,* VI (July 14, 1835), Number 2; *ibid.,* VI (July 21, 1835), Number 3; *Commercial Advertiser,* August 21, 1835.

[397] IX (August, 1835), 136-137.

[398] *Morning Courier and New York Enquirer,* September 3, 22, 1835.

Cooper's incorrigible sensitiveness; the less political *Southern Literary Messenger* thought Cooper had been more splenetic than it was like him to be, but the spleen was justified. A few neutral critics praised its descriptions with polite moderation.[399] The Whigs made up the largest number of the reviewers, and they attacked the book's politics, selecting as their targets the frequent passages on the Doctrinaires, one on the finance controversy, one on Federalists, and one which by some exaggeration they construed to be a defense of trades unions.[400] They enjoyed harping on

[399] *New York Mirror*, XIV (September 10, 1836), 82; *ibid.*, XIV (November 4, 1836), 151; *Knickerbocker Magazine*, VIII (July, 1836), 102-103; *Southern Literary Messenger*, II (May, 1836), 401-403.

[400] *New York Mirror*, XIII (June 11, 1836), 399, gives the book a recommendation as agreeable light reading but objects to the passages on insults to Americans in Europe. It says Cooper has written himself out. The *New York American*, May 28, 1836, praises the book's Americanism and its excellent descriptions. It even agrees with Cooper that newspapers often have corrupt influence, and quotes a passage on this subject. It says, however, that the book is impaired by politics. The *American Quarterly Review*, XX (September, 1836), 228-244, disapproved of Cooper's hatred of England, his discussion of the withdrawal of deposits, his "slashing right and left at aristocracies," his dislike for commercial men. It said, "It is in bad taste to write out party doctrines to the utmost verge in this manner" and "He speaks strongly . . . of the bitterness of party spirit with us . . . . Though his application of this censure, we fear, was meant to be partial, yet we are willing to let it stand against all." The *Journal of Belles Lettres, Waldie's Select Circulating Library*, VII (May 31, 1836), Number 22, called the work tame. It referred with some pique to *A Letter to His Countrymen* and objected to the reappearance of "The old idols of Mr. Cooper . . . bitterness to England, laud to democracy—now and then sublimed with a spice of Trades-unionism, and the old philippics against the time-honoured institutions of the old world. . . ." The trades-unionism here mentioned is alleged to be present in Cooper's assertion of the superiority of the lower classes in clearness of views about the great principle which ought to control human affairs. Other excerpts are given to illustrate faults of style and vulgarity. A long description of the Alps is granted praise.

Cooper's "sensitiveness." Bryant defended Cooper against the political attacks, of course.[401] Reviews from England were reprinted and made the usual stir in this country. The *London Spectator* was half favorable,[402] and the *Examiner* commended his republicanism, saying that his countrymen ought to be pleased by the justice, generosity, and candour of his remarks on the French government. The *Quarterly Review* called the book surly, referred to Cooper's hatred of the English, and dwelt at length upon the damaging things the work reveals about Americans; many people in the western hemisphere must have writhed when they read this essay reprinted in the *Museum*. In short, those who liked scenery and Andrew Jackson admired *Sketches of Switzerland*, those who did not, denounced it; and a few more turns were made by the papers in the weaving of the Cooper myth.

Gleanings in Europe: *France* was even less successful because it lacked *Switzerland's* attractive passages of Alpine description. It won a few friends,[403] but the general opinion was that it was thin.[404]

Now, what should happen, in 1838, but that the *North American Review* trundled back on the scene after years of total neglect of the author of *The Pioneers*. It printed a

Remarkably enough, this review commends Cooper for being good-humored except for some petulance on politics and the English. *The Courier and Enquirer*, October 19, 1836, takes the opposite stand on this point, sneering at Cooper's sensitiveness and professing boredom at having to read of Cooper's finance controversy again.

[401] *Evening Post*, June 25, 1836.

[402] Copied by *Southern Literary Messenger*, II (October, 1836), 720-721; *Museum of Foreign Literature, Science, and Art*, XXIX (July-September, 1836), 461-463; XXX (November, 1836).

[403] *New York Mirror*, XIV (March 4, 1837), 285; *American Monthly Magazine* (New York), III n.s. (April, 1837), 401-405; *Knickerbocker Magazine*, IX (April, 1837), 421-422.

[404] *Southern Literary Messenger*, III (May, 1837), 272; *American Quarterly Review*, XXI (June, 1837), 522; *North American Review*, XLVI (January, 1838), 1-19.

review of *France* long after the book had gone the rounds of the other journals, and it behaved in characteristic fashion by dealing out a preliminary survey of Cooper's past works and then damning *France* with faint praise and Cooper with talk about his sensitiveness.[405] The *Knickerbocker* applauded,[406] and the *Journal of Belles Lettres* was pleased but thought the Boston critic had been too mild in his rebuke of Cooper's vanity and weakness—he should have been as severe as the *London Quarterly's* recent article on *England*.[407]

This article in the *Quarterly Review* was a sensation.[408] It was written by Walter Scott's son-in-law, Lockhart, and it was taken throughout the United States as a proof that Cooper had betrayed his country to foreign criticism. "What *will* our amiable novelist say?" asked the *Knickerbocker Magazine*, and exulted in the humiliation which it supposed he must be suffering from the really cutting personal remarks to which Lockhart had descended.[409]

J. G. Lockhart had long been cordially hated by American Democrats. N. P. Willis had once called him the "most unprincipled writer of the age, a bravo in literature, a reptile of criticism," because he consistently and savagely denounced liberalism in England and Democracy in America. But though Willis hated Lockhart's behavior, there were those who loved it. An article in the London *Metropolitan* had applauded his tactics in 1836, saying that England was endangered by the democratic ideas which threatened from America.[410] The reviewer in the *North American* was sympathetic to such an English view as this, for he asseverated

[405] *North American Review*, XLVI (January, 1838)), 1-19.

[406] XI (February, 1838), 182.

[407] *Journal of Belles Lettres, Waldie's Select Circulating Library*, XI (January 16, 1838), Number 3.

[408] LIX (October, 1837), 327-361.

[409] XI (February, 1838), 184-185.

[410] *Journal of Belles Lettres, Waldie's Select Circulating Library*, VII (March, 1836), Number 9.

that we like a republic in America but a monarchy might be preferable in Europe, and Cooper ought to keep his republicanism to himself. This was consonant with all the Whig expressions of opinion.

But the vicious personalities which Lockhart introduced along with his political bias are the most startling aspect of his review.

The *Knickerbocker Magazine* culled a few of Lockhart's fine flowers of rhetoric, gleefully rejoicing that Lockhart had sneeringly questioned Charles Mathews' ever having taken pleasure in the view of Albany; that he had called Cooper's book "an extravagance of vanity, morbid as Bedlam, and impudent as Billingsgate"; that he had lied about Cooper's birth by saying the novelist had a fondness for lords derived from his having been "a common seaman, for a long period, in the merchant service," with a " 'late and scanty acquaintance with polished society' "; that he had announced that Cooper was invited to breakfasts because Englishmen gave that invitation to the socially unacceptable; that he had called one of Cooper's statements "*an infamous falsehood*" and another "*a calumnious falsehood*"; and that he had taunted Cooper to reply by sneering, "Coffee and pistols for two!"

The Whigs, of course, resented no syllable of this, but only competed to add flourishes of their own.

Lockhart showed "potent causticity" in exposing "the gangrene" of Cooper's mind "in its most foul and diseased state"—Cooper's "friends are ashamed of the universality of his cynicism"—Cooper manifests "malignant irritability . . . against everything popular" and has "out-Trolloped Fidler" in insults to America.[411]

Lockhart had justly "scarified him [Cooper] to the bone."[412] *England* is a "breviary of an egotist's woes" and

[411] *Gentleman's Magazine,* II (February, 1838), 131. The title of this journal, I can not resist saying, seems here somewhat ironic.

[412] *New Yorker,* VI (October 13, 1838), 61.

abounds with "*sottises*." It reveals in Cooper spleen, dogmatism, and ill manners. England may rest assured that we attach no value to his opinions in this country.[413] The book "is well and vigorously written" and "possesses more than common interest," but Cooper is "a marked exception to the mass of Americans, who, he says, 'care no more for a lord than for a woodchuck!' " "As for the English, heaven help them!" "Would Washington Irving . . . support these declarations" which Cooper makes about England? "Mr. Cooper's claims, as a gentleman of good manners, cannot be exalted."[414]

Harmless little *Gleanings in Europe*: *Italy* appeared in the midst of this battery, and the publisher was very fearful indeed.[415] Even though *Italy* was innocuous, hostile journals used it for an excuse to attack; one could always recall the sins of former books in order to grant that the present one was better.[416] *Italy*, they could say, is a pleasanter book than *England* because "It is no discredit to our stout and keen-eyed 'Pilot' that his Yankee-village and main-deck education has not fitted him to shine in the saloons of what in England may be esteemed 'good society.' "[417] "Were we in the habit of using forcible dictionary words to express our meaning . . . we should assert to the public,—'Mr. James Fenimore Cooper is a blackguard and a slanderer!' " *Italy* would not sell even if "unincumbered by any of his faults—such as dullness, droningness, poverty of thought garbed in loose rags of

[413] *American Monthly Magazine* (New York), IV n.s. (October, 1837), 391-393; *New Yorker*, IV (October 17, 1837), 462-463. Both these journals were Park Benjamin's and Whig.

[414] *Knickerbocker Magazine*, X (October, 1837), 350-352; copied in *New Yorker*, III (October 14, 1837), 476-477.

[415] Letter to Cooper, Philadelphia, November 12, 1835. Unpublished. Cooper collection, Yale.

[416] *New York American*, June 2, 1838; *Morning Courier and New York Enquirer*, May 30, 1838.

[417] *New Yorker*, V (June 2, 1838), 173.

expression." Cooper had said that the bas reliefs at Parma were almost as bad as those in the rotunda of the Capitol at Washington, but had hoped that our Golden Age of sculpture was to follow. "Facetious remark that! very charming! next to abusing your mother, we can conceive of no more elegant recreation than that of vilifying your country. Our author indulges constantly in this vein. . . ." Cooper had said the Bay of Naples is more beautiful than New York Harbor, adding, "if it be patriotism to deem all our geese swans, I am no patriot, nor ever was. . . ." Well, retorted the reviewer, Cooper was our best example of American geese that had been taken for swans. "His political brethren, the Loco Focos, would be induced, no doubt, for a consideration, to furnish him with a charger in the shape of a rail, and a full parade-dress of tar and feathers.[418] Now, there is an interesting coincidence connected with the journal which concocted the last remark. The *American Monthly Magazine*, conducted by Hoffman and Benjamin, had at one time refrained from comments on national affairs and had indulged only popular poems and tales. In those days, it had given *Gleanings in Europe* a friendly review. This was in April, 1837. But the leading article in the periodical in September of that very year was an announcement that the time had come when the *American Monthly* must cease maintaining its principles merely incidentally, and must begin to enter into "practical discussion." The country was at a crisis because of "The course of the past and present administration, in preaching one doctrine and practising another; in hanging out banners of Democracy while enforcing an actual Despotism; in encouraging a Foreign political influence . . . while affecting a high-toned nationality" and so forth, the other Jacksonian hypocrisies being concerned with State banks and Federal interference in local affairs. In the same issue and in

[418] *American Monthly Magazine* (New York), XII (July, 1838), 74-84.

October appeared articles on the Bank, and it was in October that a long and savage attack (briefly quoted above) disposed of *England*.

There were a good many distortions in the course of this reviewing. Lockhart distorted Cooper's book to the point of falsification, and then when Lockhart's review was copied here it was cut so that it appeared even more savage than it was. The *Gentleman's Magazine* reported Cooper incorrectly,[419] Benjamin's *American Monthly* misquoted,[420] and the *Courier and Enquirer* pounced upon a footnote of Cooper's praising Jackson's recommendation of reprisals against France, and made it the sole topic of review.[421]

There was a wave of comparisons, just at this time, with Washington Irving, and Cooper was always made to suffer in the parallels.[422] Park Benjamin advised him to "institute a comparison in his own mind" between himself and Irving as to their relative standing in the affections of the people.[423] Benjamin should have been an authority on their relative standing; he had helped powerfully to create it.

Of course, Cooper was not entirely unfriended. There was always Bryant. To him, Lockhart's article was a "tissue of petulant railing." The *Quarterly* could have been expected to make some such rejoinder as it had done, he said, but this attempt was "made pointless by its angry and malignant tone."[424] For once the *New York Mirror* stood by Bryant manfully, saying that Cooper's book had been caustic and candid but not unfair, and that any book ever published would make the author of it appear "equally hate-

[419] I (October, 1837), 290-291.

[420] *Loc. cit.*

[421] September 8, 1837.

[422] *Knickerbocker Review, loc. cit.*; *Western Monthly Magazine and Literary Journal,* V (November, 1836), 685; *Morning Courier and New York Enquirer*, November 22, 1838.

[423] *New World,* III (November 27, 1841), 349.

[424] *Evening Post,* January 31, 1838.

ful and ridiculous" if it were similarly taken to pieces and reassembled. The *Mirror* hoped the *Westminster Review* or some other paper of the liberal party would reply to the *Quarterly*. In the meantime, it said:

> however his own countrymen may unite in deploring the unhappy temper in which Mr. Cooper writes of late years; and, however they may smile when foreign or domestick criticks show up the whimsicalities of his disposition, his essential manliness of character, his haughty independence and high-toned principal [*sic*] as a republican, an American and a gentleman, not less than his unquestioned superiority of talent, and his commanding station as one of the pioneers of our infant literature, intrench him too deeply in their esteem, their pride and patriotism for a hundred reviewers, though all as clever as he of the Quarterly to shake or impair. When such ephemeral comments shall have passed away, the world will judge the writings of Cooper by their intrinsic merits, and not by the opinions which individuals or parties may have expressed concerning them.[425]

Willis must have been behind this article. Elsewhere, he expressed his complete disgust with Lockhart for having insinuated in the October article that Cooper would not have been so flattered by Rogers's breakfasts as he had shown himself to be, if he had known that in London a breakfast was a probation for persons concerning whose "manners, character, or social position, there is some *uncertainty*." Willis retorted that Lockhart was a cat and looked the part. No one, he declared, would ever ask Lockhart to breakfast, for "Would any one in his senses begin his day by sitting down opposite to such a face for a couple of hours?" Every Englishman but Lockhart would agree that a breakfast invitation was "much more flattering" than one to dinner. Willis argued that Rogers would never have

[425] *New York Mirror*, XV (January 20, 1838), 239.

wished to insult Cooper, for he admired Cooper's independence and "spoke in the highest terms of him as a gentleman and a friend," having said enough in Willis's hearing "to gratify the self-love of the most exacting," even if one allowed for any margin of kindness he might have used in speaking to the novelist's compatriot. Rogers was a charming host, Willis said, and if Lockhart had ever been invited to a single one of his breakfasts, "he would have excused Mr. Cooper for dwelling complacently on the 'breakfasts in St. James's Place.'" So Cooper's defender dismissed Lockhart with this benediction: "Heaven send him a relaxation of his facial muscles, and a little charity to leave the world with."[426]

The *Mirror* spoke a gentle word for *Italy,* also,[427] and of course the *Evening Post* was delighted with Cooper's having said in that book that the merchant class will always "oppose an administration that loyally carries out the intention of the government.[428] So Cooper had Democrats and friends in American journalism.

The supposedly "sensitive" Cooper did not behave very much in his reputed character during all this noise, for

[426] N. P. Willis, "Ephemera," *Complete Works of N. P. Willis,* New York, 1846, 788-789. Perhaps Rogers really had a little too much of both Cooper and Willis. Sumner, who thought Cooper was right about Lockhart, yet wrote to Cooper's admirer, George S. Hillard, December 4, 1838: "Cooper and Willis have harmed us not a little; and then some others of our countrymen, who have not been so extensively received in society as these two, and who have written nothing, have yet left impressions not the most agreeable. A friend told me yesterday what Rogers said the other day to him: 'The Americans I have seen have been generally very agreeable and accomplished men; but there is too much of them: they take up too much of our time.' This was delivered with the greatest gentleness." *Memoirs and Letters of Charles Sumner,* II, 23.

[427] XV (June 16, 1838), 407.

[428] August 18, 1838. The *Hesperian* defended Cooper's prejudicies against the English, I (July, 1838), 250-255; I (August, 1838), 305-315.

instead of following the reviews, he had not even known *England* was off the press until his publisher wrote him that the papers had been "regularly attacking it or rather its author." Carey had grumbled that "It would have been perhaps more honest to have let the author alone & to have said more of the book."[429]

Why, no, Mr. Carey. The journalists, in order to serve their purposes, had to attack the man, not the book. It was not even necessary for them to read the book to review it. A satire of Cooper's critics under the title "Noctes Puffianae" represents Blunt and Puff preparing "for the flourishing" at a new book. From Blunt: "I hear, it is all about monkeys. I wonder if Mr. Cooper is attacking *us*? Some of us are apes, to be sure, but I don't think any of us are monkeys. I wish Mr. Cooper would get to his sailors and Indians again, and leave reforming the world alone. It is a very wicked world, and he won't make it a whit better." From Puff: "If there's any politics in it, I intend to castigate him about it; that's fine game. I have taken the sense of the community, and I find that it is pretty generally opposed to all novel-writer's politics; and therefore I shall allow myself to be indignant. But, Blunt, you must tell me what it is about, for I don't think I shall have time to read it myself."[430] This is, alas, too close to the truth to be witty. Even Puff's last remark is a literal one; an editor who was once told that he had written unfairly of Cooper answered that he had only glanced at the book in question but would abuse anything the author wrote.[431]

Cooper was disappointed that the public liked *Italy* better than *England*; "This is a proof," he wrote to his wife,

[429] Letter, Carey and Lea to Cooper, Philadelphia, September 13, 1837. Unpublished. Cooper collection, Yale.

[430] *Journal of Belles Lettres, Waldies' Select Circulating Library,* VI (July 7, 1835), Number 1.

[431] Letter, W. Pell to Cooper, New York, August 29, 1839. Unpublished. Cooper collection, Yale.

"how completely England has her foot on this country, for there is no comparison between *England* and *Italy*."[432] This is a true statement, as far as real intellectual interest is concerned, and it is even truer as far as strength of "American principles" is concerned.

But the reviewers were spoiling with inaction. *The American Democrat* was nothing that they could make a stir about. The *Evening Post* approved of it and found quotations from it useful in replying to his Whig opponents on one thing or another.[433] The Whigs admitted there was some common sense in it, but made some political objections and some sneers at Cooper's conceit.[434] Still, there was nothing here to raise a fight.

It was a magazine article which gave them their next opportunity. Here was a spectacle made to their wishes, J. F. Cooper reviewing a book of Lockhart's, the *Life of Sir Walter Scott*.[435] Unfortunately for their desires, however, it was not a spectacle of Cooper taking revenge. There was nothing to be seen that was vicious or spiteful. But Cooper did undertake to show that both Lockhart and the American people had idolized Scott beyond all reason, and to demonstrate that even Scott had some faults as well as virtues. In a way, this was a lunatic thing to do. Everyone would cry "Envy!" naturally. But Cooper was one of those people who have such faith in logic and in words as actually to think that if they prove their points people will believe them, and that if they say they are not envious when they really

[432] *Correspondence of James Fenimore-Cooper*, I, 382.

[433] *Evening Post*, April 13, June 18, July 18, 1838.

[434] *Morning Courier and New York Enquirer*, April 19, 1838; *New York American*, April 21, 1838; *Commercial Advertiser*, May 25, 1838.

[435] *Knickerbocker Magazine*, XII (October, 1838), 349-370. In this magazine, XI (April, 1838), 380-386, Cooper had offered some corrections to things Lockhart seemed to have altered in the *Diary of Sir Walter Scott*.

are not, their good faith will be understood. Unblessed are the logical, for of such are the babes in this world's wood.

In his review, Cooper wrote justly of Scott's charm and of his ability to throw the illusion of reality over improbabilities. But he expressed a purely republican objection to the Toryism of the Waverley novelist. He said, too, that there were certain meannesses in Scott, like reviewing his own works, making secret marks on letters of introduction to indicate how much they should be discounted, driving hard bargains with the Ballantines, and drinking too much. He did not attempt to prove Scott a bad man, but he did assert that he was not a man for Americans to deify as they did, and that Lockhart's insincere manipulation of the facts made his biography an unreliable book.

Now Cooper was not the only man in the world who suspected Scott was not a saint and martyr in all that writing that he did for money's sake. Thomas Carlyle might be mentioned. But to keep to American opinion, we have Charles Sumner's comment on Cooper's very review, put into his hands by Barry Cornwall:

> I think it capital. I see none of Cooper's faults; and I think a proper castigation is applied to the vulgar minds of Scott and Lockhart. Indeed, the nearer I approach the circle of these men the less disposed I find myself to like them. Scott is not *sans reproche*; and Lockhart seems without a friend. Of course, I see the latter often.[436]

Cooper was supported in his statements by the *Refutation of the Misstatements and Calumnies Contained in Mr. Lockhart's Life of Sir Walter Scott, Baronet, Respecting the Messrs. Balantine.*[437]

[436] Letter to George S. Hillard, London, January 12, 1838, in E. L. Pierce, *Memoir and Letters of Charles Sumner*, Boston, 1877, II, 38. Sumner was not especially prejudiced either for or against Cooper; II, 23, 106.

[437] He read this book; *Correspondence of James Fenimore-Cooper,* I, 384-385.

But American reviewers were not looking for honesty in him, but for sensitiveness. This was a rich field for imagining they saw it. Lockhart had just reviewed Cooper, and Lockhart had said insulting things in this very biography about Cooper. To be sure, the insulting things were not true. Samuel Rogers had made breakfast parties popular, and the phrase about Cooper's having the "want of manners" common among his countrymen was a misprint (corrected later) for Scott's actual phrase, "want of manner." But the admixture of untruth was not a thing which ever spoiled the Whig reviewers' pleasure.

Well, *Fraser's Magazine*, Lockhart's political ally, called Cooper's review a "vile thing" drifting on a "foul current of republican abuse and calumny." Egotism, jealousy, republicanism—Cooper was compact of these, and all were contemptible. Much notice was taken of Cooper's remarks upon Scott's homage to hereditary power. The *Museum* did not fail to give this article American publicity.[438] Some of our American home-made replies to Cooper were as good retorts upon his egotism.[439] The Whig *American Monthly* and *New Yorker* were the fiercest. The latter called Cooper "low-minded and contemptible" in his "attempt to avenge himself." The climax was a formal answer to the "attack" on Sir Walter, printed in the *Knickerbocker* itself,[440] which magazine had been nervous over the trouble it had got itself into, and had already published a disavowal of responsibility for the opinions Cooper had expressed.[441] The answer it now printed was an unfair and quibbling retort which garbled Cooper's arguments and cast slurs upon him as being

[438] *Museum of Foreign Literature, Science, and Art*, XXXV (April, 1839), 529-532.

[439] *American Monthly Magazine* (New York), XII (July, 1838); Boston *Daily Advertiser*, October 18, 1838; *New Yorker*, VI (October 13, 1838), 61; *New York Mirror*, XVI (November 17, 1838), 165.

[440] XII (December, 1838), 508-520.

[441] XII (November, 1838), 471.

inhospitable, inordinately jealous, and insincere in professions he had made in *The American Democrat.*

Perhaps it would be worth while to illustrate from this review the method by which reviewers achieved their effects; not because this was one of the most rabid articles, but because it was one of the more dignified. Cooper courteously apologized for being about to break the rule, *"Nil nisi bene de mortuis,"* pleading as excuse that Scott's having authorized a biography waived all privilege except the right to abstract justice. He was answered with a groundless sneer at his grammar: "by saying 'the axiom of *Nil nisi,* he transforms his latin phrase into a latin author;" and with the testy remark that Cooper could have saved himself the trouble of saying Scott deserved mere justice, as that was "quite undisputed." One of the petty dishonesties of which Cooper complained was Scott's having written and published, for personal or political reasons, a review which, by Scott's own admission, was worthless and puffing. Cooper was making the point that Lockhart ought to have taken cognizance of these petty faults and ought not to have held Scott up as a model to all young men at the same time that his own book revealed these failings in the hero. The *Knickerbocker's* ideas on this ethical point were: "of all the men on the face of the whole earth, [Cooper] should be the very last to *complain* of the criticism which 'slurs over absurdities and enlarges upon beauties.'" In connection with a discussion of Scott's toryism, Cooper made some statements that Scott had adhered both in his Scottish and English allegiance to what were, in British phrase and custom, sovereigns or lords *de facto* instead of sentimentally clinging to the heads *de jure.* The reviewer gave another meaning entirely to the phrase, *de jure,* making out that whom Parliament recognised was sovereign *de jure*; concealing this double use of the term, he accused Cooper of hypocrisy in his republicanism and he cried that he hoped "the October number of the *Knickerbocker* will never reach Victoria's boudoir: the hammer-and-tongs logic of our critic *might* compel Her Majesty to resign." When Cooper, having mentioned something which looks like an indication of duplicity in Scott, said that it was too slight an incident to be considered without further proof and that it would not have aroused suspicion at all if Scott's probity and sincerity elsewhere had arisen superior to such an accusation, the *Knickerbocker* might well have taken exception; but it screamed: "Without more positive evidence? Without more positive *brass*! . . . *who* is this bravo of criticism? this common stabber? that presumes to suspect without occasion."

To turn back to Cooper's criticism of Lockhart after reading this criticism of him is to return to a world where the air is freer and the company is dignified. If Cooper has faults which show in his article they are his zest for considering all sides of a bit of evidence (which makes him too insistent) and an interest in honor which some might call quixotic. He did not demand of Scott behavior higher than his own performance had always been, but he did condemn in Scott dishonesties which were common enough among political journalists. At any rate, the *Knickerbocker's* article pleased the Whigs;[442] a few more strokes had been added to their Cooper myth.

The spell of the Cooper myth was removed from one influential man, however, by this very review of Cooper's. Lewis Gaylord Clark, one of the editors of the magazine and a friend of Washington Irving, discovered something about the true Cooper. Before Clark met Cooper he hated him so that when Charles Wiley once offered to introduce the novelist he refused to allow it. According to his repentant confession afterwards, this antipathy had been aroused by the accounts in the papers "of his alledged pompous and un-American bearing abroad; of his unpleasant airs; his sudden . . . usurpa-

[442] *New Yorker*, VI (December 29, 1838), 228.

tion of . . . privileges on Otsego Lake . . . of his libel suits. . . ." And, once aroused, it had been strengthened by Clark's having once overheard him say that Clark's own friend Irving was "not a true American in feeling" but enjoyed a popularity established by "influenced and directed public opinion."

But one day Clark was forced to meet Cooper; the novelist called on business, and the editor could not decline. The business was a request that the *Knickerbocker* print the review of Lockhart's *Life of Sir Walter Scott.* Clark consented. Moreover, he was immediately pleased by Cooper's cordiality. Now, though the review brought on Cooper's head half the nation's accusations of paltry jealousy, Cooper and the article itself convinced Clark that it had not been motivated by any such emotion. He got the idea that behind Cooper's review lay some offense that Lockhart had once given. He determined to learn more about Cooper, and so he took the proof sheets to Cooper's rooms in the Astor House himself. Here all was warm and pleasant. There was a cheerful grate fire, four wax candles burned on a table, a flagon of old Madeira and two wine glasses stood below them. Clark secured a few admissions from Cooper, and what he called "subsequent personal research" gave him the secret, he thought. Whatever it was that Clark discovered, it made him an intensely sympathetic friend of Cooper. He considered that "If Cooper had been in London there would have been a duel," and in regard to the charge of sensitiveness, he said that Cooper did not allude to the notorious passage about "want of manners" either in his review or at any time in Clark's presence. He thought Cooper did us a good service in overturning Scott from his American pedestal of moral example.

"Such was the style," Clark said in conclusion, "in which the gifted American novelist drove helter-skelter in a coach-and-six through Lockhart's *Life of Scott*, always citing chapter and verse in support of his charges." And such was the manner in which Cooper's magnetism and manliness won to his side those whom rumor had kept from him.[443]

It is a pleasure to know that Cooper's friends and some great men who were not acquainted with him had rallied round him during these trying years. They wrote loyal encouragement about the nobility and justice of his course.[444] Those of them who were writers defended him in articles, N. P. Willis with the strong statement already quoted, on the unfair treatment the press had given him,[445] and Dr. James E. De Kay with a biography of Cooper in the *National Portrait Gallery* which he made into a highly intelligent defense of Cooper against the allegations of conceit and snobbery. This work came out in New York in 1834, and it was not without influence.[446]

But the help of his friends, even the help of his party, could not avail against that incessant propaganda which was recreating Cooper's whole identity in the concepts of the once adoring people. The Handsome Mr. Effingham had not yet been mentioned by name, but he had already been rounded

[443] Lewis Gaylord Clark, *Lippincott's Magazine*, VIII (December, 1871), 625-629. After this visit, but before the review was in press, Clark wrote to Cooper pointing out an inconsistency of Lockhart's insult to Cooper concerning English breakfasts, and asking Cooper whether the latter could resist "so admirable a chance to make a *short* knock-down blow." Letter to Cooper, New York, n.d. Unpublished. Cooper collection, Yale.

[444] Letters, Ashbel Smith to Cooper, *New York*, March 31, 1837; William Dunlap to Cooper, New York, July 24, 1833. Unpublished. Cooper collection, Yale; Horace Greenough to Henry Greenough, Paris, October 14, 1831, *Letters of Horatio Greenough to His Brother Henry Greenough*, p. 89; to Rembrandt Peale, Paris, November 8, 1831, *New York Mirror*, IX (March 3, 1832), 279; W. R. McNally to Cooper, Paris, August 24, 1834. Unpublished. Cooper collection, Yale.

[445] *Athenaeum* (British), VIII (January 3, 1835), 11.

[446] For instance, it influenced a very good defense of Cooper in the *Hartford Pearl and Literary Gazette*, IV (August 20, 1834), 5-6. On De Kay's authorship of the article in the *National Portrait Gallery*, see *American Historical Record*, III (November, 1874), 486.

out into an effigy which Whig editors had arranged among themselves to pass off upon the public and upon posterity. Within a year or two they had succeeded almost completely in their enterprise. One souvenir of that fact is a letter to Cooper from a school teacher, Thomas Baldwin, who had written Cooper an expression of regard for his character and authorship and, having received a kind answer, replied to thank him and confess that he had been so misled about Cooper's character by press accounts that he had actually feared Cooper would publish his note as an evidence of effrontery. Baldwin had thought himself "beyond being influenced by our venal press, but it proved I did not know myself."[447]

Edgar Allan Poe wanted an article from Cooper for the *Southern Literary Messenger,* and the editor of that faithful journal assured Cooper that "all those whose opinions are worth anything" were still his friends and enthusiastic admirers in 1836.[448]

[447] *Correspondence of James Fenimore-Cooper,* II, 456, 464-465.

[448] Letter, Thomas W. White to Cooper, Richmond, August 2, 1836. Unpublished. Cooper collection, Yale. A remark which seems to indicate hostility occurs in Una Pope-Hennessy's *Edgar Allan Poe, 1809-1849,* Macmillan, 1934, p. 175: "There was a notice of Fenimore Cooper, for example, that Mr. White said might land him in a libel action." White's words are not quoted, but a reference is made to a letter from White to Poe, September 29, 1835. We know that on October 1, only two days later, White wrote to Lucian Minor concerning an article which he hesitated to print, not from fear of a libel suit, but because it seemed "unnecessarily severe on Cooper" and because he did "not like to shoot so sarcastic an arrow at poor Cooper—however much he deserves it." The article in question he refers to as "'Autography' No. 1" and says if it is printed Cooper's and Irving's names must be struck out. (For the letter, see David K. Jackson, *Poe and the Southern Literary Messenger,* Richmond, 1934, pp. 101-102). If this is the article published soon after in the *Southern Literary Messenger,* II (February, 1836), 207, 209, there seems little cause for the anxiety. Perhaps the original was altered. The published piece consists of a series of epistolary fragments, printed, with a facsimile signature appended to each. The handwriting in each signature is analyzed for indications of character.

William Gilmore Simms, fellow-novelist and fellow-Democrat, member of the legislature of South Carolina, said of Cooper's labors:

> it is to be regretted, not that our literary men do not more frequently engage in politics, but that our politicians are not more generally literary men—at all events, not so very illiterate. Some increase of political decency might be the fruit of their improvement in this respect.[449]

And James Russell Lowell added to his classic couplet about Natty his stanzas on Cooper's work in these years:

> There is one thing in Cooper I like, too, and that is
> That on manners he lectures his countrymen gratis;
> Not precisely so either, because, for a rarity,
> He's paid for his tickets in unpopularity.
> Now he may overcharge his American pictures,
> But you'll grant there's a good deal of truth in his strictures;
> And I honor the man who is willing to sink
> Half his present repute for the freedom to think,
> And, when he has thought, be his cause strong or weak,
> Will risk t'other half for the freedom to speak,
> Caring naught for what vengeance the mob has in store,
> Let that mob be the upper ten thousand or lower.
>
> There are truths you Americans need to be told,
> And it never'll refute them to swagger and scold. . .

Yet the Thomas Baldwins over the United States, people who really admired Cooper's conduct, were somehow persuaded that his personality was of the kind to which it is best to give a wide berth. In spite of Bryant and Poe and Simms and Paulding and Lowell, one James Watson Webb could create Mr. Effingham, who was even in 1837 and 1838 waiting to be born into a name in 1839.

Cooper's is said to be illegible and unformed, of a "finicky" appearance. Irving's is called commonplace, a clerk's hand, but a hint is dropped that as author Irving may have talents which as penman he does not indicate.

[449] "The Writings of James Fenimore Cooper," *Views and Reviews*, First Series, pp. 229-230.

CHAPTER VII

Mr. Effingham and Jack Cade

THE last chapter has for a few pages been indulging in half-truth. That is to say, things were twice as bad in 1837 and 1838 as has yet been told. At about the time when the fire-eating London *Quarterly* was fulminating against *Gleanings in Europe*: *England,* the Whig press discovered an opportunity for some real tormenting. They found an excuse to change their flank attack on Cooper's character through ostensible reviews of his books to direct firing on his private behavior.

The Three Mile Point controversy has been frequently described by Cooper's biographers, but a brief restatement of the case with different emphasis will be required here. Judge William Cooper had ordered in his will that a certain point of land which he owned on Otsego Lake be held in trust until the year 1850, when it was to be inherited by a descendant bearing his name. In 1837, James Fenimore Cooper was the trustee in charge of this land. He had no son named William, and no interests in the title or the occupation of Three Mile Point except those created by sentiment and the duties of his trusteeship. Three Mile Point was a place connected with the tenderest memories of his boyhood. Certain spots, and notably a certain tree, were particularly dear to him because of their association with his father. The Coopers had always allowed the village people to use Three Mile Point as a picnic place. At first everyone understood that this privilege was granted as a free gift. But while James Fenimore Cooper was living in Westchester, in New York City, and in Europe, strangers drifted into town who had never known William Cooper or the family. At length these persons took it into their heads that the village of Cooperstown owned the Point. They used the place carelessly, and they destroyed William Cooper's tree.

When James Fenimore Cooper repurchased The Hall and returned to his old home, he naturally considered that it was time to assert his trusteeship over the use of Three Mile Point. The danger which the property was in may be judged from the fact that "Shad Cam," another point on the lake, was actually lost by the Cooper family through failure to defend their ownership.[450] Cooper inserted a card in a local paper warning people that trespassers on the Point would be prosecuted. There was nothing apologetic about this notice, and it would be difficult to adduce any reason why it should have been apologetic. It was worded as any ordinary trespass notice would have been worded. Immediately, the malcontents of Cooperstown held a mass meeting and showed how much of mob spirit the little village could produce. They resolved William Cooper had devised the Point to the use of the town; that all of James Fenimore Cooper's books should immediately be removed from the library; and that the members of the gathering "will and do denounce any man as a sycophant, who has, or shall, ask permission of James F. Cooper to visit the Point in question."

Contradictory accounts of this extraordinary convocation were printed by the two local papers, the *Otsego Republican* and the *Freeman's Journal.* These different attitudes were natural, for the former was a Whig and the latter a Democratic paper. The *Otsego Republican's* account was repeated in New York by the *Morning Courier and New York Enquirer*[451] and, with some reservations, by the *Commercial Advertiser.*[452] The Democratic version was reported there

[450] James Fenimore Cooper, *Legends and Traditions of a Northern County*, p. 20.

[451] August 15, 1837.

[452] August 11, 19, 1837. The *Commercial Advertiser* deplored the resolution regarding Cooper's books, but sympathized with the villagers about the use of the land.

by the *Evening Post.* Party papers throughout the state followed this lead, and soon the Three Mile Point difficulty was a national topic of partisan discussion.

The Whig account of the affair was that Three Mile Point was expressly reserved by William Cooper's will to the use of the citizens of Cooperstown, and that the Point had been "the daily, almost *hourly* resort of some of the inhabitants" until James Fenimore Cooper had published an abrupt notice ordering them off the premises. Accordingly a meeting was held of "the industry, intelligence, and respectability of the village of Cooperstown," who in an orderly and well conducted meeting enthusiastically passed a set of resolutions which were "full, pungent, yet respectful." This was the story told by the *Otsego Republican*[453] and retold by its friends. The Norwich *Chenango Telegraph*[454] had earlier printed a summary of the affair which the *Albany Evening Journal* and the *Otsego Republican* reprinted.[455] This Whig article began by saying that Cooper, "not satisfied with having drawn upon his head universal contempt from abroad, has done the same thing for himself at Cooperstown, where he resides." It closed with the ironic hope that "perhaps Mr. J. Fenimore Cooper himself will find the occasion a good one for addressing another edition of 'Letters to his Countrymen.'" This article was accompanied by an insulting paragraph on *Gleanings in Europe: England* copied from *Blackwood's Magazine* for August.

Cooper did not oblige by writing another letter to his countrymen. Of course, as his trusteeship necessitated, he published a true history of the ownership of Three Mile Point in the Democratic *Freeman's Journal* on August 21. A week

[453] August 14, 1837.
[454] October 4, 1837.
[455] Ethel R. Outland, *The 'Effingham' Libels on Cooper*, University of Wisconsin Studies in Language and Literature, 28, Madison, 1929, pp. 42-43.

later he printed a copy of the mass meeting's resolutions, which the officers of the meeting had for some reason failed to publish. He answered the claims of the villagers vigorously, perhaps scornfully, and he printed at the head of his letter the following passage:

> There shall be in England, seven half-penny loaves sold for a penny, the two hooped pot shall have ten hoops; and I shall make it a felony to drink small beer. All the realm shall be in common, and in Cheapside shall *my* palfrey go to grass.—*Jack Cade.*

Against the spirit of Jack Cade, the *Evening Post* came to Cooper's assistance on August 23.

In due time, Cooper filed suit for libel against the editor of the *Chenango Telegraph* for his false report.[456] He immediately demanded[457] from A. M. Barber, editor of the *Otsego Telegraph*, a retraction of the falsehoods which had been published in that paper. Barber refused, and he was brought to trial in May, 1839. Cooper won a verdict of $400, but before the judgment was perfected on July 25, 1840, he generously offered to cancel the verdict if Barber would yet publish a retraction and pay the costs of the suit.[458] Barber refused. He had a better plan than retraction; simply not to pay any damages in spite of the judgment. For the sake of example, Cooper astonished him by collecting the money in February through the sheriff. Without mentioning Cooper's two offers to cancel his action and his judgment, Barber now raised a whining protest in the

[456] *Ibid.*, pp. 42-45.

[457] Letter, Richard Cooper to the editors of the *Otsego Republican*, Cooperstown, August 11, 1837. Unpublished. Cooper collection, Yale. Richard Cooper was a nephew of James Fenimore Cooper who acted as legal counsel in his suits.

[458] Richard Cooper to A. M. Barber, July 16, 1840. Unpublished. Cooper collection, Yale.

New York papers,[459] declaring that he had been forced to bankruptcy by Cooper's cruelty. He had had to sell everything, he said, except his clothes, his hairbrushes, a campaign model of a log cabin, and a picture of Tippecanoe Harrison. Cooper merely said that he had "brushed off that mosquitoe."[460]

There were other mosquitoes, however, and in a leisurely and wondrously systematic way Cooper turned his attention upon them one by one. Most of the libel suits which followed the first ones sprang from these original litigations; for during the three years which passed before the suits against Barber and Pellet were both closed, these trials were the subject of libelous articles by various editors against whom Cooper later brought action, winning indictments which in turn inspired the Whigs to new libels and drew down more suits. It is not the purpose of this study to follow these litigations. All that I wish to do is to illuminate the hoax concerning Cooper's character, and to show the spirit with which an unruffled Cooper conducted his famous law-suits.

In the Monikin country of Leaplow there was once a candidate for public office who

> had lately performed that which, in most other countries, and under other circumstances, would have passed for an act of creditable national feeling; but which, quite as a matter of course, was eagerly presented to the electors, by his opponents, as a proof of his utter unfitness to be intrusted with their interests. . . . In an evil hour, the candidate undertook to explain by means of a handbill, in which he stated that he had been influenced by no other motive than a desire to do that which he believed to be right. Such a person was deemed to be wanting in natural abilities, and, as a matter of course, he was defeated. . . .[461]

[459] *Morning Courier and New York Enquirer*, March 9, 1841.

[460] Ethel R. Outland, *op. cit.*, p. 51. *Correspondence of James Fenimore-Cooper*, II, 439.

[461] *The Monikins*, p. 367.

This sketch was not a reference to Cooper's litigations, for that war had not been declared. But perhaps we may take it to heart as all too true a description of America's unwillingness to credit Cooper with public spirit when that warfare did occur.

Newspaper readers of the twentieth century are not all aware of the nature of this Leviathan which Bryant congratulated Cooper for having hooked in the nose. We ought to understand that Cooper never answered or sued for any attacks upon himself as an author. His campaign was fought against the assailing of private character by means of lies. He was determined that the slough of libelous writing in which the editors were wallowing, and from which they unfortunately splashed others, should be drained dry; and he proposed that it be done by process of law. There is no question that American newspapers between 1830 and 1845 were violently libelous. Histories of journalism refer to the era as one of political domination and of blackguardism in the press.[462]

The language habits of American editors a hundred years ago may be inferred from the fact that James J. Brooks posted a notice on the streets of New York which said, "I publish M. M. Noah of *The Enquirer* as a coward." Horace Greeley in his paper disputed whether he or James Watson Webb took more baths,[463] and the *Morning Courier and New York Enquirer* once said that an editorial written by the author of "To a Waterfowl" was so cruel that it "would do unmerited disgrace to a cannibal."[464] A talent for coining opprobrious nicknames was a great asset to a journalist. Bennett once published a long list of the terms which he declared had been employed against him by Park Benjamin and M. M. Noah (two editors, as it happens, whom Cooper

[462] James Melvin Lee, *op. cit.*, pp. 140-163.
[463] *Ibid.*, pp. 213-214.
[464] April 7, 1841.

sued and silenced). They included some terms that are not spoken, and more speakable ones such as offal, garbage and filth, vagabond, spotted caitiff, contagious disease, libeller and assassin, daring infidel, scoffer, poltron [*sic*], leprous wretch, tainted hand.[465] Cooper's disheartening venture with Greenough's Chanting Cherubs is recalled in a comparatively innocuous title which the Whigs applied for years to two Democratic friends of Cooper and Greenough, the poet-editors Bryant and Leggett—"chanting cherubs of the Post."[466]

The amenities which editors exchanged in these days were not confined to words alone. Philip Hone gives an account, much quoted, of seeing the two most respectable editors in New York, Bryant and W. L. Stone, engage in a fight on a New York street. Bryant began the fray by striking Stone with a cowhide whip.[467] But such editorial combats were not rare. Bennett and Webb frequently encountered, afterwards writing up the affrays for their columns in a strain which managed to combine martyrdom and triumph.

It was the Whig editors whose vilification Cooper suffered. His quarrel was not with various Whig gentlemen living at ease in New York and Rye—"the Whigs," in this book, is a phrase referring to pressmen. And by 1841 the Whig editors had worked themselves into such low standing in the community that at a convention in 1841 where they celebrated their party's victory by dining and praising each other, they are reported to have discussed ways and means of making themselves socially respected.[468]

It has been frequently admitted that the United States Bank, in its efforts to survive under Jackson and Van Buren,

[465] The *Herald*, May 22, 1840.

[466] Frederick Hudson, *Journalism in the United States from 1690 to 1872*, New York, 1873, p. 222.

[467] *The Diary of Philip Hone, 1828-1851*, I, 40.

[468] *Niles' Weekly Register*, LX (March 20, 1841), 34-36, quoting the *National Intelligencer*.

subsidized and corrupted the newspapers. Beginning with Jackson's decision to remove the deposits, the editors organized what Horace Greeley called the Whig tornado, an alliance to carry the Bank and to crush its enemies by any means at hand.[469]

Thus politics, the desire for notoriety, and the mere habit of vulgar detraction made public life unsafe even for men of the highest character. Today, a speedy libel suit would silence any burst of such gross abuse as was customary a hundred years ago. Then, the newspapers were so powerful that though all men feared them few dared risk an encounter with them in the courts; for winning a suit was small satisfaction when a paper in reporting the suit would think nothing of falsifying the charge, the argument, the decision, and the law of the case. It was useless for any individual to have recourse to the law of libel unless he was prepared to go through a prolonged and systematic series of suits until the papers should be frightened away from this practice of turning rebukes into triumphal trophies.

Regarding the nature of libel the newspaper editors at this time held some curious illusions. One was that if an editor believed somewhere in the recesses of his own mind that an accusation against a man's character was true, even if he had no proof whatever, the publication of the accusation was not a libel.

For instance, in 1830,[470] long before it had become embroiled in suits with James Fenimore Cooper, the *New York American* complained that it had been martyred for having asserted during a political campaign that a certain gentleman was a drunkard. The editors had been required by a libel suit to prove their accusation and had been unable to do it; but they declared in their newspaper review of the case that they had believed and still believed the gentleman

[469] James Melvin Lee, *op. cit.*, pp. 156-159; 208.
[470] January 4.

in question to be a drunkard. Any definition of libel which required for acquittal more than the editor's belief of a statement was a danger to the commonwealth, the irate editor asseverated, for if this rule were maintained, an editor might have to suppress suspicions which "if true, it highly imports the electors to know." In the case of the gentleman accused of drunkenness, the editor said he "had even expected to prove" his charge in the near future, but if he had delayed his accusation until proof was established, the gentleman might have won an election. Such reasoning defies comment; and it was against such logic that Cooper had to contend.

Though editors filled their sheets with complaints of martyrdom when they lost libel suits, they were really delighted by the publicity which these trials created. Thurlow Weed, one of the most unprincipled of Cooper's detractors, wrote proudly in his autobiography: "During my fifty years of editorial life it was my lot to be chosen defendant in more libel suits than I can remember or enumerate. There was, or seemed to be, something in my manner or style of writing to 'make the galled jades wince.' My opponents, instead of contenting themselves with replies, frequently resorted to libel suits."[471]

Poor Ned Myers, whose life Cooper saved when they were boys together at sea, has written[472] one of the most picturesque descriptions of the situation:

> In the New World of the 25 inst. I see some remarks respecting the book written by you, called 'Ned Myers etc,' & which I conceive to be very ill natured. I had some thoughts of calling upon the editor of the paper for an

[471] Thurlow Weed, *Autobiography of Thurlow Weed*, edited by his daughter, Harriet A. Weed, Boston, 1884, I, 527.

[472] Letter, Edward R. Myers to Cooper, Sailor's Snug Harbor, Staten Island, November 28, 1843. Unpublished except in part. Cooper collection, Yale.

explanation: but concluded I would first write to you for your advice. . . . As far as I have heard from those that have read the book, it is much liked. I however do not like the idea of the fellow in his remarks calling me a *renegade.* I should not be at all afraid to smell a little more powder, but I suppose there would be no chance with such fellows, who would make lee out of any thing.

Ned Myers was right, and though the licentiousness of the press between 1835 and 1845 was notorious, the difficulty of coping with such an enemy frightened away all champions of decent speech until Cooper rose and turned in wrath upon the monster.[473]

Cooper proposed to do something more reserved, more dignified, and more effective than calling upon editors of papers to render explanations out of which they would manage to "make lee." His course of action shows in favorable comparison not only to Ned's method but to the behavior of some well libeled literary men of his day.

It is true that some might prefer the conduct of the gentle spirit of Sunnyside. Beside Cooper, Washington Irving was a petted darling of the journals, yet Irving felt the iron of the lesser criticism which he suffered enough to defend his character by a letter to the press. Moreover, long before Cooper did, he resolved to stop writing for the unappreciative American critics; and a friend wrote, not to the supposedly hypersensitive Cooper, but to the supposedly angelic Irving: "It gives me some little dissatisfaction to perceive that you suffer yourself to be influenced in the pursuit of a great object by the squibs and crackers of criticism."[474] But Irving did nothing to check the abuses which he resented, and it may be that he chose the more dignified part.

Long before Cooper's libel suits were dreamed of, a Frenchman had written that one of Cooper's novels revealed

[473] J. M. Lee, *op. cit.*, pp. 221-222.

[474] Pierre M. Irving, *op. cit.*, III, 6-12; II, 36, 39, 199-208.

in its author a high sense of honor and a creditable knowledge of when it was proper to find quarrel in a straw.[475] The dapper Nathaniel P. Willis, not a ferocious character in literature, also thought it was in a gentleman's code to know when to quarrel. When he was abroad, he actually challenged one of his reviewers to a duel, and the adversary was none other than Captain Marryat.[476] Poor Willis suffered much at home from the Whig press.[477] For saying pleasant things about his friend Cooper in the *New York Mirror,* he was teased by these enemies.[478] His biographer has written a passage which describes his situation well, at the same time that it betrays unconsciousness of the political causation of the difficulties:

Next to Cooper, Willis was the best abused man of letters in America. It is easy to understand how the former, who was pugnacious and struck hard, should have been always in hot water. But why a man of Willis's urbanity should have been a target for the newspaper critics is more difficult of explanation. 'Colonel' William L. Stone of the 'Commercial Advertiser,' and 'Colonel' James Watson Webb of the 'Courier and Enquirer,' distinguished themselves especially by their stern condemnation of Willis's literary affectations, and of what they were pleased to consider the weaknesses of his private character and life. It is suggestive, by the way, of the militant disposition of the New York press at that time, that so many editors were generals and colonels—or at least were breveted such by public consent, and graced with titular embellishments of a warlike character. Henry J. Raymond, who joined the 'Courier and Enquirer' in 1842, proved his zealous adhesion to the traditions of the paper

[475] Review of *The Prairie, Gazette de France,* copied in *New York American,* September 21, 1827.

[476] Algernon Tassin, "American Authors and Their Publishers," Part II, *Bookman,* XXXIV (May, 1914), 276.

[477] *E.g., Morning Courier and New York Enquirer,* October 1, 1834.

[478] *E.g., New York Mirror,* XV (August 19, 1837), 63, ridiculed by *Buffalo Commercial Advertiser* with a statement which was given publicity under a pretense of deprecation in the New York *Commercial Advertiser,* August 22, 1837.

by an onslaught upon Willis, in which he asserted that the latter had snobbishly represented himself as received in the best circles abroad, 'when in truth 't was no such matter.' Willis replied to this in an editorial which Poe mentioned as a clever specimen of skill at fence.[479]

Willis complained that he did not know how to stop the slanders against him. When he tried to defend himself, he declared, the press accused him of "Coopering." In England, he said, he could duel, but Americans did not have that custom.[480]

Now, it is natural that Cooper's remonstrance should take the form, not of dueling literal or literary, but of law suit. It was not dignified to wrangle with scandalmongers by letters to papers, though journals tried, for their own publicity, to tempt him into doing so.[481] To a certain extent, Cooper enjoyed conducting a suit for the legal game of it; he could pursue a piece of litigation with a long, easy stride.[482] Mr. Henry Seidel Canby has said some wise things about Cooper's Quaker inheritance. If he did not derive from his ancestors the spirit of pacifism, he did possess a strong love of the truth and of the law. Perhaps this principle had been silently reinforced in Cooper's boyhood by impulses from the frontier habits of old Cooperstown, where William Cooper complained that every man went to law on every provocation, as if litigation were both a sport and a duty.[483] Lounsbury was right in quoting as one of Cooper's characteristic

[479] Henry A. Beers, *Nathaniel Parker Willis*, Boston, New York, 1885, pp. 306-307. Willis's father had been a "Jacobin" and had been imprisoned for what he said in his paper, the *Eastern Argus*. (J. M. Lee, *op. cit.*, p. 172.)

[480] N. P. Willis, "Ephemera," *Complete Works of N. P. Willis*, New York, 1846, p. 650.

[481] *E.g.*, *New York Tribune*, November 30, 1841. Letter, Cornelius Mathews and Evert A. Duyckinck to Cooper, New York, December 4, 1841. Unpublished. Cooper collection, Yale.

[482] His typical mood is shown in a letter to his wife, *Correspondence of James Fenimore-Cooper*, II, 473-474.

[483] William Cooper, *op. cit.*, p. 33.

remarks: "So far as my means allow, insult shall be avenged by law, violence repelled by the strong hand, falsehood put to shame by truth, and sophistry exposed by reason."[484] An admirer once pronounced the following words as a toast at a table where Cooper's libel suits had been discussed in the novelist's absence: "J. Fenimore Cooper—a marvel in modern ethics—a man who is just to the laws—and who *trusts* in their justice to him."[485]

There is something marvelous, still, in this kind of faith in law. And it is a pleasure to see the *soi-disant* cranky Cooper exhibiting in his letters an amused tolerance for people of lesser faith, and to see them envying him his equanimity. When Morse got into difficulties concerning his rights to the telegraph, Cooper wrote home, "He groans over the press worse than I ever did, and seems to imagine justice deaf as well as blind. Still he is a great man, and will stand so in history; and so deserves to stand."[486] And Morse wrote Cooper, "I wish I may be able to bear it as bravely and philosophically as you have done."[487]

Not merely the good temper but the necessity and the public spirit of Cooper's libel suits have been attested by an imposing number of contemporaries whose own reputations command respect.

Perhaps it is due to Cooper's personal friends to let them head the list.

From Bryant, then, we have:

When these litigations were first begun, I recollect it seemed to me that Cooper had taken a step which would give him a great deal of trouble, and effect but little good. I said to myself—

'Alas! Leviathan is not so tamed!'

[484] T. R. Lounsbury, *op. cit.*, p. 147.

[485] Charles P. Clinch to Cooper, New York, January 20, 1845. Unpublished. Cooper collection, Yale.

[486] *Correspondence of James Fenimore-Cooper*, II, 626.

[487] *Ibid.*, II, 634.

As he proceeded, however, I saw that he had understood the matter better than I. He put a hook into the nose of this huge monster, wallowing in his inky pool and bespattering the passers-by; he dragged him to the land and made him tractable. . . . After, I believe, about six years of litigation, the newspaper press gradually subsided into a pacific disposition towards its adversary, and the contest closed with the account of pecuniary profit and loss, so far as he was concerned, nearly balanced. The occasion of these suits was far from honourable to those who provoked them, but the result was, I had almost said, creditable to all parties; to him, as the courageous prosecutor, to the administration of justice in this country, and to the docility of the newspaper press, which he had disciplined into good manners.[488]

From S. F. B. Morse:

In all your libel suits against these degraded wretches, I sympathize entirely with you, and there are thousands who now

[488] "Discourse on the Life, Character, and Genius of James Fenimore Cooper," *Memorial of James Fenimore Cooper*, pp. 61-63. Bryant openly said, also, that in his defense of a citizen's rights Cooper was not fighting against the onslaughts of personal malignity, but against the use of slander as a retort to his remarks on government. *Ibid.*, p. 61. Professor Ethel R. Outland (*op. cit.*, p. 61) has made a curious statement on this subject which may be confusing to persons who do not have at hand Bryant's "Discourse on the Life, Character, and Genius of James Fenimore Cooper." Regarding the libel suits she admits that "All three members of the famous Whig political firm of Seward, Weed, and Greely were involved," and yet she inclines to think that the charges of partisanship in the newspaper attack were false. To support her opinion of this falsity she does nothing except quote Bryant: "It will be recalled that Bryant touched upon this point, saying that he could not ascribe the attacks 'either to party or personal malignity.'" But Bryant's own sentence, as found in his discourse, reads as follows: "I cannot, however, ascribe them all, or even the greater part of them, to personal malignity." The page on which the sentence occurs makes the point that Cooper's remarks on government were a very important factor. It would have been unsuitable, on the occasion of a memorial meeting, to speak more pointedly of party malignity. Of course, on other occasions, as has been shown already, Bryant did write pointedly of that very thing.

thank you in their hearts for the moral courage you display in bringing these licentious scamps to a knowledge of their duty. Be assured the good sense, the intelligence, the right feeling of the community at large are with you. The licentiousness of the press needed the rebuke which you have given it, and it feels it too, despite its awkward attempts to brave it out.[489]

From Judge William Jay:

How piteously the Editors are squirming under the law of libel. It is certainly hard that they may not lie and slander with impunity. Why, it is by this craft that they get their living. Were they to print the truth only, their papers would be stale, flat and unprofitable. The public, I fear, would not read them, and they would be of but little use to the politicians.[490]

From Commodore William Branford Shubrick:

I am sorry you have had more trouble about the point, though you are without question right in the whole business, a bad case is made of it—but what can a man do if unprincipled blackguards assail his rights. He must defend them at all hazards.

In a later letter, Shubrick was to say:

When will your editorial war terminate? Is it to be as long as the siege of Troy? the public certainly owes you a great deal and your brother writers more for putting such fellows to writes [rights?].[491]

[489] S. F. B. Morse to Cooper, *Correspondence of James Fenimore-Cooper*, II, 461.

[490] Letter, William Jay to Cooper, *ibid.*, II, 499.

[491] Letters: W. B. Shubrick to Cooper, Newport, August 31, 1838; and W. B. Shubrick to Cooper, Gosport, Virginia, January 6, 1843. Unpublished. Cooper collection, Yale. Some qualifications of these quotations from William Jay and Shubrick may perhaps be in order. Peter Jay wrote to Cooper from New York, May 14, 1833, ten years before his brother expressed his sympathy for the novelist: "You see that poor William has had a melancholy winter. He has just published a life of my father. . . . Having commenced author he must expect criticism. I hope he will wince under it less than you do." This was deleted from the letter when it was published in *Corre-*

From J. De Peyster Ogden, a Whig friend, admissions of the licentiousness of the press[492] and the statement that

spondence of James Fenimore-Cooper, I, 316, 317. The original is in the Cooper collection, Yale. Then there is an unpublished letter, in the same collection, from Shubrick to Cooper, Norfolk, Virginia, April 7, 1841, which declares there is "more plague than profit in contending with such people"; but this is by way of complaining that Cooper does not visit Shubrick enough when the lawsuits take so much time. To complete the list of remonstrances, we may add a letter from W. Pell which said Webb was a person with whom he had years before "ceased to communicate," Webb was "not worth writing about, and I wish you thought he was not worth thinking about."—Pell to Cooper, New York, August 29, 1839. Unpublished. Cooper collection, Yale. James K. Paulding sent his congratulations to Cooper on "having gained your Point, and overcome the Philistines"; and yet he left at the end of his letter a remark which might be taken as an expression of fear for Cooper's generosity: "Use your victory moderately; remit the Damages, and grant that as a boon, which they claim as a right. A man may as well be hanged at once, as make enemies of his neighbors: or quarrel with his inferiors." As a matter of fact, Cooper before the suit had always been willing to grant the use of Three Mile Point as a boon. He did not remit the damages, but he gave the money away. J. K. Paulding to Cooper, Washington, May 20, 1839. Unpublished. Cooper collection. Perhaps it was in answer to this letter that Cooper wrote: "Certainly I *cannot pocket* money ittained [*sic*] under such a verdict, but the affair has been accompanied by circumstances that require an example, and the money must be paid The verdict has already been given away. The lesson is working famously, and much good will result from it." Cooper to J. H. [*sic*] Paulding, printed in facsimile in an article by M. A. de Wolfe Howe, *Bookman*, V (March, 1897), 20. G. A. Worth, in a letter referring to Cooper's independence and self-respect having kept him out of the Cabinet, while his "political associations and predilections" exposed him "to the censure and obloquy of the Whig press," expressed real admiration and friendship for Cooper, but protested against his tendency to champion worthless people like Elliott and declared that Cooper descended from his dignity "by even *thinking* of such *things*" as Park Benjamin, whose vituperations ought to be left to go "to the d—l where they belong." G. A. Worth to Cooper, New York, June 18, 1839. Unpublished. Cooper collection, Yale.

[492] Letter, J. De Peyster Ogden to Cooper, New York, June 10, 1839. Unpublished. Cooper collection, Yale.

under the suits "Stone . . . gets *fat*, and Webb looks well—but this only proves that they are incorrigible, and have not the fear of the law before their eyes."[493]

But we have equally strong testimony, both publicly and privately expressed, from a noted man who was not even acquainted with Cooper at the time of the suits. To the public, the lawyer George S. Hillard wrote as follows:

Timid men, cautious men, men who love their ease, will call him Quixotic, rash, imprudent, to engage in a controversy in which he had much to lose and little to gain: but the reply to such suggestions is, that if men always took counsel of indolence, timidity, and selfishness, no good would ever be accomplished, and no abuses ever be reformed. Cooper may not have been judicious in everything he said and did; but that he was right in the main, both in motive and conduct we firmly believe. He acted from a high sense of duty; there was no alloy of vindictiveness or love of money in the impulses which moved him. Criticism the most severe and unsparing he accepted as perfectly allowable, so long as it kept within the limits of literary judgment; but any attack upon his personal character, especially any imputation or insinuation involving a moral stain, he would not submit to. He appealed to the laws of the land to vindicate his reputation and punish his assailants. Long and gallant was the warfare he maintained,—a friendless, solitary warfare,—and all the hydra-heads of the press hissing and ejaculating their venom upon him,—with none to stand by his side and wish him God-speed. But he persevered, and, what is more, he succeeded: that is to say, he secured all the substantial fruits of success. He vindicated the principle for which he contended: he compelled the newspapers to keep within the pale of literary criticism; he confirmed the saying of President Jackson, that 'desperate courage makes one a majority.'[494]

To Cooper himself, Hillard sent another tribute:

I remember that some years ago you were engaged in a struggle with a portion of the press and in defense of your

[493] Letter, J. De Peyster Ogden to Cooper, New York, June 10, 1840. Unpublished. Cooper collection, Yale.

[494] George S. Hillard, "James Fenimore Cooper," *Atlantic Monthly*, IX (January, 1862), 52-68.

good name and rights against their invasion. In that contest you had my hearty sympathy and good wishes, as I have long felt that from that quarter—from an unprincipled and irresponsible press—our greatest danger was to follow.[495]

But it is something of a task even to read the roll of the other men who sent Cooper warm expressions of their support in his press war and who viewed that war as one of public service.[496]

[495] Letter, George S. Hillard to Cooper 1850. Unpublished. Cooper collection, Yale.

[496] Fitz-Greene Halleck to Cooper, *Correspondence of James Fenimore-Cooper*, II, 490; J. E. De Kay (the naturalist) to Susan Fenimore Cooper, Syosset, September 20, 1850. Unpublished. Cooper collection, Yale; the same to Cooper, *Correspondence of James Fenimore-Cooper*, II, 566-567; Richard Henry Dana (the editor) to Cooper, *ibid.*, II, 558; William Gilmore Simms (the novelist) to Cooper, Charleston, South Carolina, September 27, n.d. Unpublished. Cooper collection; Horace Greenough (sculptor) to Cooper, October 8, 1839. Unpublished. Cooper collection; Theodore Sedgwick, Jr., to Cooper, *Correspondence of James Fenimore-Cooper*, I, 394-395; D. D. Barnard (New York Assemblyman and United States Minister to Germany) to Cooper, *ibid.*, I, 392-393; the same to Cooper, Albany, November 27, 1841. Unpublished. Cooper collection; the same to Cooper, House of Representatives [Albany], June 20, 1842. Unpublished. Cooper collection. Barnard's strong approval of Cooper's suits in an address made at Amherst College is mentioned by I. W. Stevenson to Cooper, Albany, September 7, 1839. Unpublished. Cooper collection; George Lippard (editor of the *Home Journal*) to Cooper, Philadelphia, May 21, 1844. Unpublished. Cooper collection; J. L. O'Sullivan (editor of the *Democratic Review*) to Cooper, New York, June 22, 1842. Unpublished. Cooper collection; Edward D. Ingraham (editor) to Cooper, Philadelphia, July 5, 1839. Unpublished. Cooper collection; Henry D. Cruger (land holder in Herkimer County, New York) to Cooper, Great Western steam ship, December 4, 1838. Unpublished. Cooper collection; Captain Conner (Navy Commissioner) to Cooper, Washington, November 22, 1841. Unpublished. Cooper collection; Charles P. Clinch (dramatist) to Cooper, New York, January 20, 1845. Unpublished. Cooper collection; Joseph Ransom to Cooper, *Correspondence of James Fenimore-Cooper*, II, 451; Thomas Baldwin (teacher) to Cooper, Philadelphia, *ibid.*, II, 464; Henri D. Brackette to Cooper, Kaskaskia, Illinois, August 5,

After five years in which he had kept his word and produced no new writings, and during which the impressions of his return from Europe had been seasoning, Cooper began a novel based upon the homecoming of an American family after a protracted visit abroad. His fearful publishers insisted upon a sea story. To please them, the westward journey of the Effinghams was prolonged by a long sea chase. But this cut down the space available in *Homeward Bound* for impressions of American manners, and so a sequel was necessitated, *Home as Found*. Cooper wished these fictions to be novels of manners, or what he termed useful glances in the direction of *Roman de Société*.[497] They turned out to be realistic novels embodying in fictionized form almost all those opinions of America which had been exhibited in his books ever since *A Letter to His Countrymen*. Fictionized, these opinions were even more offensive to Americans than they had been in their expository shape. Steadfast Dodge in the ladies' cabin on the packet ship, Aristabulus Bragg at dinner with the Effinghams in New York, or the insolent ball-players on the lawn in Templeton are only too real and too discouraging. The more realistic these novels were, the smaller was their chance of being well received by a vain and sensitive nation. Besides, the narrative form led Cooper into allowing his characters to make speeches which would have been said with better grace about them than by them. An illustration is Eve Effingham's notorious piece of self-

1842. Unpublished. Cooper collection; Thomas Randall to Cooper, Belmont, Florida, August 27, 1844. Unpublished. Cooper collection; L. Foot to Cooper, General Hospital, St. John's Bluff, Florida, August 10, 1841. Unpublished. Cooper collection; A. Danyan (writer and editor) to Cooper, New York, March 27, 1841. Unpublished. Cooper collection; Frederick Howes, Jr., to Cooper, *Correspondence of James Fenimore-Cooper*, II, 592-593; Parke Godwin (writer and editor), *Cyclopaedia of Biography: a Record of the Lives of Eminent Persons*, New York, 1878, Supplement, pp. 71-72.

[497] *Homeward Bound*, Preface, iv.

description: "Miss Effingham has been grieved, disappointed, nay, shocked, . . . but still she will not despair of the republic."[498]

The two novels which Cooper wrote under these dangers are dominated by the theme of American subservience to Europe. Three kinds of American Doctrinaires are sketched, in three characters who are intended to represent types. The first is of the highest type of doctrinaire, John Effingham, a man in whom good natural parts have been damaged somewhat by false training. The history of John Effingham's development in the Doctrinaire persuasion[499] is a remarkable description of the evolution of the Whig party from the Federalist as Cooper had observed the process.

John and Edward Effingham, as the story runs, were the children of brothers, one of whom, John's father, inherited the personal property of the family, while the other, Edward's father, took his inheritance in land. John's father had plunged into speculation and had grown rich. He had also (and Cooper implies that this is a failing of speculators in general) "entered warmly and blindly into all the factions and irreconcilable principles of party." The two cousins, like Cooper, were educated in the early years of the century, "under the influence of the British opinions that then weighed (and many of which still weigh) like an incubus on the national interests of America." Edward Effingham had escaped from the incubus, and John Effingham had not:

> The Effingham family had started Federalists, in the true meaning of the term; for their education, native sense, and principles, had a leaning to order, good government, and the dignity of the country; but as factions became fiercer, and names got to be confounded and contradictory, the landed branch settled down into what they thought were American, and the commercial branch into what might properly be termed English Federalists. We do not mean that the father

[498] *Home as Found*, p. 240.

[499] *Homeward Bound*, pp. 53-56.

of John intended to be untrue to his native land; but by following up the dogmas of party he had reasoned himself into a set of maxims which, if they meant anything, meant everything but what had been solemnly adopted as the governing principles of his own country, and many of which were diametrically opposed to both its interests and honor.

In other words, John Effingham developed into a commercial man, a Doctrinaire, and a Whig. Travel did something to moderate his prejudices, but enough of English coloring remained to throw "a species of twilight shading over his mind." Throughout the novel and its sequel, the twilight shading continues to cloud John Effingham's remarks about America. In this characteristic cynicism he serves constantly as a foil to his brother and his brother's daughter Eve, who are compounded of hope and affection for their native land.[500]

It is one of the ironies of Cooper's reputation that the contempt for America which he portrayed as a serious blemish in an otherwise noble character became mysteriously identified with his own opinion, as if Cooper were the very John Effingham whom he wrote two books to condemn. Another piece of irony is the fact that though Cooper complimented the Whigs in John Effingham, the Whig critics ignored the compliment. By portraying a gentlemanly Whig, Cooper implied that a gentleman's nature was not incompatible with Whiggism; but John Effingham's political party, instead of contemplating this tribute, concentrated their energies upon resenting Cooper's portrait of an ungentlemanly Whig, the editor Steadfast Dodge.

Cooper's libel suits have made it common knowledge that the portrait of Steadfast Dodge stirred resentment among American editors. But no one has observed since Cooper's time that Whig editors, not all editors, harbored this sentiment. When it has once been noticed that the resentment lay among the Whigs and not among the Democrats, the

[500] *E.g.*, pp. 4, 203.

reasons for this phenomenon must be found; and they were probably apparent to Cooper's contemporaries, though they escaped Professor Lounsbury and later critics. Steadfast Dodge's paper was an Anti-Jackson sheet. With one of those sly strokes which make his satires more diverting than some modern readers think them, Cooper designated Dodge's politics and at the same time touched the conservatism of old-style Federalists with a palpable hit. Dodge is asked[501] whether his paper is not called the *Active Inquirer.* He answers: "That is the name, Sir George. 'The Active Inquirer' is the present name, though when we supported Mr. Adams it was called 'The Active Enquirer,' with an E." Dodge's paper is an Adams sheet, and Dodge is a Whig of the contemptible order, just as John Effingham is one of the respectable class. Dodge also is a Doctrinaire, but on a lower plane than Effingham. His sycophancy towards English opinion, especially English aristocratic opinion, is a principal theme of the novel. He is fooled at the outset by a renegade English criminal posing as a baronet, and none of his adventures can teach him to distinguish true aristocracy from false show, or principles appropriate to America from European conventional fustian.

A third type of Doctrinaire is presented in Mr. Howel, of *Home as Found.* Mr. Howel was one of nature's gentlemen, a homebred man. In Templeton he had "dreamed away his existence in an indolent communication with the current literature of the day." This literature was imported from England, and having much good faith and no contentiousness, Mr. Howel had become a reservoir of British opinion. He had, in fact, become too English to suit even John Effingham: " 'American, quotha! The man is no more American than the "Times" newspaper, or Charing Cross!' "

It is not surprising that with three strong protagonists of Doctrinairism among their characters, *Homeward Bound* and

[501] *Homeward Bound,* p. 176.

Home as Found are obliged to pause frequently for parlor debates on Americanism. One of the conversations near the close of the second volume seems to offer the thesis of the two novels. It repeats *The American Democrat's* warning against doctrinaires and chauvinists alike. Mr. Wenham speaks for the latter class in a silly rebuke to Mr. Howel, of the former. The wiser persons in the audience act for Cooper by killing Wenham with a smile.

The possibilities for dispute among Cooper's critics over the topics of "aristocracy" and doctrinairism were unlimited in 1839, the very year when Harrison's log cabin campaign was launched. The party implications of an attack on commercial interests must have been known to Cooper, for he wrote to a United States senator in 1838,

> The present political struggle, in this country, appears to be a contest between men and dollars, and it is a bad omen for the first that they are so easily duped by the arch enemy, to their own injury. I think, however, that New York will soon return to a better state of things. Our autumn election will be close, but I believe the quack whigs will be beaten.[502]

As for the editors, if the Whiggishness of Steadfast Dodge had escaped the notice of any of them, Bryant did not fail to broaden Cooper's hint; when he wished to contradict a certain political rumor which the Whig papers had circulated, he did so by saying there was not a syllable of truth in the tale, and citing Mr. Dodge as so typical of "a large class of newspaper editors" that his character was not overcharged "by a single touch of the pencil."[503] R. W. Griswold, himself an editor, testified that there were Steadfast Dodges in the world,[504] and William Gilmore Simms, author and journalist, called this character a "very just portrait."[505] But he

[502] Letter to United States Senator Bedford Brown, Cooperstown, March 24, 1838, North Carolina Historical Society Historical Papers, Section VIII (1908-1909), 1-2.

[503] *Evening Post*, June 27, 1839.

[504] *Op. cit.*, p. 179.

[505] *Op. cit.*, p. 179.

was a Democrat. The Whig editors did not attempt to deny that the sketch had truth in it, but they howled in unison because Cooper had not assured a suspicious world that some editors were not quite so bad. Cooper had once in a former unappreciated book praised the American press more than it deserved,[506] and in another he had said it was composed of men "good, bad, and indifferent," concerning whom one could not generalize justly.[507] The truth is that this time he *had* limited the generalization to a certain class of editor; but the Whigs were that class. Moreover, the drawing was a significant likeness, and everybody knew it.

Homeward Bound was published in August, 1838, and *Home as Found* in November of the same year. The former was received by the newspapers with a confessed conspiracy of silence.[508] The *Morning Courier and New York Enquirer*,[509] however, was not quite able to contain itself; it came out with a decidedly unfavorable notice, declaring that the reviewer had not read the novel, but knew Cooper was a better novelist than politician and ought to keep to his proper field. The *Knickerbocker Magazine* endorsed the newspapers' campaign by suggesting that the novelist's countrymen exercise charity, suffer long and be kind by keeping silent about Cooper's books and not buying them until he reformed.

The only major journal which gave *Homeward Bound* a favorable review was the *New York Mirror*, and in keeping with the behavior of this sheet divided against itself, the favor was promptly revoked in later statements. In August the *Mirror* was praising the novel's characters. its narrative interest, and its description, and putting Cooper "at the head of the nautical novelists of the day, simply because he is the most natural and true." In September it was objecting to Cooper's denial of the stories that Louis Philippe had taught

[506] *Notions of the Americans*, II, 132-139.
[507] *A Letter to His Countrymen*, p. 39.
[508] *New Yorker*, VI (October 27, 1838), 94.
[509] August 7, 1838.

school in America and that William the Fourth had been beaten by American sailors. In December, it pleased to refer to Cooper in a headline as "The Great Used-up."[510] Sometimes a magazine review would pronounce the book readable for its sea pictures, but with large reservations. The satire of Steadfast Dodge was exasperating to many, and Cooper's presumption in criticizing America in books that were popular abroad was a bitter draught to almost all—a fact which might stir in us memories of *The Traveling Bachelor's* reception. Quotations from England said Cooper's "political discussions on America and federalism" were "becoming bores."[511]

Of course, there was more to say on the subject of Cooper's sensitiveness. Here is an example of how the *North American Review* continued that process; Cooper's work, this journal said, had for the last three or four years abounded in:

> uncalled-for political disquisitions, filled up with expressions of the bitterest scorn and hatred. They are deformed by perpetual outbreaks of a spirit, which might be expected to show itself in the pages of a ruthless partisan, careless of truth in aiming at the reputation of an opponent whom he wishes to ruin; but from which the writings of the poet and the man of letters sitting apart. . . ought to wholly exempt.[512]

[510] *New York Mirror,* XVI (August 18, 1838), 63; (September 8, 1838), 87; (December 15, 1838), 200.

[511] *Albion,* August 18, 1838; *Knickerbocker Magazine,* XII (September, 1838), 263-267; *Journal of Belles Lettres, Waldie's Select Circulating Library,* XI (June 26, 1838), Number 26; XII (August 14, 1838), Number 7; *North American Review,* XLVII (October, 1838), 488-489; *Gentleman's Magazine,* III (September, 1838), 216-218; *Southern Literary Messenger,* IV (November, 1838), quoted in the *New Yorker,* VI (October 27, 1838), 94, and the *New York American,* October 27, 1838.

[512] The *New Yorker,* VI (October 13, 1838), 61, expressed delight that "Funnymore Cooper" had been suitably treated in the *North American Review's* "rich morceau of criticism."

And yet someone was mistaken in this reviewing; for the publishers wrote that sales were satisfactory, and within a month they proposed a new stereotyped edition of two thousand copies. English approval was grudgingly recognized.[513] Upon the shores of Lake George in August the inhabitants met and passed a resolution to call their lake the "Horicon," a title which Cooper had introduced to the national imagination and vocabulary.[514] Outside of the papers, evidently, Cooper had a following still.

Then in September Cooper brought suit against Pellet of the *Chenango Telegraph* and Barber of the *Otsego Republican* for their libels on the Three Mile Point difficulty. In November Cooper gave his country *Home As Found.*

The Whig tornado swooped in from three sides. Cooper was a vile aristocrat highly contemptuous of America; he was hostile to freedom of speech; he was a disgusting splenetic crank. Such accusations are difficult to answer. Of course the Whigs' master stroke was the personifying of all three obnoxious qualities in the Handsome Mr. Effingham.

The Whigs were almost beside themselves for fear *Home as Found* would be believed abroad as well as read. Captain Marryat had not helped their peace of mind by saying in *A Diary in America* that Cooper's book on England absolved him from any obligation to treat America tenderly, and by quoting native American authors about the United States in order to use American authorities against themselves. "Why authorities *against* themselves?" shrieked one journal. "Who will recognize, for instance, as a true picture . . . the caricature . . . in 'Home as Found?' "[515] Unfavorable reviewing in England was noted and quoted with alarm, and great

[513] Letter, Carey, Lea and Carey to Cooper, Philadelphia, August 18, 1838. Unpublished. Cooper collection, Yale. *Commercial Advertiser,* October 18, 1838.

[514] *New York Mirror,* XVI (September 1, 1838), 79.

[515] *Journal of Belles Lettres, Waldie's Select Circulating Library,* XIV (September 24, 1839), Number 13.

relief was felt in New York when a violent statement about Cooper in the *Morning Courier and New York Enquirer* was actually copied in the London *Times*; the splash of vitriol, they hoped, would give the British an understanding of "the public sentiment of our countrymen in regard to this miserable libel on their character and manners."[516] Any reader could have seen, if the *Knickerbocker Magazine* had not told him, that the novel was "full of nuts for the tories of England, and all enemies of republican equality and institutions, everywhere."[517] But the suspicion was cast upon Cooper that he was not really a friend of republicanism, withal. "If such are the friends of Republicanism, she may well pray Heaven to save her from them," the *North American Review* had said in reviewing mere *Homeward Bound.*

Now on all sides was raised the outcry against the egotism of "I, Mr. Cooper, my family, my history, my books, my enemies, my squabbles . . . my prejudices, my opinions, my everything." The nation was warned of Cooper's spleen as if he were a mad dog, and one journal hinted at a "deeply seated disease" which had caused a dense "mental obscuration" and produced the ill temper, puerility, prejudice, arrogance, and fatuity of which *Home as Found* was compact.[518]

The "self-love of an imagined *arbiter elegantiae*" was alleged by one journal,[519] which included a backward sweep in its view, to have motivated the review of Lockhart, and *The Bravo* was brought up again and was said to have commented severely and discourteously upon every person the author had seen. The Cassio business was revived, Cooper

[516] *New Yorker*, VI (February 23, 1839), 356; (February 9, 1839), 323-324.

[517] XII (December, 1838), 539; *New York Mirror*, XV (December 15, 1838), 200.

[518] *New York Mirror*, XVI (December 8, 1838), 192; *Knickerbocker Magazine*, XIII (June, 1839), 539; *Gentleman's Magazine*, IV (January, 1839), 64-66.

[519] *New York Review*, IV (January, 1839), 209-221.

was told that the press in America was so high morally that we ought to rejoice it was no worse, and *Home as Found* was said to have a fling on every page "at something which belongs to us, our architecture, our literary institutions, our scientific associations, our political anniversaries, our foreign ambassadors, our laws, our liberties, and our modes of life." Cooper's manner in the book was labeled ungracious and sneering. "And then it is arrogant in the extreme; Mr. Edward Effingham, whom he has placed in his house, and made to father his quarrel with the people of his village, must be regarded as intended for himself, and he and his are the sole judges of taste, refinement, manners, and elegance."

The effect of this kind of reviewing was to make Cooper's social criticism appear to be microscopically petty. Sometimes it is as ludicrous as a musical comedy. For instance, this same review said Cooper ought to judge politeness by laws which originate in the heart and a sense of the fitness of things instead of by such trifles as whether we eat eggs from shells or from cups. Now the only thing Cooper ever judged politeness by was the spirit and fitness of actions. It is because he showed that bad American manners often revealed badness of head and heart that these two novels have such power. But of course such things as table manners do come into novels; and eggs can find their way to the table there without the novel's becoming a disquisition on them. The comedy element in this criticism is that for years American papers had been debating with foreign critics whether the native habit of drinking eggs from a cup without fork or spoon was as revolting as visitors unused to the practice declared it was.[520] I will not claim that there was any political division here, as with the big and little ends of the Lilliputian eggs; but the egg-eating was a ridiculous national quarrel. Cooper did mention it; and so his novel is dubbed a disquisition on the subject. Even Lounsbury

[520] *New York Mirror*, X (June 8, 1833), 392.

included a solemn criticism of Cooper for having descended to argue about how to eat eggs.[521]

But besides conceit and pettiness, this review drew a picture of monstrous malice. Steadfast Dodge was said to be an example of Cooper's "Prejudice, ill humor," "extreme disingenuousness," which together with a recent "venomous and almost rabid attack upon Sir Walter Scott" indicated "a strong determination to tarnish with the breath of calumny, every mirror which does not reflect the object of his own imagination, as comely as it appears to himself." *Home as Found* it adjudged a still more malicious work than its companion novel, in fact a "bursting out of superabundant bile, and that after the manner of a general deluge." These floods the reviewer attempted to illustrate by selected quotations, all of which he printed out of their context, and none of which were attributed to the characters who said them, or were answered, as the book answered many of them, by retorts from other speakers. Some of them (for example, the remarks about Eve Effingham's surprise at the coldness of New Yorkers towards liberal sentiments when she had been accustomed to the warmth of liberal Europeans) were made to imply very different things from those they implied in the novel. No mention was made of the American institutions which Cooper praised, of course, and there was no recognition of Cooper's truth. (It is a curious thing that several reviewers said in bitterness that the book was Hogarthian and showed no suspicion that this was anything but blame of it.)

How little this particular reviewer understood the scope of critical problems in literature may be judged from what he reveals as his idea of real literary criticism in his parting shot:

Had we aimed at a literary criticism of these works, we should have had frequent occasion to point out verbal inaccuracies, such as the use of *understandingly,* which does not

[521] *Op. cit.*, p. 169.

belong to our language; of *bluff*, which is known only as a maritime word; of *imperious*, instead of imperative, and many others; and we should also have had occasion to contrast the flat, feeble, vapid, and unmeaning character of Mr. Cooper's productions, since his self-love and vanity have corroded his heart and bedimmed his understanding, with the lofty, spirited, and delightful ones of his earlier days. But the literary offences seemed to be so completely merged in the moral one, as to be undeserving of notice.

The *New York Review* was not strictly partisan but "was whiggish in politics."[522] Its judgment on Cooper was hailed with applause by other Whig or Whiggish periodicals,[523] and all this seems foolish enough now, in a new season when America is beginning to consider *Home as Found* the greatest of Cooper's books.[524]

But these were not the libelous reviews. "Colonel" James Watson Webb set out to show what he could do.[525] Before he finished his astonishing article he had managed to say that *Home as Found* had been designed to repair the European market for Cooper's books by praising "every thing that is *English* at the expense of everything that is *American*." He quoted the description of Aristabulus at the dining table, adding that Aristabulus was represented as a lawyer, and flourishing off with: "This much for the manners of American *gentlemen*." (Of course, any reader of *Home as Found* knows that Cooper never breathed the lightest hint that Aristabulus was a gentleman or a lawyer, nor that any American gentleman would take him for either.) Besides Truck, only the Effinghams, Webb said, were treated with respect, and Effingham was Cooper. Then a handful of

[522] F. L. Mott, *op. cit.*, p. 671.

[523] *Morning Courier and New York Enquirer*, January 23, 1839; *New Yorker*, VI (January 5, 1839), 243-244; *Knickerbocker Magazine*, XIII (February, 1839), 172-173.

[524] Fred Lewis Pattee, "James Fenimore Cooper," *American Mercury*, IV (March, 1925), 289-297.

[525] *Morning Courier and New York Enquirer*, November 22, 1838.

epithets Cooper used for Effingham were thrown into print: "handsome," "thoughtful," "mild," "Philosophical," "up-right," "clear-headed," "just minded," and "liberal." "MR. EFFINGHAM," quoted Webb with italics, "across whose *mild* and *Handsome* face a smile was gradually sliding!!" and Webb sneered, "Reader, did you ever see Mr. *Cooper*? if not, do not delay getting a peep at him if only for the purpose of admiring the *modesty*, depicted in his '*handsome face*.' "

Webb asserted that Cooper had claimed a family equal to the noblest of England, a claim that was "part and parcel of the system by which he endeavors to heap contempt upon every American." Now, what Cooper had actually done was to have the traveled Eve Effingham assure her untraveled cousin that the latter ought not to feel inferior to a young English baronet merely because she was American and untitled; the best families in America ought to recognize themselves as being on the social level of the best families elsewhere, not degraded necessarily to the place of the untitled at the foot of the table; the place of a Jay or a Washington was not beneath some paltry count. Bryant had had to fight with Europeans for republican principles of precedence on his own soil, even for his right as host to give the signal for leaving his own table; Cooper was not the only person interested.[526]

But Webb saw something he could do to make Cooper's stand on this matter disgraceful. He launched the following:

It is certainly a matter of no importance to the public to know who MR. COOPER'S father was; but inasmuch as he has endeavored to deceive them, and in doing so has exhibited both weakness and a want of proper respect for the *truth*, we take the liberty of saying that Mr. C. is the son of a highly respectable WHEEL-WRIGHT of *New Jersey*, who has frequently been heard to declare that he was proud of his

[526] Parke Godwin, *op. cit.*, II, 367, note, and John Bigelow, *William Cullen Bryant*, Boston and New York, 1890, 294-295.

occupation and only regretted that while he labored at it, he was unable to manufacture as good *waggons* as his brothers in the trade.

At the end, the political hook shows through the worm: "Another object of this selfish book is to enable MR. COOPER to abuse the public for having laughed at his political address to the people in behalf of General JACKSON, when he hoped to be appointed Secretary of the Navy."

Webb was cheered for this by his Whig allies.[527] Cooper was in New York. What caught his eye in the tirade was a statement that he had insulted American ladies in his novel and that he had once been heard to declare that there were not three ladies in America. This he said was a libel he was unwilling to let pass uncontradicted while waiting for a trial of Webb to put it to the proof; and so he wrote a brief denial of having spoken ill of the ladies, a denial somewhat touching in its open simplicity, which was published the same day in the *Evening Post*.[528] He declared his intention to sue, and he gave a rebuke to Webb's conceit by flatly repudiating the latter's strutting references to himself as a personal acquaintance of the novelist. "This I deny;" said Cooper, "he is my junior, and I knew him slightly when a boy, and slightly when a young man." This must have deflated many a brag of the journalist Colonel. He had no more sense than to attempt on November 27 to prove an acquaintanceship. On November 23 he reprinted Cooper's simple letter, dubbed it an "effusion of mortified vanity," implied that one could never believe what Cooper said, and swaggered that Cooper would never sue him. On November 30, there was another letter from Cooper in the *Evening Post*, anxiously repeating his denial of having jested about the ladies of America. Poor Cooper; what a ridiculous thing that a man who was such a combination of domesticity and chivalry should ever

[527] Ethel R. Outland, *op. cit.*, 77.
[528] November 22, 1838.

have been shocked into making such a protestation! On December 1, Webb repeated the story about the ladies and mocked at Cooper for taking a long time to sue.

Meanwhile (we can smile, now) *Godey's Lady's Book* considered that even the harshest statements were insufficient punishment if Cooper was really guilty of this offense.[529]

Park Benjamin howled with delight that Webb had annihilated Cooper's "absurd pretensions," and exhibited his own inventive and invective powers by calling Cooper "a superlative dolt" and "the craziest loon that was ever suffered to roam at large without whip and keeper."[530] But Benjamin, like Webb, was brought under action for libel in 1840. After being forced to pay three hundred and seventy-five dollars in damages, he learned to restrain his verbal impulses.[531]

There was no literary criticism of *Homeward Bound* or *Home as Found* in 1839 and 1840. Cooper's name was constantly in the papers, to be sure, and as the author of these books; but the subjects with which it was connected were whether he really was a fish hawker's son, how he had libeled the American people, and why he had attempted to throttle by lawsuit the freedom of the brave American press.[532] New

[529] XVIII (January, 1839), 48.

[530] *New Yorker*, VI (December 1, 1838), 173; *New World*, I (August 29, 1840), 193-195; I (August 29, 1840), 205; I (September 5, 1840), 210-215.

[531] Ethel R. Outland, *op. cit.*, pp. 66-68.

[532] *E.g.*, *Morning Courier and New York Enquirer*, May 24, 1839; September 6, 1839; September 13, 1839; May 14, 1840; May 16, 1840; July 10, 1840; August 28, 1840; September 22, 1840; October 10, 1840; October 23, 1840; April 17, 1841; November 19, 1841; November 22, 1841; December 31, 1841. *New Yorker*, VI (December 1, 1838), 173; VI (February 23, 1839), 361; VII (March 30, 1839), 29; VII (June 8, 1839), 179-180; VII (July 6, 1839), 255; VII (August 31, 1839), 381. *New World*, I (July 18, 1840), 97-100, 108; III (September 25, 1841), 204. *New York American* (Semi-weekly), July 2, 1839; September 10, 1839. *Commercial Advertiser*, quoted by *Albany Evening Journal*, May 30, 1839, Ethel R. Outland, *op. cit.*, p. 15.

Whig allies appeared. Thurlow Weed, head of the party and through the *Albany Evening Journal* the controlling power over Whig papers of the state, arranged his libels of Cooper in a regular column, and was repeatedly convicted at the novelist's suit. His most famous editorial is his allegation that Cooper had libeled New York and New Yorkers and had "disparaged American Lakes, ridiculed American Scenery, burlesqued American coin, and even satirized the American Flag!"[533] But other assaults of Weed's which are less famous than this were more malicious, attacking Cooper as cruel, selfish, and untruthful. Weed grew more and more violent under suit, trying to make a test, evidently, of the real power of the law. He was worst in 1842, but he was eventually muzzled. Horace Greeley in the *New York Tribune*[534] was almost as loud and as foul of speech as the rest of the tornado, but Cooper's persistence showed him, too, that for once he had met a better man.

How honest this supposed "reviewing" was as literary judgment can be estimated by an anecdote Weed later told of himself. On his way to one of the libel trials, he bought Cooper's latest, *The Two Admirals.* "I commenced reading it in the cars, and became so charmed with it that I took it with me into the court-room, and occupied every interval that my attention could be withdrawn from the trial in its perusal."[535] Why not say so in your paper? we feel like asking in reply; admit that though Cooper is a Democrat he has written an absorbing book. Paul Cooper did say something similar years later when he told the anecdote to him; as Weed puts it, Paul expressed regret that the incident had not come to the knowledge of his father. Weed seems not to have suspected Paul of any irony, or to have dreamed that

[533] *Albany Evening Journal,* November 22, 1841.

[534] November 20, 30, 1841; December 12, 1842.

[535] *Autobiography of Thurlow Weed,* edited by Harriet A. Weed, Boston, 1884, I, 527.

it is dishonest to admire an author's works in secret and decry the same works in public.

Weed was a sensational weeper. He said over and over that when Cooper's first case against him was called, he was prevented from attendance by the serious illness of his wife and the dangerous illness of his daughter. He whined that his lawyer "made . . . an appeal to Mr. Cooper's humanity" for postponement, but "that appeal of course was an unavailing one." He claimed, too, that the case had been at the foot of the calendar. He never printed the truth, as Cooper stated it, which was that the case was thirteenth in a list of forty, and came up the first day; that Cooper's own recommendation procured a postponement for one day, directly in opposition to the ruling of the court and the advice of counsel; that not only Weed but Weed's lawyer failed to appear when the postponed case came up again; and that Judge Willard told the lawyer who had asked for postponement that it would be granted if he would himself make affidavit that he believed the report of sickness in his client's family to be true, and the lawyer declined to make the affidavit. Besides, Weed had already been granted six months' postponement on the wonderful plea of having forgotten the case.[536]

The editors' accounts of their own trials are not to be trusted. Their impudent representation to the public that a libel consisted in a truth, "the greater the truth, the greater the libel," is notorious. Webb gave an inaccurate account of his first trial at Cooper's suit, and when Cooper published a

[536] For Weed's account, see his *Autobiography*, I, 521; *Albany Evening Journal*, November 22, 1841; Ethel R. Outland, *op. cit.*, pp. 111-114. This was circulated in many Whig journals, *e.g.*, Boston *Daily Advertiser and Patriot*, November 22, 1841; *New World*, III (November 27, 1841), 348-349; *Morning Courier and New York Enquirer*, November 29, 1841. For Cooper's account, see *Cincinnati Gazette*, clipping, Cooper collection, Yale. The Democratic *Albany Argus and Rough Hewer*, quoted by the *New York Tribune*, November 30, 1841, told the truth. See Ethel R. Outland, *op. cit.*, pp. 255-256.

correction in the *Evening Post* on December 3, he replied by saying Cooper was a liar and a monomaniac.[537] Horace Greeley printed such an unfair report of one of the novelist's triumphant suits against him that Cooper brought new charges of libel and won again.[538] Judge Willard once wrote the novelist that Webb had printed an untruthful account of his charge to the jury in the trial of Temple versus Webb, but it was not customary for a judge to correct newspaper accounts, and he preferred to suffer injustice rather than depart from custom.[539] This is the kind of opponent Cooper had engaged.

The widely held supposition that against this unprincipled Whig tornado the Democrats put up no defense for Cooper is utterly unfounded. Both sides admitted that the quarrel was partisan. Cooper was afraid of Whig juries, and the editors were no less afraid of Democratic ones.[540] The leading Democratic papers of the country not only supported Cooper during the libel suits but protested against the Whig system of attacking his private character for a political reason. The *Boston Post*, which was the Democratic opponent of the *Advertiser*, said:

> Before Mr. Cooper came out as a friend to Democratic principles and the Democratic party, his writings were read, praised, and admired by everybody. Since then every effort is made by the Whigs, or by a portion of them, to ruin his literary reputation, to prevent the sale of his books, and *even to injure his private character.*[541]

[537] *Morning Courier and New York Enquirer*, November 23, December 4, 1841; *Evening Post*, December 3, 1841.

[538] *New York Daily Tribune*, December 12, 1842.

[539] Letter, Judge John Willard to Cooper, Saratoga Springs, December 8, 1841. Unpublished. Cooper collection, Yale.

[540] *Correspondence of James Fenimore Cooper*, II, 459; *New York Weekly Tribune*, September 2, 1843, quoted by Ethel R. Outland, *op. cit.*, p. 57; *Morning Courier and New York Enquirer*, May 24, 1839.

[541] Quoted, *New World*, May 30, 1840. See Ethel R. Outland, *op. cit.*, p. 60.

Therefore we are not surprised to find that the *Evening Post* praised the truth and the courage of *Home as Found* (January 11, 1839); expressed its opinion that the attacks on Cooper were made from personal pique, and agreed with the *New Era* that the political tinge in his writings was not such as to merit persecution (January 29, 1839); gave an honest report of the Point litigation and congratulated Cooper on it (May 18, 1839); and opened its columns freely to letters from Cooper (November 3, 1838, March 20, 1841, October 15, 1841, October 18, 1841, December 3, 1841). Besides this old ally, the *Philadelphia National Gazette*[542] and the influential Albany *Argus* were on the side of the Boston *Post*. So were the small Democratic sheets.[543] But the petty Whig journals imitated the larger ones by calling Cooper a fool and a "malignant, avaricious, and mean-spirited man."[544] Some of these papers hoped for the notoriety of a libel suit, and the editors sent Cooper marked copies, penciled on the margins with challenges to sue.[545] One intrepid honest man who had somehow got a job on a Whig paper gave the world a paragraph acknowledging that his editor had told him some remarks about Cooper in a former issue were opposed to the journal's editorial policy, but insisting that he still thought his former statement was truthful, and he had inserted it in the earlier issue because he had innocently supposed "that in the defence or condemnation of

[542] *E.g.*, October 22, 1839; May 15, 1840; August 21, 1840. Ethel R. Outland, *op. cit.*, pp. 114-255.

[543] *Niagara Democrat*, answered sneeringly by the Whig *Niagara Courier*, June 26, 1839; Cooperstown *Freeman's Journal*, July 1, 1839; Philadelphia *Weekly Ledger*, September 26, 1840; *Onandago Standard*, cited with a sneer by *Albany Evening Journal*, December 11, 1841.

[544] Oxford (Chenango County) *Times*, June 19, 1839; *Wayne County Whig*, August 11, 1841; Philadelphia *Weekly Messenger*, January 30, 1839; *Niagara Courier*, July 17, 1839.

[545] *Baltimore Commercial Chronicle and Daily Marylander*, June 27, 1839; Syracuse *Morning Signal*, May 28, 1840. Cooper collection, Yale.

Mr. Cooper, rested not a test of political orthodoxy." The remarks which had been so obnoxious to the editor, so indicative that that journalist had not passed the test of political orthodoxy, were simply that Cooper was not conducting libel suits against hostile literary criticism, but against personal abuse, and that he was giving a salutary check to the licentiousness of the press.[546]

After reading three years' reviews of the two Effingham novels, with the Democrats hailing their Democrat hero and the Whigs crying in derision, "aristocrat Cooper," we can not wonder at reading in a letter from a friend of the novelist, "I am going to try an experiment that will puzzle the world to find out whether I am a Republican or royalist as much as 'Home as Found' & 'Homeward Bound' do Mr. Cooper's readers *all but me*."[547]

A book which Edgar Allan Poe considered the best American satire[548] gave a contemporary summary which we may better adopt here for ours than any opinion of later biographers. This satire was Laughton Osborn's *The Vision of Rubeta*,[549] and Osborn understood the situation very well. The Whig newspapers, he said, had deliberately set about defaming Cooper, a part of their system being discrimination against Cooper in favor of Irving in their reviews. They reprinted from *England*, he said, such passages as would "set the merchants of New York, that is, nearly all the city, against their once favorite author." They disgustingly dragged the Cooperstown dispute by main force into a story on Captain Marryatt and were willing, as Osborn put it, to defame Sir Walter Scott in order to father the defama-

[546] *Madison County Eagle*, December 22, 1841.

[547] Letter, Harriet Douglas Cruger to Mrs. Cooper, Richfield Springs, September 12, 1845. Unpublished. Cooper collection, Yale.

[548] Edgar Allan Poe, *The Literati, Works of Edgar Allan Poe*, Chicago, 1895, VII, 45-50.

[549] *The Vision of Rubeta, an Epic Story of the Island of Manhattan*, Boston, 1838, pp. 347-352.

tions upon Cooper. This hypocritical conduct, the satirist said, had two causes: anger at Cooper's having spoken contemptuously of the press (with which contempt Osborn had sympathy); and a partisan desire to make Cooper the successor of Clinton as the principal target for political vituperation. Osborn touched off (as "Petronius") the editors who claimed to be defending the freedom of the press against what they called Cooper's "persecutions":

> Yet who dares say PETRONIUS is unjust?
> Are not his own words worthy of all trust?
> Hark, how he prates of candor! with such zeal
> As 'twere a superfluity to feel.
> So ladies, crack'd of virtue, cry out *Jade,*
> And rail at hussies who are such by trade.
> Candor? What strumpet can be more sincere?
> What damm'd-up dike his current rolls more clear?

The poet's prose footnote on this passage reads: "The N. Y. American, as everybody knows who reads it, and wishes it were silent on this point, is day after day ringing fresh changes on the same tune of its own magnanimity. *Verbum sap.*: It would puzzle the Devil himself to extract bowels from a drum."

In spite of the papers, Osborn said, Cooper was still admired by the judicious few. A newspaper editor once wrote Cooper an admiring letter avouching that he was sending a copy of his own journal to Cooper, "to be placed among your family archives, that your grandchildren may have at least one more proof, that you are not the *cold hearted man*, some of yr cotemporaries would have us believe."[550]

Yet without the witness of these indignant allies, our generation has means of knowing that the Cooper myth was a mere manufactured shadow. We can tell from James Fenimore Cooper's own behavior that though the Whig cabal

[550] Letter, Samuel Williams to Cooper, Waterloo, August 7, 1844, speaking of *Tubbs Journal*. Unpublished. Cooper collection, Yale.

knew how to "make lee" for themselves, they could not spoil Cooper's character along with his reputation. While Barber and Weed were sobbing out their woes, Cooper's letters indicated a healthy interest in the world in general and no more than a businesslike interest in his lawsuits as they came up. He wrote to his friend Theodore Sedgwick, who was interested, a careful history of the suits, and another, in answer to inquiries, to Hunt, who published it.[551] But his usual letters simply refer to his suits in passing. He will mention to his wife that he has won a suit against Weed and is opening one against Stone, and then say, "It is warm and pleasant, but very little rain. I never saw the country more lovely. My best love to all—yours tenderly, J. F. C." Or when Benjamin attacks him vilely he merely writes, "Benjamin is down-derry-down—character understood, and sinks fast to Webb's level."[552] Lounsbury opened his eleventh chapter with a summary of the events in Cooper's life which might have embittered him. To offset the effect of this list, he offers only one feeble subordinate phrase: "without having his whole nature soured." The implication is that Cooper's nature, if not wholly soured, was nearly so. The inescapable fact of Cooper's persistent sweetness in *Pathfinder* and *Deerslayer*, written during the period of Cooper's libel suits, Lounsbury had to dismiss as an inexplicable phenomenon.

It is an inexplicable phenomenon, and so is Cooper's self, if we accept the Whig myth. But if we accept the evidence of Cooper's writings and contemporary testimony to his lovable nature, the sweetness of *Pathfinder* and *Deerslayer* will not be inexplicable as we follow the next years of Cooper's life; instead, the Effingham legend will be incredible.

[551] Both items are in the Cooper collection, Yale. See Appendix B.

[552] Quoted from the original letters to Mrs. Cooper, New York, May 13, 1842, and New York, March 29, 1841. Cooper collection, Yale. These letters have been altered in the published correspondence.

CHAPTER VIII

"Whose Name Is with His Country's Woven"

WHEN Commodore J. D. Elliott was in charge of the navy yard at Charleston, he placed a likeness of Andrew Jackson as a figure head on the sacred old Constitution. Boston Whigs were scandalized. As soon as they could, they removed the offending effigy. In vain; the prow of Old Ironsides soon flourished with a new and finer likeness of Old Hickory. Whig and Democratic papers advertised these outrages for years. Typical of Whig comments is an editorial in the *Commercial Advertiser* which said this dispute recalled the fact that Elliott had been a coward in the Battle of Lake Erie.[553] Typical of the Democratic version is this from the *Evening Post*:

It gives us sincere satisfaction to learn that the dastardly outrage committed by the whigs of Boston on the figure head of the frigate Constitution has been repaired in this city, and that she again shows at her prow the venerable features of our illustrious Chief Magistrate. . . . The whigs of New York, who are a brave set of men, as their heroic courage at the Arsenal a year ago, when they undertook 'to kill the damned Irish,' must bear eternal witness, will hardly undertake to mutilate again the reverend image of the greatest man of modern times. We should like to see a battalion of smooth faced clerks set out on an expedition of that kind. . . .

But it is a different game which they intend to pursue. The prowess of the valiant whigs is to vent itself, not in an attack on a wooden figure, in imitation of the whigs of Boston, but in an expression of public insult to Commodore Elliot, for having obeyed the orders of the Navy Commissioners in replacing the head. So at least we infer from the sentiments of a paragraph in the Courier and Enquirer of this morning. That journal, in pretending to dissuade the whigs from going to the Bowery theatre to-night to hiss Com-

[553] August 31, 1834.

modore Elliot, (who, it is understood, means to visit that theatre) in reality designs to stir them up to commit that most atrocious public indecency.[554]

And what has all this to do with James Fenimore Cooper? Strange to say, a great deal. Cooper in May, 1839, became the author of the *History of the Navy of the United States.*

The years 1838 to 1842, supposed to have been so troubled, were Cooper's best period as a writer, and he was aware of it. Cooper's readers are familiar with his belief that if posterity cherished any of his novels it would be *Pathfinder* and *Deerslayer,* and he "always regarded [The History of the Navy] . . . as his great work, and . . . often said, the day would come, when his country would do justice to it . . ."[555]

At that gay farewell banquet when Cooper was sailing for France, the announcement that the author of *The Pilot* had undertaken to write the history of his country's navy was hailed with enthusiasm. His experience, tastes, and talent would all contribute, and the prediction was that his work would be "one of the standard histories of the age."[556] His friends did not allow him to forget his country's high expectations of this work while he was abroad,[557] and his correspondence shows that he worked over the details of the history as he never labored with a novel. When his book appeared after ten years' toil, among the first to send their congratulations on its excellence were Richard Rush, one time ambassador to England, and James K. Paulding, Secretary of the Navy. The best contemporary historian, George Bancroft, who was an admirer of Cooper's "genius, manly character and great career," said before the New York Historical Society that the *History of the Navy* was "the most

[554] March 14, 1835.

[555] Letter, Mrs. Cooper to "Frederic," December 13 [1851]. Unpublished. Cooper collection, Yale.

[556] *Southern Review,* II (November, 1828), 351; *Connecticut Observer,* March 1, 1825, quoting the *National Gazette.*

[557] *Correspondence of James Fenimore-Cooper,* I, 245.

admirable composition of which any nation could boast on a similar subject."[558] Even the publishers were surprised into pleasure at the sales; they not only printed a second edition at the end of 1839, but enlarged the new edition from a proposed two thousand copies to three thousand.[559]

When it came to reviewing, Willis and Bryant were as loyal as ever; the book was charming, brilliant, engaging in its narrative and "written in a manifest spirit of fairness and truth."[560] Willis even dared to reply to the British. Of course, the latter were prolific with accusations of partiality in the history, and if any journalism ever deviated from book reviewing into personal and libelous calumny, these British reviews did it. Take as a sample this slur upon Cooper's birth:

> Mr. Cooper is incapable of one generous—one manly thought. . . . Time and his extended travel might have eradicated the early prejudices of his youth and education, and in some slight degree qualified him for the various tasks he has imposed upon himself. Alas! Mr. Cooper is another proof how very hard it is to wash the blackamoor white, and stalks before us a living confirmation of the saying—'That it requires a whole generation to eradicate the weeds which are nurtured, in the ungenerous soil of a low estate.'[561]

The same article said that in Cooper's book there was not "one account given in good faith—with the liberality of a gentleman, or the truth of an historian." Willis assured the alarmed natives that Americans simply could not conceive

[558] *Correspondence of James Fenimore-Cooper,* II, 397-398, 402; letter, J. K. Paulding to Cooper, Washington, May 20, 1839. Unpublished. Cooper collection, Yale; *Memorial of James Fenimore Cooper,* pp. 16-17.

[559] *Correspondence of James Fenimore-Cooper,* II, 400.

[560] *Evening Post,* October 28, 1841; May 16, 1839, quoting the *Pennsylvanian*; *Corsair,* I (May 25, 1839), 168-169.

[561] *United Service Journal,* quoted here by *Museum of Foreign Literature, Science, and Art,* XXXVII (December, 1839), 449-455; XXXVIII (January, 1840), 52-62.

of the firmness with which British policy had implanted in English minds the belief that no British vessel had ever been defeated. Cooper's "manly style and plain figures" must triumph in the end, he said, against the "special pleading or angry invective by which his reviewers would fain invalidate or overpower them."[562] The *Democratic Review* gave two unusually long leading articles to defending the accuracy of the book against the *Edinburgh Review*.[563] This was loyal, but intrinsic worth and Democratic praise were slight help to a book against a Whig tornado. Other reviews were for the most part so timid in their commendation as to arouse the suspicion that their inditers had not read the book. Some of them, though admitting that the *History of the Navy* was in itself spirited and reliable, insolently reminded the world that Cooper was recovering from "promptings of Satan and the spleen," and that Americans had grown ashamed of Cooper in late years because of his peevishness and conceit. One of them suggested that even though Cooper was in a literary pillory it was not becoming to "every man to hurl an offensive missile" at him and to scream small errors into great sins.[564] The new edition moved slowly, after all,[565] for the Whigs found a great many damaging things to say, and eventually they managed to precipitate the history into the most interesting of all the political lawsuits.

Here is the story. One of the most popular events of American history had always been the Battle of Lake Erie,

[562] *Corsair*, I (July 27, 1839), 316.

[563] *United States Magazine and Democratic Review*, X (May, 1842), 409-435; (June, 1842), 513-541. Cooper seems to have been the author.

[564] *Knickerbocker Magazine*, XIII (June, 1839), 538; *Journal of Belles Lettres, Waldie's Select Circulating Library*, XIII (May 28, 1839), Number 22; (June 5, 1839), Number 23; (June 18, 1839), Number 25; *New Yorker*, VII (May 18, 1839), 141; *Albion*, July 13, 1839; *Gentleman's Magazine*, V (July, 1839), 56-58.

[565] Letter, Lea and Blanchard to Cooper, Philadelphia, February 11, 1840. Unpublished. Cooper collection, Yale.

and of that battle Commodore Perry was in Cooper's day the hero. Now, reviewing that action in the original records, Cooper became convinced that Commodore J. D. Elliott had been treated with gross injustice in reports of the engagement. Perry's heroism had been exalted by the allegation that Elliott had been too cowardly to bring up his vessel as promptly as he should have done. The documents indicated to Cooper that Elliott had acted as quickly as was physically possible, considering the position of the ships and the state of the wind. Naturally, he presented this evidence and this conclusion in his history. He did not treat Elliott as the hero of the battle. He simply ignored the gossip concerning Elliott's alleged cowardice and recorded the facts as he found them; no, not quite as he found them, for he made of them a masterly narrative of winds, sails, gun shots, and manoeuverings of vessels.

No one liked Elliott much, personally. He was widely considered a whining incompetent,[566] and he caused Cooper some embarrassment by his too abundant gratitude for what he chose to interpret as a championing of his cause instead of a mere disinterested statement of truth.[567] In the July after the *History of the Navy* was published, Elliott actually was court martialed. He was acquitted on every important count, but the publicity was unfortunate.[568] Then, too, Elliott had

[566] Letters, G. A. Worth to Cooper, New York, June 18, 1839; G. A. Worth to Cooper, New York, July 11, 1839; J. De Peyster Ogden to Cooper, New York, June 20, 1839; W. B. Shubrick to Cooper, Washington, November 23, 1843. Unpublished. Cooper collection, Yale; *Correspondence of James Fenimore-Cooper*, II, 507-508.

[567] W. B. Shubrick, *loc. cit.* For an account of the medal which Elliott had struck in Cooper's honor, see T. R. Lounsbury, *op. cit.*, pp. 224-225. Elliott suggested distributing among the members of the New York and Pennsylvania legislatures copies of an article which Cooper wrote in defense of his *History* and which Elliott considered a vindication of himself. J. D. Elliott to Charles R. Grayham, February 3, 1843, R. W. Griswold, *op. cit.*, p. 136.

[568] *Correspondence of James Fenimore-Cooper*, II, 399.

got himself embroiled in the party conflicts at Harrisburg, Pennsylvania, in 1838.[569] What with this and the Boston troubles, it is no wonder that one of Cooper's Whig friends wrote him that he had been unfortunate in some of his "*historical* friendships" as well as his "political associations," mentioning Elliott for an example of the former as flatly as he gave Cooper's having committed himself "to the chance of Mr. Van Beuren's success, and consented to share his political fate" for an instance of the latter.[570] Ogden wrote as if defending Elliott and supporting Van Buren were calamities. But how could Cooper have helped doing either?

And what could be expected of the *Courier and Enquirer*, now, except the following?

James Fenimore Cooper.—This traducer of his country and his countrymen—this common slanderer of his fair countrywomen, and all that is honorable, honest and intellectual in the land of his birth—is now in Philadelphia, writing a Naval History of the United States, and bolstering up the tottering character of Commodore Elliott!! He not only declares that Elliot is an ill-used gentleman—a declaration which is untrue in every respect, for he is neither ill-used nor a gentleman—but what is far worse, he intends to prove that he Elliott, did not disgrace himself in the battle of Lake Erie! This part of the work is, we understand, to be dictated by Elliot; and if so, the fame of the gallant, Perry will doubtless be blackened and injured to the full extent that two such congenial spirits can detract from it. Our only hope is, that a naval history of the United States, from such a source, will meet with the silent contempt to which the general character of the author for truth and veracity, where his country and countrymen are concerned, so richly entitles it. To expect a faithful history of our Navy, by one who has devoted the last five years of his life to the indiscriminate abuse of every thing American, would be quite as reasonable, as to look for

[569] *New York American,* December 26, 1838.

[570] Letter, James De Peyster Ogden to Cooper, New York, August 4, 1840. Unpublished. Cooper collection, Yale.

an honest record of the battle of Lake Erie, from one who skulked from the dangers of that day, and had nearly converted a glorious victory into a disgraceful defeat.[571]

Of course the *Commercial Advertiser*, which had been attacking Elliott frequently since 1834, printed two long articles on June 8 and 9, attempting to discredit not only the whole narrative of the action of Lake Erie, but Cooper's integrity. These articles were written by William A. Duer, ex-president of Columbia College, but Cooper held W. L. Stone responsible as editor of the paper. For nearly a year the *Commercial Advertiser* boasted of these articles and of its immunity from lawsuit, but when Cooper in his calm course got around to Stone, a process was served upon him in May, 1840.

The account of Cooper's suit against Stone has been written in so masterly a way by Professor Lounsbury that nothing need be said about it here except to mention a few details which escaped the biography.

Not the least interesting aspect of the trial is Cooper's absolutely unshakable confidence in his book. Such a phenomenon as a historian who never made errors "the world never yet saw," he said, "Moses excepted." But he believed he had presented all the ascertainable facts and presented them fairly. He could not demand from Duer and Stone any justification for their own criticisms, "for that is out of the question," he said; he asked them only to make "*any apology for them.*"[572]

In the Yale Cooper collection is preserved a report of the Supreme Court proceedings which reproduces the *Commercial Advertiser's* libel of Cooper's probity. The libelous matter is

[571] January 26, 1839.

[572] Letters, Cooper to Captain Dobbin, Cooperstown, May 20, 1843. Unpublished. Buffalo Historical Society; Cooper to James De Peyster Ogden, Cooperstown, June 11, 1839. Unpublished. Maine Historical Society, Portland. Cooper to the Editors of the Naval History. Unpublished. Yale.

closely annotated in Cooper's hand with indications of its false statements. At the end of a page of notes for use at the trial, Cooper has written: "Is the interest of the public in Commodore Perry, greater than their interest in truth?"

Stone made the complaint that he was a helpless and unwilling victim of Cooper's persecution. Ogden wrote to Cooper like the persistent Whig he was, warning his friend not to distrust the Whigs so much, and saying Stone had expressed regret over the dispute and wished to settle the matter by some agreeable arrangement.[573] Now, Stone had been sneering at Cooper ever since the days of "Something Strange"; his regret had evidently come upon him suddenly. It left him even more suddenly, for as soon as the suit on the *History of the Navy* was over, he renewed his libels and brought upon himself a second and richly deserved litigation.[574]

A typical mishandling of the truth in connection with this trial is the representation by Stone that he was being sued for legitimate literary criticism. Stone claimed that his demurrer was a test of the freedom of an editor to make "fair or honest" literary criticism, and this he advertised widely.[575] Of course, the claim was not in the least true. Cooper never in his life sued for literary criticism, but only for false aspersions upon his own character. Judge Esek Cowen explained perfectly clearly in his decision the difference between attacking a man's character and attacking his book. If a man chances to be an author he is no more to be subjected to

[573] Letter, J. De P. Ogden to Cooper, New York, March 23, 1841. Unpublished. Cooper collection, Yale.

[574] Stone died before this litigation was over, and his widow wrote a sentimental, self-pitying letter to Cooper asking that the case be dropped, though there is no indication that Mrs. Stone made any effort to have a retraction published. She, like Weed and Barber, preferred to sob. *Correspondence of James Fenimore-Cooper*, II, 539-540. Cooper always dropped prosecutions upon printing of retractions. See, for instance, *ibid.*, II, 541.

[575] *E.g.*, *New Yorker*, IX (August 8, 1840), 335.

malicious attack upon his personal reputation than any other man, Judge Cowen declared; in fact, he ought to be more carefully defended from such attacks than other men. Cowen found, in this case, that "It is difficult to read the articles . . . without seeing at once that they are direct and undisguised attacks upon the moral character of the plaintiff by name."[576]

Cooper once wrote a careful and good-tempered explanation of this point to an editor who had been urged by friends to denounce Cooper's suits. He wrote to Cooper before denouncing, and Cooper replied that as his inquiry was "written with an apparent desire to learn the truth" he would answer its questions "quite cheerfully." His answers are both cheerful and dignified. One passage only exhibits a little spirit:

If the editors of the papers I have mentioned, knew that they were circulating ridiculous falsehoods, they might understand how much I care for their strictures. One of these papers has just reached me, coming all the way from Illinois. It speaks of my having persecuted the 'amiable and gentlemanly Horace Greely, Esquire,' for criticism. Now, I never sued 'Squire Greely for any such thing. I sued him, some time since, for *calumny*, and beat him; and I have just sued him a second time for calumny, and depend upon it, sir, I shall beat him again; as I have every man I have sued, who has not retracted his libels.

I have never even sued for ridicule. Every action brought by me, has been brought for direct and palpable *calumny*. I have brought these suits because I am sick of being a Freeman in name only. The man is a slave who lives in dread of calumny, and I choose to struggle for my liberty.

As for money, not a human being who knows me, has the smallest idea, it, in any manner, influences my course. If *money* were the object, I own too much literary property, not to understand how important it is to my pockets, to make friends among the newspapers. I have lost a fortune by the hostile influence of the American press; but its power has never induced me to court it in any shape, or yield to it a

[576] Ethel R. Outland, *op. cit.*, p. 224. It is remarkable that Miss Outland does not stress the falseness of Stone's claim.

single privilege. The calumny in connection with the battle of Lake Erie, has, of itself, cost me many thousands. It destroyed the sale of a work that ought, and otherwise would have put into my pocket a very large sum; whereas, I am now five or six thousand dollars poorer than if I had never written it. The injury is irreparable. I have refuted that calumny, but much of its moral effects will remain, long after I am dead; and, as for money, the loss once made, is made forever. This is a people that never yet repaired a wrong; bodies of men seldom do; the American people less than common. It will scarcely inforce justice as between man and man; much less will it, at its own cost.

To conclude, therefore, criticism *cannot* be a libel, while purely criticism. I have never sued for mere strictures on a book, and in only one case, that of Mr. Stones, for any thing connected with a book.[577]

Most of the letter is an exposition of the legal differences between literary criticism and calumny. When Hunt had read it, he printed it instead of a denunciation, and when Cooper died, Hunt sent it to another paper with the request that it be printed again in order that the matter of Cooper's prosecutions be "placed before the world in its just and proper light. . . . A great man has departed; and generosity demands that all his redeeming qualifications should be placed upon record; that his errors, (and who is devoid of them?) should be 'interred with his bones.' "

The naval history case was tried before a board of arbitration because Stone objected that no jury was competent to consider the technical points involved. This board met on May 16, 1842, and Cooper defended himself in a spectacular address which must have been something astonishing to hear. Henry T. Tuckerman was there, a prominent literary figure of Boston, who did not know Cooper and who went to the trial with his sympathies inclined towards the defendant. He

[577] Letter to J. Hunt, Jr., Cooperstown, New York, February 28, 1843, printed in the *Cincinnati Gazette*. Clipping in Cooper collection, Yale. See Appendix B.

has related how Cooper's magnetism and energy won him over in spite of himself.

"A more unpopular cause never fell to the lot of a practiced advocate," Tuckerman said, for Cooper was "almost alone in his opinion,—the tide of public sentiment against his theory of the battle, and the popular sympathy wholly with the received traditions of that memorable day." If Cooper had been a petty, a selfish, or a bitter man he could never have overcome this barrier. Evidently he was not such a man, for Tuckerman says that he commanded admiration as soon as he began examining witnesses, and that his account of the movement of ships in the battle was "like a chapter in one of his own sea-stories." His zest for the argument and his dogmatism were something marvelous to behold, and "He quoted Cooper's 'Naval History' as if it were 'Blackstone.'" Yet Tuckerman admired, for "his self-complacency was exceeded by his wonderful ability." At length Tuckerman surrendered to the "manly, firm, yet not unkindly spirit" of the man who stood before him, so that his final word on Cooper as he saw him conducting a libel suit was this:

> As we gazed and listened, we understood clearly why, as a man, Cooper had been viewed from such extremes of prejudice and partiality; we recognized at once the generosity and courage, the willfulness and pride of his character: but the effect was to inspire a respect for the man, such as authors whose errors are moral weakness never excite.[578]

Washington Irving read this description of Tuckerman's and "pronounced it a very fair, discriminating article."[579] What Tuckerman felt, another witness of the trial said the audience felt, moving from unfriendly prejudice to delight.[580]

[578] *North American Review*, LXXXIX (October, 1859), 305-306. Quoted, Lounsbury, *op. cit.*, pp. 217-218.

[579] Pierre Irving, *op. cit.*, III, 261.

[580] Letter, J. D. Elliott to Cooper, Philadelphia, January 10, 1842, quoting a friend who was present. Unpublished. Cooper collection, Yale.

Of course, Tuckerman cultivated an acquaintance with the man he had thus discovered, and he found that the bringer of law suits was himself a person unusually ready to own an error and make restitution for it. He learned, too, that "it was needful but to approach him candidly, to meet him on his own ground of frank utterance, in order to find him at once a most interesting companion and a noblehearted gentleman." As for himself, he found Cooper "absolutely refreshing."

The outcome of this trial, as everyone knows, was that Cooper's history was upheld on all of the eight points disputed, and Stone was required to publish a retraction.

Another incident connected with the *History of the Navy* serves as a revelation of Cooper's quickness in springing to self-defense and equal quickness in releasing his enemy generously. One Alexander Slidell Mackenzie, Lieutenant in the navy, wrote a criticism of Cooper's history for the *North American Review*.[581] This article was a family affair; Mackenzie was a nephew of William A. Duer and a brother-in-law of Commodore Perry's brother. This brother, M. C. Perry, had tried to influence Cooper's history before its publication.[582] Mackenzie was not, like William Duer, insulting, nor did he squander all his space on the Elliott case. He praised Cooper for careful research, spirited narration, and liberality towards England. But he succeeded in giving a strong impression that the history was seriously damaged by a false account of the Battle of Lake Erie, and he produced his effect by facile and shallow reasoning. Cooper wrote his wife that the article was "superficial and jesuitical," not personally abusive, but false. "He wants candor and a sense of right."[583] It was true; and considering that Mackenzie had repeatedly called Cooper deliberately unfair, Cooper spoke mildly. Cooper published a very interesting article in

[581] XLIX (October, 1839), 432-467.
[582] *Correspondence of James Fenimore-Cooper*, I, 386-387.
[583] *Ibid.*, II, 404.

the *Evening Post*,[584] answering Mackenzie with nautical explanations. Early in 1841, Mackenzie published a life of Perry which was intended to silence Cooper's account of the Lake Erie battle for all time. The Whigs welcomed it as an answer to the *History of the Navy*[585] and the Democrats regretted that it was extremely controversial.[586]

About this time John C. Spencer, Superintendent of Schools, told a bookseller he would not adopt an abridged edition of Cooper's history for use in New York schools because it was controversial. Cooper did not need the sales, for he had already decided to sell the book in Philadelphia instead of New York. But to have his work called controversial was too much. He wrote privately to a friend:

> Now, in the first place, it is the *want* of controversy in the *History* that has made the clamor about it—my abstaining from accusing Elliott, etc. But the d—d scoundrel had actually put in Mackenzie's life of Perry, which is *all* controversy, which avows itself to be controversy in its preface, and controversy on the Battle of Lake Erie, too, several months before he wrote that letter! I pledge you my honour to these facts. I have lately been told that the biographies he mentioned as having been rejected on account of their controversy, he had officially admitted, but, on receiving a notice from Gen. Dix, his predecessor in office, informing him that they contained deliberate attacks on the democratic party, and that if published in the series, the abuse would be exposed, he withdrew them. The last I give you on respectable information—the first I know to be true. I wonder if there is such a thing as an honest politician?[587]

Cooper set to work on a pamphlet which Catharine Sedgwick referred to ironically as one that would "grind M'Kenzie to powder."[588]

[584] March 29, 1841.
[585] *Morning Courier and New York Enquirer*, November 26, 1840.
[586] *Evening Post*, March 13, 1841.
[587] *Correspondence of James Fenimore-Cooper*, II, 455.
[588] Mary E. Dewey, *op. cit.*, pp. 285-286.

But Cooper never ground Mackenzie, after all. Mackenzie got himself into some rather shocking trouble, and so Cooper suppressed the pamphlet, even buying the right to do so from the printer. "The poor fellow," he is reported to have said, "will have enough to do to escape the consequences of his own weakness. It is no time to press upon him now."[589]

Instead of his pamphlet, Cooper printed a report of Mackenzie's court-martial and acquittal, so liberal a report that one reader complained that it made Mackenzie out to be better than he was,[590] and another, that Cooper seemed "to have a sort of hydrophobia [*sic*] dread of thinking Mackenzie a *villain*. He is to be reduced to a mere ill-reasoner. . . ."[591] William Gilmore Simms wrote to Cooper expressing his faith in the latter's honesty in this matter, and hoping that Cooper would not be denounced for it by the "hard master" (the public) which they both served.[592]

Mackenzie's offense was having hanged Midshipman Philip Spencer on his ship without a trial, and with him two seamen. This young Spencer was the son of the very Superintendent of Schools who had befriended Mackenzie's book.

This was the end of the navy troubles for Cooper. Or shall we mention Tristram Burges? This gentleman was a Rhode Islander who had once delivered a lecture on the Battle of Lake Erie before the Historical Society of his state, and who hastened to print and circulate this *magnum opus* when the excitement rose over the *History of the*

[589] George Washington Greene, *Homes of American Authors*, pp. 209-210.

[590] Letter, W. H. Norris, addressee unnamed, Baltimore, December 16, 1843. Unpublished. Cooper collection, Yale.

[591] Unsigned and undated letter. Unpublished. Cooper collection, Yale.

[592] Letter, W. G. Simms to Cooper, Woodland, North Carolina, April 10. Unpublished. Cooper collection, Yale.

Navy.[593] One of its brave statements, marked in Cooper's copy, runs as follows: "Every Yankee is an axe man; and all the companions of Perry were of the full blood; and most of them were of the best of that blood, the Rhode-Island stock." More examples could be culled from it of Burges's intellectual gigantism. Cooper indulged himself in some laughter with Mrs. Cooper over the gem.[594] There was no need to answer. Oh, of course the Whigs talked as if Burges had said something,[595] but what of that?

Thus Cooper perfected his vindication of the *History of the Navy*, a vindication highly creditable to his courage and his veracity. "I see with much pleasure that you have confined your defensive to the proper subject—viz. the impartiality and integrity of your history," wrote G. A. Worth, who was a Whig, who in general thought Cooper was too sensitive to the attacks of the press, and who had feared Cooper would get drawn into a defense of the character of Elliott.[596] According to Elliott, Democrats, from the Tammany society to President Jackson, were delighted with the outcome.[597] Simms was pleased that the Perry faction was most effectually demolished,[598] and Greenough rejoiced that one man dared tell the truth in the teeth of the "aristocrats."[599]

Cooper was doubtless pleased, also; but he must have been far more interested in writing *Pathfinder* and *Deerslayer* while all this was going on than he was in his suits.

[593] *Battle of Lake Erie with Notices of Commodore Elliot's Conduct in That Engagement*, Philadelphia, 1839, p. 20.

[594] *Correspondence of James Fenimore-Cooper*, II, 404.

[595] *New York American*, semi-weekly, October 15, 1839.

[596] Letter, G. A. Worth to Cooper, New York, July 11, 1839. Unpublished. Cooper collection, Yale.

[597] *Correspondence of James Fenimore-Cooper*, II, 529-531.

[598] Letter, W. G. Simms to Cooper, Charleston, South Carolina, September 27. Unpublished. Cooper collection, Yale.

[599] Letter, Horace Greenough to Cooper, October 8, 1839. Unpublished. Cooper collection, Yale.

He had brought out the former in March, 1840, and the latter in August, 1841. There was *Mercedes of Castile*, too, in November of 1840. *Mercedes* was a failure, but *Pathfinder* and *Deerslayer* were remarkable successes. Cooper was delighted. He wrote home: "Lea has sold near 4000 of *Pathfinder*. It has great success, in the worst of times. Indeed, it is the only thing that does sell."[600] Like the old wildfire triumphs, *Pathfinder* was dramatized, coming on the boards at the Bowery Theatre in April, 1840.

The Whigs made quite a point of not reading these latest books, though they reported hearsay that Cooper's power was lost.[601] They were delighted to use C. F. Hoffman's new *Grayslaer* as an excuse to say how bad Cooper's frontier novels were,[602] though such a critic as Edgar Allan Poe still treated Cooper as the standard,[603] and Balzac wrote a famous piece of admiring criticism for the *Revue Parisienne*.

But when the *cacoethes scribendi Whigium* was really upon a reviewer, he wrote in one of the following styles:

> [The book has only one merit; it contains no] political, philosophical, and philological ravings.
>
> His wand is broken; and he can never again charm 'the judicious' with its waving.
>
> [Cooper tried to avenge himself on Sir Walter Scott by] the childish attempt to cast odium on a Scotchman, *as such*, in the Quarter Master.
>
> If any one besides ourselves has read the book through, we give him joy—he has had a tough time of it. . . . We do not imagine that any other mere man has accomplished the

[600] *Correspondence of James Fenimore-Cooper*, II, 414.

[601] *New York American* (Semi-weekly), March 28, 1840; *New Yorker*, X (March 6, 1841), 397; XI (September 4, 1841), 397.

[602] *New World*, I (July 11, 1840), 94; *Morning Courier and New York Enquirer*, July 2, July 10, May 14, 1840.

[603] Review of W. G. Simms, *The Kinsmen*, in *Graham's Magazine*, XVIII (March, 1841), 143. For Poe's connection with this review, see W. P. Trent, *William Gilmore Simms*, New York, 1892, p. 159.

task; and we hug . . . the hope that in after days, as we walk along Broadway, we shall be ranked with *the two* other distinguished personages of the nineteenth century. . .

The Man in the Claret-Colored Coat;
The Man who read the Monikins;
The Man who read the Pathfinder[604]

[To convince readers that he is not over-sensitive] will require not a few upturnings of the nose and dignified sneers.

[In drawing the portraits of historical persons, with] really great men, Mr. Cooper seems to us uniformly unfortunate. His attempt, in 'The Spy,' to bring in Washington . . . is an instance . . . . Perhaps, however, the character of Mr. Effingham . . . is so illustrious an exception, as completely to nullify our general rule.[605]

[It was hoped that when Cooper put by] his insufferable egotism [he would write a good novel, but] Of all the novels in which Mr. Cooper has not introduced himself and family, this [*Mercedes of Castile*] is the most vapid, stale and worthless.[606]

'If Mr. Cooper is writing any new work which he intends shall appear shortly, we humbly beg permission to inform him that we consider it good. We are delighted with it; in fact we are amazed; it surpasses, we think, all he ever has written and all he ever means to write, and is emphatically *the* book of the age. There is no further use for pen and ink, for there is nothing further to achieve in literature. The ink manufacturers are all bankrupt, and the paper mills must stop. The man at last breathes who proves the possibility of human perfection, and the rest of mankind must gaze in silence and admire . . . . All the excellences of all other authors, and even all the perfections of *Cooper,* on which the public have hitherto been graciously permitted to gaze, are in this work ten times trebled, and in one overwhelming cataract of sublimity the whole now bursts upon the reader . . . . We are awe-struck, paralysed, petrified, macadamised. . . .'

[604] *New York Evening Signal,* March 19, 1840.
[605] *New Yorker,* X (November 28, 1840), 173.
[606] *Morning Courier and New York Enquirer,* November 27, 1840.

[Added note:] There—we trust John Doe and Richard Roe will be satisfied with that. . . . It certainly is laid on pretty thick, which is the chief consideration.[607]

[The downfall of Cooper's popularity was not due to his] folly, his egotism, and his slanderous assaults upon his country and its institutions, [but simply to his complete incompetence as a writer, which the people had discovered at last in *Deerslayer*].[608]

[While Weed stood] watching over the bed of his dying child . . . his heart . . . pained to bursting—and his brow wet with the dew of anguish, [Cooper had exacted the last legality from the sorrowing editor. Let Cooper ask himself whether he was not, twelve years before, as much as Irving the pride and pet of his countrymen, and let him say:] alas, yes! But why did I defend my countrymen while abroad, to abuse them when I returned home? Why did I exhibit such repulsive harshness? . . . . Was this a proper return for all the kind praises I had received? And how has Irving behaved? . . . Has he kept himself in boiling water as I have . . .? Has he quarreled with the citizens of his native village, engaged in undignified newspaper warfare, made himself as notorious as a ballad-monger's wench, brought libel-suit after libel-suit against editors of newspapers, and failed so absurdly that his name, once smothered with laurels like a bifteck aux ognons, is now synonimous with every thing that is funny. . .?

Mind, reader, every word we have said refers to Mr. Cooper as an author, not as a man. In fact it must: there can be no doubt that he *is* an author—but as has formerly been logically remarked by the learned Smellfungus . . . 'a man to be a man must be a man and not an'—the quotation is somewhat musty.[609]

So the Whigs were impudently learning their lesson, that they dared no longer attack Cooper's character, and must limit themselves to advertising the death of his talent. But the evil they had already done to his personal reputation was

[607] *New Yorker*, IX (June 27, 1840), 283, quoting *Picayune*.
[608] *Morning Courier and New York Enquirer*, September 3, 1841.
[609] *New World*, III (November 27, 1841), 348-349.

well enough sown to live after them. So even the *Knickerbocker Magazine,* which printed three notices highly favorable to *Pathfinder,* could not resist referring to assaults which "have evidently stung him into madness."[610] The *New York Mirror* had to call Cooper "that prince of egotists" in a review that ridiculed him and Heckewelder together,[611] after having avouched in an earlier number that *Pathfinder* was "a good book, and it gives us great pleasure to say so."[612]

The loyal *Evening Post* was the only journal which gave *Pathfinder* two perfectly serene and satisfied mentions.[613] It reprinted Balzac's noted review, and August Danyan, a friend of Cooper, prefaced Balzac with remarks to the effect that Cooper had "at last found one of his peers to sit in judgment upon him" in France, whereas in his own country he had been "assailed by critics, who, lacking even the inspiration of envy, have made themselves the servile echoes of some British reviews hating our great novelist with the combined fervor of tory and national antipathies." Danyan sent a copy of these remarks to Cooper with a letter which refers to the former's "assiduous toils in the cause of Democracy during the last Presidential election," discusses the beauties of *Pathfinder,* and says that while he can produce such canvases Cooper need not care for "the hissings of the Vipers wreathing" under his feet.[614]

[610] *Knickerbocker Magazine,* XV (April, 1840), 344; (May, 1840), 449; XVII (January, 1841), 72-77.

[611] XVIII (July 4, 1840), 12.

[612] *Ibid.,* XVII (March 21, 1840), 305.

[613] March 14, 26, 1841.

[614] Letter, A. Danyan to Cooper, New York, March 27, 1841. Unpublished. Cooper collection, Yale. There were other notices of these novels, on the whole favorable, some with condescending or even insulting "forgiveness" dominating the praise: *Ladies' Companion,* XII (April, 1840), 296; XIII (May, 1840), 47; (August, 1840), 207; XIV (January, 1841), 148; *Casket,* XVII (August, 1840), 96; *Godey's Lady's Book,* XX (May, 1840), 239; XXII (January, 1841), 47; *New York Review,* VI (April, 1840), 479-480; VIII (January, 1841), 271; *Gentleman's Magazine,* VI (April, 1840), 200;

So when the New Haven *Daily Herald* (Whig) boasted that its editors had never admired this egotistic and foppish author and that the first two sentences of *Mercedes of Castile* contained two "gross violations of syntax,"[615] the New Haven *Columbian Register* (Democratic) cried "Pish"[616] and let it go at that. With *Deerslayer,* the reviewers who could not resist making patronizing allusions to the fabulous Effingham qualities of character still worked up real enthusiasm about the new novel.[617] The friend of old times, the *Democratic Review,* was pleased to find "good old" Natty again and asked for another book about him with a Mrs. Bumpo and a Nathaniel Jr. The public was pleased again, the politicians were unmasked, the Webbs, Weeds, and Greeleys were learning their lessons and watching their pens.

Cooper had never minded the adverse reviews even of *Pathfinder.* "The opposition reviews are laughed at," he had written his wife at the height of their abuse, "They have done me no harm, and themselves a great deal."[618] And now he did not settle down in a retreat of old age or of romantic

Iris, I (January, 1841), 137; *Evening Post,* November 25, 1840, quoting the *Pennsylvanian.* Unfavorable reviews, some with insult, were: *New Yorker,* VIII (March 14, 1840), 413; X (October 24, 1840), 94; *New York American* (Semi-weekly), December 1, 1840; *Arcturus,* I (January, 1841), 90-92, quoted as to its adverse criticism but as to none of its favorable comment, in *New Yorker,* X (January 2, 1841), 253; *Morning Courier and New York Enquirer,* November 27, 1840.

[615] November 26, 1840.

[616] November 28, 1840.

[617] *New York Mirror,* XIX (September 11, 1841), 295; *Knickerbocker Magazine,* XVIII (October, 1841), 349-352; *New York Review,* IX (October, 1841), 537-538; *Godey's Lady's Book,* XXIII (October, 1841), 189; *Ladies' Companion,* XV (October, 1841), 310. But the *Southern Literary Messenger,* VII (October, 1841), 742-743, thought *Deerslayer* a "poor thing" "beneath the dignity of a criticism." *United States Magazine and Democratic Review,* IX (October, 1841), 404-405.

[618] *Correspondence of James Fenimore-Cooper,* II, 414.

Glimmerglass. He kept right on dealing with social problems, alternating them with idyllic visions of the forest. The Chain Bearer series, dealing with the anti-rent struggles, is an example. Hillard thought these books perfectly sound, disinterested, vigorous, and courageous,[619] and so did many other men. As a lawyer, Hillard said that *The Ways of the Hour* was so sensible a criticism of the jury system, and its legal points were so well taken, that the professional reader could not follow them without admiration. The anti-rent war tore New York into new factions, many Democrats uniting with the Whigs on the new issue. "I am a Whig," a friend of Cooper's wrote to him, "but I am sorry Young has been elected gov. of N. Y. because he favors Anti-Rentism. I wish your party had elected their gov., though Mr. Wright is not so opposed to Anti-Rent as I wish."[620] This is how it happens that C. A. Bristed wrote, in an official Whig organ, of the Chain Bearer trilogy, "We were glad (for the first time in our lives) that he was a 'Democrat,' for many men will listen to a Democrat who will not think of hearing a 'British Whig.'"[621] So Cooper proceeded on his way as an author, exercising his hard-won right both to criticise and to entertain.

Cooper's works left those readers who were real literary figures feeling the inner greatness of the man who wrote such novels as his. *The Prairie*, Bryant said, gave him an "undefined sense of sublimity"; *Mercedes of Castile* and *Pathfinder* were precious tokens of the eternal summer of Cooper's spirit and of the novelist's continued interest in his

[619] George S. Hillard, "James Fenimore Cooper," *Atlantic Monthly*, IX (January, 1862), 52-68. George Stillman Hillard, LL.D., was a lawyer, state senator in Massachusetts, United States District Attorney, editor, lecturer, and author.

[620] Letter, Joseph Salkeld to Cooper, Naugatuck, Connecticut, November 13, 1846. Unpublished. Cooper collection, Yale.

[621] "Cooper's 'Indian and Ingin,'" *American Review: a Whig Journal of Politics, Literature, Art and Science*, IV (September, 1846), 276.

fellow-beings, no less "large and free" than in his earlier works.[622] "They may say what they will of Cooper; the man who wrote this book is not only a great man, but a good man" and "it has given me a still higher opinion than ever of Cooper's head and heart," said Washington Irving after reading *Pathfinder*.[623] Hillard thought the truth, courage, and affection in Cooper's characters were the best indication that their creator had the same qualities himself, and Herman Melville wrote: "it is certain that he possessed not the slightest weaknesses but those which are only noticeable as the almost infallible indices of pervading greatness. He was a great, robust-souled man, all whose merits are not seen, yet fully appreciated. But a grateful posterity will take the best care of Fenimore Cooper."[624]

As for posterity, it needs to begin this grateful work. Donald G. Mitchell long ago warned us that Lounsbury's biography, though fair, created the impression of an irascible Cooper which the novelist's best friends could not recognize as the man.[625] Mitchell said this, perhaps, because he had known Cooper in his last years—he has left us his own pleasant description of that acquaintanceship, and indeed it is not like the biographer's.

This was the Cooper of the time when, Bryant said,

> his personal appearance was remarkable. He seemed in perfect health and in the highest energy and activity of his faculties. I have scarcely seen any man at that period of life on whom his years sat more lightly. His conversation had lost none of its liveliness, though it seemed somewhat more gentle and forbearing in tone, and his spirits none of their elasticity.[626]

[622] "Discourse on the Life, Character, and Genius of James Fenimore Cooper."

[623] *Ibid.*, pp. 63-64; James Grant Wilson, *Bryant, and His Friends*, pp. 237-238.

[624] *Memorial of James Fenimore Cooper*, p. 30.

[625] *American Lands and Letters*, New York, 1897, p. 249.

[626] *Memorial of James Fenimore Cooper*, pp. 67-68.

It was near this time that George Palmer Putnam, thinking of *Homeward Bound*, felt "surprise and delight" to see the cordiality and animation with which Cooper greeted Irving and gossiped for an hour one day.[627] It was near the time, too, when George Washington Greene saw a stir on a New York street as if there were something there to be looked at, and discovered Cooper "walking leisurely along, with his coat open, and a great string of onions in his hand"; a friendly Cooper who stopped and spoke as kindly as ever of Greenough, of Italy, and of his own country.[628]

This was the Cooper of whom the younger generation growing up at Cooperstown, young people who had never known the old Cooper of *The Spy's* heyday, thought he maintained a household the most "charming in unity and love" they had ever seen; the Cooper whom they were glad to have present at the dances and snapdragon games at the Hall, for he "never, by one forbidding word or look, cast a damper on the party."[629]

He was the Cooper to whom William Gilmore Simms wrote a charming letter from South Carolina because a mocking bird's song reminded him of his friend in the North and prompted the wish that Cooper could be with him for the spring.[630] Perhaps if Simms had visited Cooper instead of inviting him, he would have had such an experience as another novelist had, J. P. Kennedy. Kennedy got into a rain storm at The Prospect, with all the sightseers drenched. "Cooper was gay, and his daughters extremely kind and obliging" when the party had set out, and the good spirits were proof against rain. The party returned to The Hall to dry their clothes, and the guests spent the evening masquerading in borrowed garments. "Cooper was in his happiest mood—

[627] George Haven Putnam, *George Palmer Putnam, a Memoir*, New York, 1912, p. 264.

[628] George W. Greene, *Homes of American Authors*, pp. 199-200.

[629] G. P. Keese, *op. cit.*, p. 709.

[630] Letter, W. G. Simms to Cooper, Woodland, South Carolina, April 10, n. d. Unpublished. Cooper collection, Yale.

he told all manner of stories and brought out all his pleasantries."[631]

Or if the day had been one of bright midsummer sun instead of shower, a guest might have had Hillard's experience:

we walked together about the village and around the shores of the lake. . . . His own aspect was as sunny as that of the smiling heavens above us; age had not touched him with its paralyzing finger: his vigorous frame, elastic step, and animated glance gave promise of twenty years more of energetic life. His sturdy figure, healthy face, and a slight bluffness of manner reminded one more of his original profession than of the life and manners of a man of letters. He looked like a man who had lived much in the open air,—upon whom the rain had fallen, and against whom the wind had blown. His conversation was hearty, spontaneous, and delightful from its frankness and fulness, but it was not pointed or brilliant; you remembered the healthy ring of the words, but not the words themselves. We recollect, that, as we were standing together on the shores of the lake,—shores which are somewhat tame, and a lake which can claim no higher epithet than that of pretty,—he said: 'I suppose it would be patriotic to say that this is finer than Como, but we know that it is not.' We found a chord of sympathy in our common impressions of the beauty of Sorrento, about which, and his residence there, he spoke with contagious animation. Who could have thought that that rich and abundant life was so near its close? Nothing could be more thoroughly satisfying than the impression he left in this brief and solitary interview. His air and movement revealed the same manly, brave, true-hearted, warm-hearted man that is imaged in his books. Grateful are we for the privilege of having seen, spoken with, and taken by the hand the author of 'The Pathfinder' and 'The Pilot': 'it is a pleasure to have seen a great man.' Distinctly through the gathering mist of years do his face and form rise up before the mind's eye: an image of manly self-reliance, of frank courage, of generous impulse; a frank friend, an open enemy; a man whom many misunderstood, but whom no one could understand without honoring and loving.[632]

[631] Henry T. Tuckerman, *The Life of John Pendleton Kennedy*, New York, 1871, pp. 365-367.

[632] George S. Hillard, *op. cit.*

This appears to have been the reputation of the man, Cooper. But, as Webb was forced to admit, Cooper was an author. Perhaps even a book about the man ought to include a glance at the contemporary non-partisan opinion of the novelist. After dieting upon the Whig journalists' smart remarks, one is likely to lose sight of the profound effect which Cooper had upon authorship and authors in this country. Francis Parkman once wrote that several of Cooper's novels were stamped so deeply upon his mind that he could scarcely distinguish them from recollections of his own frontier experiences. Though he later came to repudiate Cooper's Indians, he always believed in his frontiersman and in *The Pioneers.* He always retained, too, a genuine enthusiasm for Cooper as a romancer. Cooper had an influence, he said, in determining his life and pursuits.[633] William Gilmore Simms was especially vigorous in emphasizing America's direct debt to Cooper for the sudden literary activity in this country after the appearance of *The Spy*; he was sure that Cooper's debut as an author was not simply a concomitant of this quickening, but a cause of it.[634] Even the scornful John Neal referred to Cooper's "exceedingly attractive 'Spy' " as the inspiration of his own *Seventy-Six*, and he sent manuscript to Cooper to get criticism or assistance.[635]

The tributes which Cooper's fellow authors paid to his genius are a revelation, after an era of the smart, superior journalistic critic who has no taste for the simple and bold.

[633] *Memorial of James Fenimore Cooper*, pp. 34-35; *North American Review*, LXXIV (January, 1852), 147-161; Charles H. Farnham, *A Life of Francis Parkman*, Boston, 1900, pp. 52, 68, 143, 199.

[634] William Gilmore Simms, *op. cit.*, pp. 210-238.

[635] John Neal, *Wandering Recollections of a Somewhat Busy Life*, Boston, 1869, p. 224; letter to Cooper, Baltimore, October 18, 1822. Unpublished. Cooper collection, Yale. Perhaps Neal was scornful of Cooper at times only because he thought no one could equal himself. At any rate, his letter indicates that when he was asking assistance from Cooper for one book, he enclosed with it *Randolph*, which spoke of Cooper sarcastically (*Randolph*, 1823, II, 213-216).

It reduces one to a proper state of humility towards the author of *The Pioneers* to read that one of America's first poets said he was "in the highest sense of the word, a poet; his imagination wrought nobly and grandly, and imposed its creations on the mind of the reader for realities." A paragraph like the following is refreshing to read even though it draws its freshness at second hand from Cooper's novel:

In the *Pioneers,* as in a moving picture, are made to pass before us the hardy occupations and spirited amusements of a prosperous settlement, in a fertile region, encompassed for leagues around with the primeval wilderness of woods. The seasons in their different aspects, bringing with them their different employments: forests falling before the axe; the cheerful population, with the first mild day of spring, engaged in the sugar-orchards; the chase of the deer through the deep woods, and into the lake; turkey-shootings, during the Christmas holidays, in which the Indian marksman vied for the prize of skill with the white man; swift sleighrides under the bright winter sun, and perilous encounters with wild animals in the forests; these, and other scenes of rural life, drawn, as Cooper knew how to draw them, in the bright and healthful colouring of which he was master, are interwoven with a regular narrative of human fortunes, not unskilfully constructed; and how could such a work be otherwise than popular?[636]

Middle-aged gentlemen now inclined to wonder at their own long-cooled enthusiasm for the Leatherstocking Tales may be pleased to hear that Irving called it absurd to deny that "Cooper is a man of genius of the first order," and believed there was "hardly any American prose that will live except Cooper's";[637] that Fitz-Greene Halleck said Cooper was "colonel of the literary regiment; Irving, lieutenant-colonel; Bryant, the major; while Longfellow, Whittier, Holmes,

[636] W. C. Bryant, "Discourse on the Life, Character, and Genius of James Fenimore Cooper."

[637] R. W. Griswold to Cooper, Philadelphia, August 6, 1842. Unpublished. Cooper collection, Yale.

Dana, and myself may be considered captains";[638] and that Emerson said, "I have, in common with almost all who speak English, an old debt to him of happy days, on the first appearance of the Pioneers."[639]

Herman Melville did not scorn Cooper's late works, but on the contrary warmly recommended *The Sea Lions* in 1849, and said, "even those who more for fashion's sake than anything else, have of late joined in decrying our national novelist, will in this last work, perhaps, recognise one of his happiest." He loved Mary in this novel for a "fine example of womanly affection, earnestness, and constancy," admired Roswell as a noble fellow, was delighted with the Deacon, "intent upon getting to heaven, and getting money by the same course of conduct," took pleasure in the singularly plain, downright, and truthful style, and thought the description of the winter spent in the ice jam was magnificent: "Few descriptions of the lonely and the terrible, we imagine, can surpass the grandeur of many of the scenes here depicted."[640]

Melville was affectionately amused at the resemblance of Stimson to Natty—"an old acquaintance. . . . But who would have dreamt of his turning up at the South Pole?" This kindly amusement recalls James Russell Lowell's phrases about Cooper's Indians, who are "just Natty Bumpo, daubed over with red," and his Long Tom, who is Natty again, "Rigged up in duck pants and a sou'wester hat." But these lines recall in turn:

> The men who have given to *one* character life
> And objective existence are not very rife,
> And Natty won't go to oblivion quicker
> Than Adams the parson and Primrose the vicar.

[638] J. G. Wilson, *Bryant, and His Friends*, pp. 238-239.

[639] *Memorial of James Fenimore Cooper*, pp. 32-33.

[640] Review of *The Sea Lions, Literary World*, IV (April 28, 1849), 370. Mr. Meade Minnigerode attributes this article to Melville and says the latter is known to have written a review of a late edition of *The Red Rover. Some Personal Letters of Herman Melville and a Bibliography*, New York, 1922, p. 191.

Similarly, Halleck considered Leatherstocking, Long Tom, and Uncas the first characters in American fiction, and agreed with Thackeray's famous appreciation, first spoken to Halleck, that Leatherstocking was "one of 'the great prize-men' of fiction, better perhaps than any of Scott's men," ranking with Uncle Toby, Sir Roger de Coverley, and Falstaff.[641] What Lowell really thought of Cooper's creation of characters is this:

> Cooper first studied from the life, and it was the *homo Americanus* with our own limestone in his bones, our own iron in his blood, that sat to him. There had been pioneers before him, like Belknap and Breckenridge. . . but he found new figures in the forest, autochthonous figures, and on the ocean, whose romance he was the first to divine, he touched a nerve of patriotic pride that still vibrates. I open upon my boyhood when I chance on a page of his best.[642]

Readers who are inclined to titter at Lowell's "sappy as maples and flat as a prairie" for Cooper's female characters will be interested in Hillard's theory that Cooper was slow in understanding what women really are, because he was a highly chivalrous man, and chivalrous men learn these things late in life. Hillard thought the women in the later novels excellent, and for that matter, against Lowell's catch phrases may be set this tribute from Irving:

> Let no one say, after reading 'Mabel Dunham,' that Cooper cannot draw a female character. It is a beautiful illustration of the female virtue under curious trials—some of the most terrific, others of the most delicate and touching nature. The death-bed scene, where she prays beside her father, is one of the most affecting things I have ever read; and yet how completely free from any overwrought sentiment or pathos! The proof to me of the great genius displayed in this work is the pure and simple elements with which the author has

[641] J. G. Wilson, *Bryant, and His Friends*, pp. 238-239.

[642] Horace E. Scudder, *James Russell Lowell, a Biography*, New York, 1901, II, 361-364.

wrought out his effects. The story has nothing complicated: it is a mere straight-forward narrative, and the characters are few.[643]

Francis Parkman, on the other hand, in his objection to the "shambles" in *Deerslayer* betrays such an insatiable desire for propriety that one wonders how Cooper dared unbend his lady characters as much as he did.

Cooper's ruggedness, his highmindedness, his creation of some strongly conceived characters, and his recording of the details of the American scene as in a historical preserve for a life fast growing extinct[644]—these are the things for which men of Cooper's craft chiefly admired and praised him.[645]

When the novelist J. K. Paulding was Secretary of the Navy in 1839, he chose the *History of the Navy* and four of Cooper's sea tales to form part of the small library with which he fitted each vessel in the service, writing to Cooper that he did not know "where our young officers may find better practical instruction of seamanship than they contain." These novels were the only pieces of fiction in the library. *Homeward Bound* was among the number. It was there

[643] James Grant Wilson, *Bryant, and His Friends*, pp. 237-238.

[644] Henry T. Tuckerman, "Cooper as a Novelist," *North American Review*, LXXXIX (October, 1859), 289.

[645] Richard Henry Dana, Sr., *Correspondence of James Fenimore-Cooper*, II, 90-94; Francis Parkman, *North American Review*, LXXIV (January, 1852), 147-161; Charles Fenno Hoffman, W. M. Griswold, *op. cit.*, p. 154 (but Hoffman is different from the others in thinking Cooper "makes a Nature of his own that you are willing to substitute for real Nature" instead of recording things as they were); John Esten Cooke, *Appleton's Journal*, XII (August 29, 1874), 264-267; Fitz-Greene Halleck, in J. G. Wilson, *Bryant, and His Friends*, pp. 238-239; Edgar Allan Poe, *The Literati, Complete Works of Edgar Allan Poe*, Chicago, 1895, VIII, 51; *Minor Contemporaries*, *ibid.*, VIII, 263; Review of *Wyandotté*, *ibid.*, VII, 3-18 (but Poe consistently believed Cooper a mediocre writer who owed his popularity to early exploitation of fortunate subjects; he never seemed to see that this striking of the fortunate subject was Cooper's act of creative genius). Emerson thought Cooper "feminine, no character," but enjoyed *The Pioneers*; *Journals*, VIII, 267, IV, 108; *Memorial of James Fenimore Cooper*, pp. 32-33.

because when Paulding had read that book he could not "go by thanking" Cooper in a letter "for the most agreeable recreation it has afforded me . . . in the loneliness of my situation. . . . You, I am sure will not suspect me of insincerity when I assure you of my most hearty approbation of your Book. There is something singularly fresh and original about it, and the situations incidents & characters are in my opinion in the highest degree interesting and well conceived and constructed. The chase, and the adventures with the Arabs, keep up a perpetual interest throughout, and are admirably managed, with a nautical skill highly honourable to your professional experience. As to Captain Truck, he is unique, and if you will only point him out to me, I will certainly promote him."[646] Paulding admired the truthfulness of *The Pioneers*, and when he heard two smart young fellows pronounce that novel vulgar, low, and commonplace, he reflected on the phenomenon. He concluded that with some persons "A worthy farmer or mechanic, in a clean white frock" is vulgar because not fashionable, and therefore "ought not to be introduced into a novel." Such false refinement was "the offspring of ignorance and vulgarity combined," he decided.[647] Cooper had said things like this in some of his prefaces in the days when he chose to be the bundle of hay between the asses.

Of course, James Gates Percival raised a famous dissent from this approval by literary men: "I ask nothing of a people who could lavish their patronage on such a vulgar book as 'The Pioneers.' They and I are well quit. They neglect me, and I despise them."[648] Percival's fuller description of the vulgarity of this novel is well known, having been quoted by Lounsbury. George Hayward invited Percival to criticize *The Prairie* for the *North American Review*, assur-

[646] Letter, J. K. Paulding to Cooper, Washington, September 4, 1838. Unpublished. Cooper collection, Yale.

[647] A. L. Herold, *James Kirke Paulding, Versatile American*, New York, 1926, p. 119.

[648] Percival to J. L. Yvonnet, New Haven, April 17, 1823, J. H. Ward, *op. cit.*, pp. 154-155. See also *ibid.*, pp. 157, 158-159, 170.

ing the poet that the editors wished Cooper "to have justice done him and no more."[649] But this is evidence of the character of the *North American's* use of "justice" towards Cooper, rather than of any great impartiality as a critic in James Gates Percival.

"We are among those who regard Mr. Cooper as a wronged and persecuted man," announced William Gilmore Simms in no uncertain ink:

We conceive that his countrymen have done him gross injustice—that they have not only shown themselves ungenerous but ungrateful, and that, in lending a greedy ear to the numerous malicious aspersions which have assailed his person and his reputation, they have only given confirmation and strength to the proverbial reproach of irreverence and ingratitude, to which countries, distinguished by popular governments, have usually been thought obnoxious. We do not mean to regard him as wholly faultless—on the contrary, we look upon Mr. Cooper as a very imprudent person; one whose determined will, impetuous temperament, and great self-esteem, continually hurry forward into acts and expressions of error and impatience. We propose to compare sides in this question:—to put the case fairly between himself and countrymen, and show where the balance of justice lies.[650]

Simms proceeded with a fair analysis in this vein, not pleading sentimentally for Cooper, but showing that the balance of justice lay with him, though he had written his satires at a moment when "an angel from heaven would have spoken . . . in vain." Cooper was not an angel from heaven, and Simms said he wrote in anger. But with all his faults, Simms reiterated, Cooper acted from good motives, and if personal feelings were sometimes a stimulant to his patriotic efforts, it is the heart's cooperation with the head that gives such men their rare power. As for the newspaper critics, hoping to raise themselves by being seen "worrying any more majestic form . . . half the two-penny sheets, of dirty yellow,

[649] *Ibid.*, p. 275.

[650] William Gilmore Simms, *Views and Reviews in American Literature, History, and Fiction*, First Series, pp. 210-238.

from Squam Beach to Little Harkaway Swamp, on the elbow of Oregon, were eager in squirting out their little supplies of storm. . . ." The "pretender critics," Simms avouched, were one of the greatest evils threatening civilization, for quack literature is as dangerous to an unlearned people as quack medicine. Steadfast Dodge, he said, was a "very just portrait," and Cooper courageously gave the quacks what they deserved.

At Cooper's death his daughter Susan, grasping at Rufus Griswold's friendly comfort, wrote to him in feminine sorrow, "You allude to the *affection* he merited. Ah, there indeed, Sir, he was sorely misrepresented! No man had warmer sympathies, stronger affections, or a more social temper. Yet with the exception of those who knew him intimately he was no doubt usually considered as a gloomy, disappointed cynic—, a character wholly foreign to his nature, as you must be well aware, from your own intercourse with him."[651]

But it was not quite so bad as Susan Cooper felt at that moment. Cooper said that the American people never repair a wrong. Perhaps they will. Halleck once wrote some verses about Cooper in a mood which is not unsuitable for the present generation, unless we must now-days omit the noble savage at the close. It is a mood of tolerance, of affectionate amusement at Cooper's republican enthusiasms, of serious gratitude and admiration:

> Cooper, whose name is with his country's woven,
> First in her files, her *Pioneer* of mind—
> A wanderer now in other climes, has proven
> His love for the young land he left behind;
>
> And throned her in the senate-hall of nations,
> Robed like the deluge rainbow, heaven-wrought;
> Magnificent as his own mind's creations,
> And beautiful as its green world of thought;

[651] *Passages from the Correspondence and Other Papers of Rufus W. Griswold,* p. 277. Griswold's letter, unpublished, is in the Cooper collection, Yale.

And faithful to the Act of Congress, quoted
As law authority, it passed *nem. con.*;
He writes that we are, as ourselves have voted,
The most enlightened people ever known.

That all our week is happy as a Sunday
In Paris, full of song, and dance, and laugh;
And that, from Orleans to the Bay of Fundy,
There's not a bailiff nor an epitaph.

And furthermore—in fifty years, or sooner,
We shall export our poetry and wine;
And our brave fleet, eight frigates and a schooner,
Will sweep the seas from Zembla to the Line.

If he were with me, King of Tuscarora!
Gazing, as I, upon thy portrait now,
In all its medalled, fringed, and beaded glory,
Its eye's dark beauty, and its thoughtful brow—

Its brow, half martial and half diplomatic,
Its eye, upsoaring like an eagle's wings,
Well might he boast that we, the Democratic,
Outrival Europe, even in our Kings!

Or suppose that Americans now take for their platform some of the words of Hunt, who planned to denounce but printed to support:

With a fame extending to the outer bounds of civilization, Mr. Cooper has nothing to fear from a press, devoted in the main, to the diffusion of certain political principles and prejudices. Mr. Webb, Mr. Stone and Mr. Greely were Mr. Cooper's political opponents, and if the truth was made manifest, I am inclined to believe that their restrictions were meted out more to effect mere party purposes, than for the actual discovery of an untruth contained in any of his statements. . . . A man, therefore, who sinks to his tomb, leaving behind him such an enduring monument of greatness, as Mr. Cooper, by his own industry and genius, has been the means of rearing, we who survive him, should feel in duty bound, to guard the same, unharmed against the encroachment of every Goth or Vandal, who dares to molest it. To this sentiment, gentlemen, I am confident of receiving your sanction and amen.

APPENDICES

APPENDIX A

Some Forgotten Letters by James Fenimore Cooper Printed in the "Evening Post" over the Signature A. B. C.

[From the New York *Evening Post,* March 14, 1835:]

To the Editors of the Evening Post

GENTLEMEN: I have the misfortune to be one of those who do not put implicit faith in the constitutional doctrines of Mr. Webster. I dissent, in particular, from most of that which he has lately told us in his speech on the right of the Executive to remove from office. In this argument he appears to me to be reasoning against his own convictions. Mr. Webster gives a brief analysis of the Constitution, in which he maintains that, because no *general* legislative or judicial powers can be attributed to the legislature, or the judiciary, it follows that no general executive powers can be attributed to the President. Now, this conclusion is by no means legitimate. The legislative power is the pivot on which the whole character of the government rests. There is what may be termed a conflicting legislative power in the States, and, unless that of the Federal Government were distinctly defined, it would be impossible to say where the one terminated and the other commenced. It becomes necessary, therefore, that the Federal Government should have no legislative power beyond that which is directly named in the Constitution, or that which is necessary to carry out the defined powers. No such reasoning applies to the Executive. In the nature of things, the Executive is to execute only the laws of the Union, and his authority, or duties, are necessarily limited by the limitations on the powers of the legislature.

General Executive powers might just as safely be attributed to the President as to the executive of any other government, for the circle of his duties is obvious, but, in the case of Congress, all that is not expressly given is expressly withheld, to prevent unutterable confusion. The instance of the right to remove from office is a case in point. We will suppose this point to be left as an inference from the principle of Executive authority. What harm can come of it? No fair inference would lead men to suppose that the chief of one government would so construe his authority as to appoint officers for another government, whereas Congress, unless restrained would, in the exercise of its powers, completely overthrow the state governments. We hear daily complaints from the states, that Congress interferes with their rights, but the executive can only interfere in the rights of the states in *effecting the intentions of the legislature.* As has just been said, the limitations of the legislative branch of the Federal Government, are all the limitations that, in the nature of things becomes necessary as general limitations, on the Executive. That we have limited the Executive more than this, is owing to a desire to bring him more within what was deemed a safer rule for the exercise of executive authority in a confederated republic.

Mr. Webster is mistaken when he intimates that the removing power has only been used by the exercise of the appointing power. In most civil cases this may be true, for the public service requires that the duties shall not be intermitted; but it has never been true in the numerous instances that have occurred of removals in the army and navy, where there is always a successor ready to fill the vacancy. In the latter, when a captain is removed, another captain is ready to fill his place, and Captain V. Morris, Captain McNiell, Captain Angus, &c. &c. were all removed by direct acts of the Executive. I could enumerate many civil cases also in which this has been the practice, and it is a little singular that Mr. Webster did not see a very important instance that was immediately before his eyes while speaking. Mr. Livingston and Mr. Barton are both ordered home (which is in effect removing them from office) in a certain contingency, without a probability of any new appointments to supersede them.

One of two things is certain. The constitution either intends that the officers of government are to be removed by some authority in the state (apart from impeachment) or that they are to hold their places during good behaviour. That it does not contemplate the latter is sufficiently apparent by the exception that is expressly made in favour of the judges. It is therefore plain, that the Constitution intends all other officers to hold during the discretion of some power in the state. We all know the practice of the Government; the only question is whether this practice has been right.

The Constitution itself makes an essential and an eloquent distinction in principle, in granting its authority to the Legislative and Executive branches of the Government. As respects the first it says:—"The legislative powers *herein granted* shall be vested, &c. &c.," while as respects the second, it says, "The Executive power shall be vested in a President, &c." The convention knew that the latter was essentially limited when it limited the former.

I conceive that the removing power, as abiding solely in the President, is fairly to be inferred from an honest comparison of the different clauses of the Constitution. It is justly inferred from the general signification of Executive power. It is a legitimate and technical consequence from the right to *commission,* else would this right be reducing the President to the duties of a mere clerk, a degradation that is opposed to all the notions that naturally attach themselves to the extent of Executive authority. The right to commission carries with it, in the case of so high a functionary, the right to recall that commission, or it is a power wielded equally without discretion or responsibility. Such a state of things may have existed in some of the aristocratical governments which have maintained Executives frauds, but it is not to be inferred without special provisions to that effect since it is not in unison with either general theory or general practice. The particular practice of the colonies and of the states, which in this instance must have been kept in view by the convention, was, I believe, pretty uniformly, in favour of the rule. Even the phraseology of the Constitution in another clause appears to make the essence of the appointing power abide in the power to commission, for it says that the President may fill vacancies in the recess, by granting commissions. If the power of the President to commission is purely a ministerial power, it stands as a solitary instance of such irresponsible duty, in the range of his functions. I do not conceive that the Senate, in the cases of treaties and appointments, has anything more than a negative. The President is not obliged to commission, or to ratify, their consent obtained, unless he judge it expedient. Such has certainly been the practice. Now, a negative power can never imply an affirmative power, and the right to remove is affirmative. The power of advice and consent in the Senate, in the cases of treaties and appointments, is not enumerated among the powers of that body, but it appears as checks upon the powers of the President.

But, gentlemen, there is one fact that I hold to be unanswerable as an argument. It is a contingent of general Executive power, but it serves to shew the working of the principle. The constitution orders the President "to see the laws faithfully executed." This high trust was clearly intended to be efficient and prompt. There would be extreme puerility in supposing that the Executive was merely to *scold* the delinquents. Now there is no possible manner in which the Executive can compel the execution of a law, *unless by the exercise of the removing power.* The laws define the duties of the agents, else a marshal might claim to do the duty of a collector, and vice versa. The President cannot execute process from the Supreme Court, in his own person, and yet he is bound, at need, to see that process is executed

The marshal refuses to act, and in what manner is the President to acquit himself of this important trust? By asking the "advice and consent" of the Senate to remove the marshal! But the Senate is not forced to "see the laws faithfully executed," and two thirds of the time it is not in session? It was unquestionably intended that there should be a power in the state to apply to for redress, as in all other governments, and the expedient of the constitution for the protection of the people against the abuse of such an authority, is not in any law like this proposed by Mr. Webster, but in the elective franchise, and in the legal responsibility of the Executive. What would be true of a marshal, would be true in the case of any other *executive* officer of the government. The intentions of the constitution are to be judged of by a general comparison of its ordinances, and it results from an examination of those just named, that the Executive has the right to remove, or that duties are rigidly exacted of him in terms, which he has no means of discharging.

This law of the Senate is every way offensive. If the President has no right to remove, without the advice and consent of the Senate, it is superogatory while it is setting a very dangerous precedent, and if he has, it is downright usurpation. The American *doctrinaires* formerly attempted to effect their objects, by the cry of anarchy, and finding themselves unsuccessful, they now appear disposed to effect their objects, by raising that of tyranny!

When a Council of War was deliberating on a new uniform for the Neapolitan army, the good old King, Don Francisco, who knew his subjects from long experience, exclaimed—"Ah! Dress them as you please, they will run." Let aristocracy take what aspect it may, it is still aristocracy.

A. B. C.

[From the New York *Evening Post*, March 21, 1835:]

To the Editors of the Evening Post

GENTLEMEN: It is alleged by some of those who support the vote of the Senate on the subject of removals from office, that there is an essential difference between the authority of the President and a *prerogative.* Even Mr. Webster tells us in substance, that this authority is no prerogative, but a delegated and an especial trust.

A prerogative is "a peculiar or an exclusive privilege." As applied to political power it usually means no more than power which is the peculiar property of a sovereign. Most sovereigns ruling by what is termed a divine right, being entirely irresponsible, in fact as well as in theory, the idea of inalienable authority also attaches itself to a prerogative. This latter distinction, however, is not strictly true, for, in the cases of the English Kings, the prerogative has frequently been shorn of its authority by acts of parliament. The Kings of England formerly possessed, for instance, an absolute and an unlimited pardoning power, which is now so restricted that they cannot pardon in cases of impeachment.

There is no difference, that is available for the purposes of this argument, between a general definition of a prerogative and of our own executive powers. A prerogative may be instituted by the vote of a convention, or a parliament, as well as a constitution, else the King of the French has no prerogative, for he clearly reigns without any other authority than that which is derived directly from the charter of 1831. In France and the United States the fundamental law proceeds equally from an acknowledged constituency, and the essential point to be ascertained, is not what the respective executive trusts are *called,* but what, in truth, they *are.* It follows that no legitimate argument can be drawn from the mere circumstance that the authority of the President is not *termed* a prerogative, while that of King is. The authority of the President is so far a prerogative that no other branch of the Government can constitutionally interfere with it, until such interference shall be authorized by the general constituency of the States. This constituency has instituted the office of President with a view to the public good, and any unlawful attempts to diminish its powers, is an attack upon the sovereignty of the nation, and not on that of the incumbent. Admitting that an incumbent is ambitious and disposed to abuse his trust, his constitutional existence is very brief, and his time will soon pass away, carrying with it the dispositions and errors of the man; but innovations, like this of the Senate's, will remain, and saddle the nation with a change that has emanated from an insufficient source. It is better to submit to a thousand unjust or impolitic removals from office, allowing them to have been made, than silently to acquiesce in an attempt of Congress to curtail *our* prerogative—if there is a prerogative at all it is *ours*—by a vicious legislation.

Mr. Webster admits in terms, while he appears to doubt the justice of the construction of the constitution, that his law supposes a right in the President to remove from office. The law, indeed, would be a dead letter without this supposition, for all its enactments are consequent on such a right. Now it is to be tolerated in a nation of freemen, who have delegated distinct political powers, to distinctly separate agents, that one set of their servants shall coolly arrogate to themselves a right to curtail another of their servants of his trusts!

It is, also, alleged that the power to commission is purely a ministerial duty. If this be true, the constitution uses the word "to commission" in its most contracted signification, or in a manner entirely unsuited to the nature of his office, and to the other duties of the high functionary, of whose authority it is treating. To commission is "to empower, to appoint;" and as applied here, it means to grant the technical or written authority under which the agent is empowered. The Constitution itself recognizes the necessity and validity of such a form, by saying that the President shall fill vacancies in the recess "*by granting commissions which shall expire*" at the end of the next session of the Senate. By this phraseology the form of a commission is acknowledged to be the test of authority. The Constitution does not say that the President shall *issue* commissions, which might indeed be interpreted into a ministerial duty; but its language is—"he shall *commission* all the officers of the United States."

The practice of the government from the commencement has been, I believe, strictly in conformity with this construction. Mr. Jefferson went much further. He even refused to *deliver* a commission which had been signed by his predecessor. If I recollect the case, the Supreme Court decided that the officer was entitled *to receive his commission,* but failing of means to obtain it, owing to a want of the necessary legislation as relates to forms, he could not qualify. This case or cases—for I think there were more than one—goes to show that the commission is indispensable to the consummation of the appointment, else the nominee of Mr. Adams might have simply taken the oaths and become a judge.

It is idle to say that it is improper to refer to our own history, or to that of the country from which we are derived, for precedents, explanations, and constructions, in instances that do not affect the distinctive principles of the government, and which are not at variance with our own ordinances. The errour on this head arises from confounding those cases which ought not to be admitted as authority with those that ought. According to English law—which is in its leading principles our own, except when it conflicts with statutes or these distinctive principles—the delivery of a commission, patent, or other written authority has always been held to be the consummation of an appointment, the Executive retaining its controul until the title has actually passed, the whole being rigidly subjected to forms. I think it is in my power to cite a case in point. A peer's patent was made out, (and if I am not greatly mistaken, it was complete—the delivery excepted) in favour of the Lord Chancellor Yorke, (not the Earl of Hardwicke): but he committing suicide before the delivery, it was held that there was no creation, and the party in remainder continued a commoner. When the convention of this country framed the Constitution of 1787, although it certainly brought into existence novel and peculiar political institutions, it did not frame a new language. The text of the compact is to be understood by terms that already had fixed significations. Mr. Webster asks whom we are to regard as authority, in setting the general principles of Executive power. De Lolme, Montesquieu or Burlamaqui? Neither. These are commentators or essayists, not jurists that we acknowledge. We may search them for reasons, but not for authorities. The latter are to be sought in our own previous practices. In some important particulars we are obliged to appeal to the past for the justification of the exercise of even the legislative powers. Whence comes the practice of permitting a majority of the members present to enact laws? The constitution settles the point of a quorum, but it does not expressly say that a majority shall give its virtue to an enactment. Is this an incident of the right of each house to establish its own rules? If so, each house may establish a different rule; or either house may say that any given number of votes, although a minority, shall enact. The practice comes from our ancestors—not from the Chinese, nor the French, nor the Tartars, but from recognized rules and usages of our own. We are to look to ourselves, and to our own understanding of terms for authorities, and not abroad. In the Polish Diet unanimity was required. Different modifications of this power have existed in different countries, but with us and our ancestors, a majority has long, if not always, been considered as the test of legislative opinion, and was so understood, as a matter of course, when the Congress of 1789 first assembled.

The limits of a daily paper require brevity, and I shall take another occasion to return to the subject.

A. B. C.

[From the New York *Evening Post,* March 25, 1835:]

To the Editors of the Evening Post

GENTLEMEN: The constitution clearly intends three stages to the completion of an appointment—the nomination, the appointment, and the commissioning. The first originates, the second agrees upon, the third consummates the act. With this statement before us, and no one can dispute its justice, since it is sanctioned by the letter of the law, we will examine the necessary definitions. To nominate is "to name;" to appoint is "to settle any thing by agreement;" to commission is "to empower." These are the definitions of Johnson that come nearest to the matter in hand. It is not easy to convey shades of meaning by the use of synonimes, it is true, but I presume all will understand the above. I will only remark that there appears to be a prevalent error on the subject of the meaning of "commission" as a verb. In a political sense it means to grant the power, by which the agent is authorized to act. To sign a commission, or attest a commission, are very different things from "to commission." Commission is a verb active, and of necessity, something is transferred from the party that grants to the party that receives. This something is power.

We will now look to the language of the Constitution. *He* shall *nominate*, and by and with the advice of the Senate, *appoint* ambassadors, &c. &c. By the grammatical construction of this sentence, *he*, or the President, both *nominates* and *appoints*. He *nominates* of his own free will, and he *appoints* restricted by the advice and consent of the Senate. An appointment is merely to settle the preliminaries. It is a usual political expression to say that the Pope has appointed a Cardinal, *in petto*, or in his own mind. Advice here means consultation; consent, agreement. This consultation has its limits; the Senate can not pretend, for instance, a right to suggest names of itself, for this would directly invade the right to nominate; to advise therefore means that the parties shall take counsel together only on the measures already proposed. Consent, though always affirmative in form, is merely negative as to efficiency. He who consents to the proposition of another does not perform his acts, but simply permits them to be performed. The father that consents to the marriage of his child, does not marry himself—he merely acquiesces in the act of another. "*He* shall appoint" is the strict grammatical meaning of the appointing clause, although restricted by the suggestions and consent of the Senate. "To commission" is to complete the act. Now we will suppose the President to refuse "to commission," after the consent of the Senate has been obtained, is it reasonable to imagine that the constitution intends to deny a discretion to the Executive, in this stage of the appointment, that is so freely accorded in another? The nomination is originated in the mind of the President; without his intention, no one can be even placed in a situation to receive the approval of the Senate; and, as the national compact does not impeach motives like party, it is not easy to discover a reason why he who is clearly possessed of the right of refusing to name a candidate in the commencement of the procedure, should not retain this right to the end. The legal presumption is that this power will not be abused, or it would not have been conceded at all; nor does it put the President in a bit better situation, or one to be more distrusted, or the country in a worse situation, at one period than at the other. One can understand why the power of the President should be limited by rendering the consent of the Senate necessary, but we cannot conceive why the country which confides the sole power of nominating to the President, should withhold from him the power to retract that nomination at any time before the appointment is complete. The public weal is presumed to be the object in every stage of the proceedings. But the Constitution furnishes of itself a clause to its own meaning. I quote its words: "*He* shall have power, by and with the advice and consent of the Senate, to make treaties, provided two-thirds of the Senate present concur. This clause precedes that of the appointing power, and has precisely the same grammatical construction. They are parts of the same sentence. *He* or the President, is the nominative of both the verbs, or of "appoint" and of "make." The President *appoints* ambassadors, and he *makes* treaties: though restricted by the consent of the Senate in each case; that is to say, he cannot appoint an ambassador, or make a treaty, without the consent of the Senate, while with its consent he can do both. Now a treaty is an interest regulated by international law, a fact that enables us to step beyond the limits of our own constructions for authorities. A treaty is a contract that is not binding until it is *ratified,* and it is ratified only by the power that *makes* it. It will not be pretended that the Senate has a right to propose alterations in a treaty; that, after inserting or omitting clauses, it can approve; and then set up the extravagant claim that the treaty is ratified! If this were true, the power of the President, or of that branch of the government which is to *make* the treaty, can be entirely annulled, for by altering, or omitting all the clauses, an entirely new bargain would be made. The Senate can give a conditional or a qualified assent, certainly, which merely refers the whole matter back to the mind of the executive for further consideration, leaving him to accept of the terms or not. The President, and not the Senate, *makes* the treaty.

It the constitution intended that the Senate should *ratify* a treaty, why did it not say so? It would have been both shorter and simpler than the course that was taken. No one will say that the Senate can make a treaty of its own suggestion; its power is confined simply to an approval. An approval, however, is very far from a ratification. He who signs a treaty approves of it at the time as a matter of course,—executives often *counter-signing* treaties, and still withhold the *exchange of the ratifications,* or the delivery. A treaty is a grave matter, and international law reserves (from considerations of the highest magnitude,) to each of the parties its original rights to the last moment. Thus the President may clearly, by all usage, according to our own practice, in conformity with the letter of the constitution, and in compliance with common sense and the right, refuse to ratify a treaty that has been approved; the approval being a matter between him and his own government, the ratification a matter between his own government, of which he is the agent, and a foreign state.

I see no essential difference between the cases of appointments and treaties. The power of the Senate is the same in both, and so do I conceive to be the power of the President. "To commission" and to ratify are the respective consummations of the two acts. The President nominates, the President appoints (though under restrictions) and the President commissions. The legitimate inference, in the absence of especial provisions to the contrary, is that the President recalls the commission. The authority to commission, if it were not held in conjunction with the authorities to appoint and to nominate, would not necessarily infer this power, perhaps, but being so held, I think it does. It will not be denied that the President has the right to withdraw a nomination, and under such circumstances it is not easy to give a good reason why he should not withhold a commission. The political consideration in granting these powers is the public good; the legal supposition is that the exercise of this authority will always be discreet, and it is contrary to legitimate argument to found a legal deduction on a different hypothesis. The constitutional protection of the constituency is in their own power, and in the penalties of impeachment. Let us look at the other side of this picture. The Senate appoints, (the Senate does not appoint but consents) and therefore the Senate ought to have a voice in removing. In this case, who is to suggest the removal? The President—why? The right to suggest a removal is not an incident of the simple right to nominate.

If the door is once opened, we shall soon see the Senate taking the *initiative* in removals, and, therefore, eventually in appointments.

I believe as little in *the principle* of the construction of the Congress of 1789, as stated by Mr. Webster, as in that of Mr. Webster himself. The former is carried too far. An *argument* in favour of the right of the President to remove may be drawn from the general nature of Executive power it is true; but if this principle is carried out in other matters, it would conflict with other fundamental principles of the government. It is a strong corroborative reason in favor of the inferences to be deduced from other parts of the Constitution, but it does not strike me as being irresistable authority.

The President has general executive powers, qualified by especial ordinances, and by general distinctive principles. He nominates, he appoints (restricted by the Senate's consents), he commissions. All these powers are executive and not ministerial. As respects the powers conceded, the rights of the President are equal to those of what are termed a prerogative. He is compelled to "take care that the laws be faithfully executed," a duty that can be discharged in no other manner than by exercising the power to remove, and the power to appoint. Analogy, reason, practice and language are all in favor of the President's strict right to appoint, and by generally admitted inference to remove, while the whole pretension on behalf of the Senate is founded on a mere consultative power—a power that is of great importance under a confederation certainly, but one that would be completely destructive of the executive energy of the state, if extended beyond its due limits.

In my next, I shall take a review of the relations of the executive and the legislature of the constituency, and of the dangers that are to be apprehended from each.

A. B. C.

[From the New York *Evening Post*, March 28, 1835:]

To the Editors of the Evening Post

GENTLEMEN: The practice of the government, from its commencement to the present time, has been opposed to the reasoning of Mr. Webster. It may be worth our while to enquire why, at this late day, so many rude attacks are made on the Executive authority. It is not difficult to understand the motive for the personal assaults on the incumbent, but this law, with much similar legislation that has been attempted of late, are so many direct attacks on the office itself.

It is pretended that the President has too much authority for this form of government. This may be true—it is true in certain particulars—and yet it is no justification of the course taken by one portion of our politicians. The maintenance of the principle that the authority which formed the constitution shall alone alter it is of far more importance than any trifling reform that might be obtained through the agency of a vicious legislation. I am one of those who believe that the executive should be shorn of a portion of the removing power. I do not think it in conformity with the general objects of this government—though quite in conformity with its legal principles—that the President should have the power to recall the commission of any military officer. Such a power is not necessary to the execution of the laws, for by the very nature of a military organization, the public service need not suffer, since there is always a successor to discharge the duty, while, on the other hand, it is a power that is liable to great abuses, and which has been occasionally abused. The institution of especial military tribunals for the trial of professional offences, would appear to be sufficient to meet all the exigencies of the state, and it is as much unsuited to the nature of the institutions, that they who wield the sword should be so absolutely dependent on the will of any branch of the government as this power reduces them to be, as it is unsuited to our habits of justice to render the services of an entire life, subject to any other final decision than that which ought to follow accusation, trial and conviction.

Cases might be named in which it would probably be better were certain civil officers independent of the Executive will. A question might also be raised as to the extent of Executive authority on the subject of treaties. Congress can declare war, but does it so clearly follow that Congress can make peace? War is the act of one nation, peace the act of two. The necessary mode of making peace is by treaty, and, circumstances might occur in which this nation would be seriously divided on the question of where the power to make peace resides. If in the treaty-making power—as is the most plausible, then can this nation be legally kept in a state of war for four years, by the will of one of its own citizens. These are questions of great theoretical importance, and although there is little probability just now that circumstances will make them of much practical interest, yet the time cannot be distant when the immence resources of the country will cause its alliance to be of so much moment, as to bring into activity, so far as foreign intrigue can effect its objects, every latent principle of the government. Impeachment is an insufficient remedy against the abuse of so grave an exercise of authority.

Notwithstanding these and perhaps a few other similar defects in the national compact, I cannot believe that the principal cause of apprehension is to be found in the power of the Executive. On the contrary, I think that all theory and all practice go to prove that it exists in the power of the legislative branch of the government.

It is a principle of human nature that power should be diverted from its true objects. It is also a very obvious truth connected with this fact, that where the greatest power resides, there are we to look for its greatest abuse. If this is true as a general principle, it becomes additionally so, when this maximum of authority is exercised with the minimum of responsibility and risk, as is the case in our own legislative bodies. The very diffusion of responsibility in a legislative corps, to say nothing of the impunity under its privilege, would of itself create a distinction on this point, against its rigid respect for fundamental ordinances. But, practically, there is no legal punishment for such a transgression, since, admitting that a legislator may be impeached, the majority that committed the abuse would neither impeach nor condemn itself. These remarks apply to all legislatures that have an equal available right in the enactment of laws. There is scarcely an instance in which such bodies have not trespassed on Executive authority. In England it has completely perverted it; and in France, short as has been the representative career of that nation, we see the legislative branch of its government openly invading the constitutional right of the King, in withholding the indemnity under our own treaty.

In our own case there are many additional reasons why this peculiar form of danger to the institutions should exist, and our legislative history is already replete with legislative abuses. The union exists chiefly through its legislative powers, and, under its peculiar character, it is self evident that there must be a never ending collision between this legislative power and those of the states. When, from local interests, the states themselves sustain measures that are of doubtful legality, we know from experience, that the barriers of the constitution are not sufficiently respected. The same may be said of party. When party objects are to be obtained, its excesses, as a matter of course, are exhibited through the power of the legislative branch of the government. The recent attacks on the executive are purely of this character.

Even this disputed appointing power is, in fact, more wielded under the authority of the legislature, than under that of the President himself. Legitimately, the legislature designates the officers, limits the salaries, and assigns their duties. In practice, the legislators crowd the departments, and perhaps the real nominations of two-thirds of the incumbents, emanate from a legislative source, and as a direct consequence of the abuse of legislative power.

We have before us a disgraceful and a lamentable effect of legislative irresponsibility, in the defenceless state of the country, at this moment, one of the utmost gravity. The statute books are filled with the boldness of legislative authority, and of the timidity of the different executives, under a system like ours.

In former ages, when executive power was a divine right, inalienable, hereditary and formidable, there was a necessity for checking it by such legislation as could be procured. But no sane man will compare such a state of things with ours. Here the constituency is, in the end, its own protector; but, so far as checks and precautions have been contemplated in the *machinery* of the government itself, the Executive and the Judiciary have evidently been intended more as checks upon the Legislature, than the Legislature has been intended as a check upon them. That the judiciary sits in judgment on all the acts of Congress no one will deny. The veto of the President is a Constitutional device to curb vicious legislation. It is not a distinct legislative power that appertains to the executive, as executives were formerly instituted, for it is not complete. This veto is qualified, being simply and obviously a check. Public opinion must be in an unsound state, indeed, when a cry is raised against the use (in the abstract too) of such an authority—an authority so indisputably created in the interest of the rights and liberties of those very freemen, who rail at its exercise, as at an act of tyranny. The constitution has not provided a single legislative check on the exercise of the assigned duties of the Executive, while it has given this check to the President on every act of the legislature! The publicity and manner in which the veto is to be used, its limitation, and all that belongs to it, prove conclusively, that the constitution intends it to be a check on legislative abuses. Where are we to look for its counterpart, if the executive authority is so dangerous? The right of the Senate to advise and consent, in the cases of treaties and appointments, is conceded on principles connected with the peculiar construction of a confederacy, and is not, in any manner, legislative.

They who made the Constitution must have been singularly dull, to concede the use of this check to the most dangerous power of the state, and to cause it to act on another power, which was intended to be the especial guardian of our liberties!

I do not say that the Executive of this Union is not checked in his authority. He is restrained by the very relations between the two powers of the state, the legislative and the executive; it is this fact which renders him so impotent to injure our liberties, but I do affirm that, considered as they are instituted, the constitution has taken especial care to enable the latter to restrain, while it does not control the former. If this restraint were an absolute and an equal power in legislation, then indeed would the whole character of the executive be changed, and we should possess a chief of, to say the least, a very embarrassing amount of authority. It is this absolute union of the legislative with the executive functions that have rendered other executives so potent, and so difficult to reduce, and yet so much more potent is representation when resorted to in an advanced state of society, that the victory almost always remains with the legislature.

A. B. C.

[From the New York *Evening Post*, March 31, 1835:]

To the Editors of the Evening Post

GENTLEMEN: You will now permit me to illustrate my position by a few examples. I write under the disadvantage of not possessing the journals of Congress, or the laws of the United States to refer to, but I think it will be in my power to establish all I aim at without quoting the text of either.

The Attorney General not long since, and in reference to the passage of this law to restrain the President in the exercise of the removing power, made a report from which I shall select the fact I want. This officer refers to a law of Congress which prescribes that certain receivers of the public monies shall periodically settle their accounts, and in failure to do so, *that they shall forthwith be removed from office.* This law, like that supported by Mr. Webster, assumes that the removing power is where it has always been practically, or in the President. It is a necessary consequence of this assumption, that the law supposes the Executive to be invested with such an authority by a just construction of the constitution.

This single case will supply much of the illustration that is wanted. It furnishes an instance of the insidious and dangerous manner in which the legislature is constantly trespassing on the duties of the Executive, by dictating the mode and motives under which that officer shall perform one of the most distinct and independent of his functions. It furnishes an occasion to show what I conceive to be the principle of general executive authority, as applied to this government, and it will enable me to demonstrate what I mean by saying that we are to look to our own understanding of terms, in interpreting the Constitution; and also to point out the great difference that exists between executive and purely ministerial duties.

If Congress has a right to prescribe these definite cases, in which an incumbent *must* be removed, it also has authority to prescribe definite cases, in which citizens shall be appointed to office. This is an unavoidable inference, since it is admitted all round that the removing power is but an incident of the appointing power, and the accessory must be dependent on the principal. What limits are to be set to this interference with the appointing power? Can Congress say no man shall be a collector until he is fifty—if so, they may also say no man shall be a collector until he has fulfilled this or that other condition, and thus, by narrowing down the qualifications, it may, in some case of peculiar importance, effectually compel the Executive to appoint an individual of its own selection. The Constitution makes no allusion to the appointing power, in enumerating the powers of Congress. This power, on the other hand, is expressly enumerated among those of the President. Nothing can be more certain than the intention that the three branches of the Government were to exercise their duties, independently of each other, except in cases that are specifically named. In no way is *Congress* connected with the exercise of the appointing power. The *Senate,* which has a negative on appointments, is not *Congress,* nor can it legislate. The law, is a law of *Congress.* We shall look in vain into the Constitution for any authority under which it has been legitimately enacted.

Congress has a general authority to enact all laws that are necessary to carry into execution the powers vested in any department *or officer of the Government.* This authority, however, does not warrant Congress in passing laws to *impede* the exercise of powers thus vested, but, by implication, would seem to recognize the existence of an exactly opposite principle.

The provision of the act in question invades the executive authority, by reducing it to be a purely ministerial authority. This is a point in which I conceive the general principles of executive power are to be referred to, in construing the fundamental law. Assuming the fact that the President is vested with the power to remove, (and this much the law assumes) the question presents itself, in what manner, and under what responsibilities and duties, is this power to be exercised?

On one point the Constitution is explicit. Its language cannot be misconceived. "The *executive power* shall be vested in a President, &c." Then follows the enumeration of the duties of his office. Among these duties are those connected with the appointing power. It is quite clear, therefore, that all these trusts are to be discharged as executive, and not as ministerial trusts. The difference is essential. One implies a general political discretion, the other a discretion limited by precise enactments. One is a consequence of legislation, the other has been instituted in its particular form, for the express purpose of being placed in a situation that is independent of legislation. The case before us will furnish an example. If the receiver of the public monies is in arrears, the officer possessing full executive authority, can view all the legitimate considerations of the case; he has an equitable discretion; he considers the interests of the state, in all their bearings, and decides to retain or remove on certain recognized general principles of public law and public policy. On the other hand, the discretion of him to whom is confided a merely ministerial authority, is bounded by the precise contingency contemplated in the law. He must remove the moment he is apprized that the receiver has failed to account, whereas the President can suspend his decision, and eventually act on the principles I have named. The Executive sees the laws executed it is true; but the laws meant by the Constitution, are the laws authorized by the Constitution and this law is not one of them. The general executive powers expressly granted in the Constitution of 1787, must, of necessity, be deemed independent of the provisions of a law enacted in 1828, unless it can be shown that the instrument contemplated such a dependence on Congress. The Constitution neither directly, nor by any just implication, enacts any such dependence. It says just as distinctly that the President shall have power to appoint, as it says that Congress shall have power to legislate. In the absence of especial provisions in each case, we are driven to general principles to discover under what limitations both are to act. In short we are to inquire what is understood—not by Montesquieu and De Lolme—but under our own conventional signification by certain terms. In the one case we are to ask what are the moral and legal liabilities of the executive trusts; in the other to ask what constitutes legislative authority. The liabilities of general executive trusts are limited by a political equity and political discretion that, apart from especial provisions, are bounded by the public weal. Legislative authority, as understood in America, abides in the majority of a quorum. The Constitution has created especial exceptions to both these principles, and like all other exceptions they go to prove the existence of the rules.

The President has the power to pardon. The mode and motives of the exercise of this trust being undefined are, like that of the appointing and removing power, to be interpreted on these general executive principles. Will it be pretended that Congress has a right, by law, to declare in what cases the President shall, or shall not, pardon? This is a branch of executive authority with which Congress has not yet meddled, and still it would be easier to make out a plausible connexion between the general powers of Congress and this right to pardon, than between those general powers of Congress and the right of the President to appoint and remove. But the pardoning power is without advantage, in either a pecuniary or a political point of view. I believe it will be found that the whole difference between the natures of those two powers, is confined to this naked fact.

It is no answer to this parallel, to say that the President appoints, restrained by the consent of the Senate, and pardons, without any such expressed restriction. The law in question supposes an absolute removing power in the President (its own provision excepted) and under this supposition, it undertakes to prescribe the contingency in which that power shall be exercised. It is true the law says the defaulter shall be removed, without saying by whom; but no one pretends that this power to remove is in Congress, and merely changing or modifying the depository of the power, in a measure alters the character of the legislative innovation, which it is my object to expose. Congress has full power to enact laws punishing defalcation, under certain limitations, by conviction and trial, but it has no right to dictate to another branch of the government, when and how it shall exercise any of its exclusive authority. This does not mean that Congress shall not say when there shall be a judge or a general, for this act does not touch the authority of the President; but it means that having so pronounced, all authority of Congress on that particular subject ceases.

It is a solecism to confound the powers of an executive with those of a mere ministerial agent. The duties are totally distinct, depend on entirely different principles, and are to be estimated by different rules. No distinct power, that is conceded to the President by the Constitution, is ministerial. They are all, by their nature, as well as by the terms of the Constitution itself, executive. In other words, they are powers to be executed under certain general political principles, independently of all legislation, or they are useless where they stand. In a government like this, in which the executive authority is directly delegated by the body of the constituency, to one of their own number, and for a limited period, it is not only just, but it is wise to sustain the incumbent by all lawful and proper means, in the strict performance of his legal duties, for he is acting in our name, at our dictation, and in our behalf. He is also strictly our representative. In theory, he is as much representative as Congress, and when we descend into the examination of personal motives, local interests, and the history of legislative deputations, he is far more the representative of the entire nation than either house of Congress, even both together. Congress, after all, is but the aggregate of local representations, whereas the President derives his authority from a general representation, and by no combination of parts of a general representation. To deny these facts, and to sustain half of what has been said lately on the other side of the question, is to affirm that the Convention of 1787 was guilty of the egregious folly of creating a political master, who requires our utmost vigilance to prevent his annihilating our liberties instead of creating a useful and necessary public servant.

The law of Mr. Webster is even less to be defended than the law quoted by the Attorney General. The former, in effect, imposes a restriction on the right to nominate, while the latter dictates to the removing power. Now, there is a question concerning where this removing power resides, while no one will deny that the power of the President to nominate, is as clearly bestowed by the Constitution, as the right to fill a vacancy in the recess of the Senate. Are we to have a law regulating the manner in which these vacancies are to be filled also?

A. B. C.

[From the New York *Evening Post,* April 14, 1835:]

To the Editors of the Evening Post

GENTLEMEN: As usual, the opinion of the trading streets of the town is in the extreme on the subject of the French treaty. It may be worth the trouble to inquire with what reason.

The Duc de Broglie is made the President of the Council and Minister of Foreign Affairs. In effect we have very much the same ministry this year, as we had last year when the indemnity was refused. In both cases the king is *premier.*

In 1834, the Duc de Dalmatie was, nominally, the head of the ministry; now, the head of the ministry is a *doctrinaire,* or one of a party that is cordially disliked by every other shade of opinion in France. To get rid of this ministry, all parties may unite, and we may lose the indemnity as a consequence. This is one chance, and by no means a small chance, against the passage of the bill at all.

What is this bill? · It is a law giving the ministers a credit in the years 1836, 7, 8, 9, '40, '41, by means of which credit they are to pay the 25,000,000 of the treaty. This is the law in its terms, but it is very far from being the treaty in its terms. By the latter, on the 3d of February, 1836, France will owe this country near 20,000,000 f., while the law will authorize the payment of less than 5,000,000. By the treaty, the entire sum of 23,500,000, with the stipulated interest, ought to be paid on or before the 3d February, 1838, while by the law, the sum of 23,500,000 will not be paid before the year 1841. Putting the most favourable construction on the law, there will exist a difference of near 3,000,000 in the amount, and of three years in the time of its payments, as compared with the stipulations of the treaty.

There is no use on concealing these facts from ourselves. Who is there, in this country, to accept less than the conditions of a treaty?—Congress? Congress is less powerful than a treaty. It can neither alter, nor authorize the alteration of a treaty. There are only two ways in which the conditions of a treaty can cease to be "the supreme law of the land;" a declaration of war, or by having recourse to a new treaty.

A new treaty can be made only by the agency of the President, sustained by a vote of two-thirds of the Senate. Will the President make a new treaty in this case? We have, in effect, his own declaration to the contrary.

Under these circumstances, it will be wise to wait the course of events before we consider the French question as settled. Too much importance is attached to the opinions of letter writers from the other side. Had circumstances called for it, the same letters would have been written, and the same confidence in the result expressed in 1833, when the law was thrown out without the formality of a vote, and in 1834, when it was absolutely and deliberately rejected. I do not believe that even the Duc de Broglie will tell the Chambers, he so interprets the prerogative, that they have only to vote the 25,000,000 *in literal compliance with the treaty*; or if he should, I do not think he will be sustained by a majority. The majority will be disposed to consider its own vote as the *only* ratification of the compact.

France has been misled by the course of Congress and by

the language of the press. She thinks that a few millions of interest and a few years in time will be forgotten in the desire for peace. She believes this country to have less public virtue than the event will probably show, because she knows this country only through its commercial towns. The delay is a bad symptom, though it will give us one advantage. The Constitution will probably have arrived before the Chamber act, and as the correspondence has preceded her, France will know that the whole legation is to be withdrawn, should the indemnity be again denied. This may have a strong effect in preventing an entire rejection of the law, but it remains to be seen if it will produce such a law as we can accept.

I have little doubt that an ordinary French ministry would, at need, comply with the conditions of the treaty, under the law as proposed, but I do not believe that a ministry of the *doctrinaires* would. Least of all do I believe that the Duc de Broglie, under a credit of less than 5,000,000, will pay 20,000,000 in 1836. Will he then present a new bill?—or, if a new bill is presented, will it pass?

I fear that the noble stand taken by the President has been too much weakened by subsequent events to produce an event so desirable.

A. B. C.

APPENDIX B

Two Unpublished and One Forgotten Letter by James Fenimore Cooper which Illustrate His State of Mind during the Libel Suits

A Letter from James Fenimore Cooper to J. Hunt, Jr., published in 1851 in the *Cincinnati Gazette.* Clipping in the Cooper collection, Yale University Library.

For the Cincinnati Gazette.

James Fenimore Cooper

Messrs. Editors:—The recent demise of the distinguished individual, whose name stands at the head of this article, will, in all probability, form the theme of some able reviewers, both in this country and Europe. During his long literary career, no man, perhaps, has been more villified and praised than has Mr. Cooper; however, I am inclined to the opinion that the voice of praise did little to sway him from his ordinary calmness; but the grumbling tones of censure, seemed to divest him,—while they yet rung in his ear,—of all that philosophy which displayed itself in his published works.

As a novelist, I never looked upon Mr. Cooper, as a man of such superior abilities, as the world, in general, awarded to him; but in the matter of fact delineations, few stars have shown with brighter brilliancy, in the literary firmament. No man can read his "Lives of the Naval Heroes," without experiencing in his bosom, the true emotions of patriotic zeal; elevation of language is discernible in nearly every paragraph; and the patience which must have been employed to sift the purely historical, from the false and fabulous, has no greater parallel.

For the sake of American literature, it is my wish, that Mr. Cooper had never plowed in the fields of fiction. Had the many precious moments of his literary life, been spent in the development of historical facts, which were otherwise lavished on the unpeopled domains of romance, a prominence would have been given to our past annals, which will now require years of unmitigated toil over the desk of study, to place in a tangible shape. That Mr. Cooper's imagination ranked with the highest order, would be folly to dispute; that his genius, however, in this respect, equalled that of Dumas, or Eugene Sue, every man of judgment knows, is far from being the case. His language was expressive, in fiction; still, the "lively interest" which renders the "Wandering Jew" famous, was not in Mr. Cooper's power to give. But as above stated, whenever he touched upon a subject which had its foundation based in reality, we find his diction clear—his arguments full of conclusive proofs. I have not the leisure, necessary to descant upon Mr. Cooper's virtues and failings as every man should have, who professes a critical ability. My sole object is to give you a statement made to me by Mr. Cooper himself, at a time when some of the most influential presses of the country were arrayed against him, for his prosecutions against those, whom it was generally understood, dared to speak in any other than tones of praise, of his literary labors.

These prosecutions will, undoubtedly, form the groundwork of many bitter remarks against him, unless the matter is placed before the world in its just and proper light. A statement, therefore, from Mr. Cooper, giving his reasons, *why* these prosecutions were instituted, needs to be published, and widely circulated. A great man has departed; and generosity demands that all his redeeming qualifications should be placed upon record; that his errors, (and who is devoid of them?) should be "interred with his bones."

The letter, which I have copied from the original, now before me, was published, at the time of its date, in a paper of my own, the circulation of which, however, was narrowly confined. My friends urged upon me the necessity of denouncing Mr. Cooper's course of conduct, relative to those prosecuting suits; and I came to the conclusion to address him personally, on the subject, promising, at the same time, that whatever he saw proper to write me, should be kept inviolably a secret. I wished him to give me, what he termed, a distinction between Libel and Criticism—or in other words, whether he considered Criticism a Libel.—In due time, his answer was received, and as the same will show, he seemed anxious that I should make his statement as public as possible. Without further remarks, then, I will give you the letter:

COOPERSTOWN, N. Y., February 28th, 1843.

J. HUNT, JR.—*Sir*:—Your letter has been received, and as it is written with an apparent desire to learn the truth, I answer your questions quite cheerfully. So far, however, from holding you to your pledge of secrecy, you are at liberty to show this reply to whom you please, or should you see proper, to publish it in your journal.

Your direct question is, whether I consider "Criticism a Libel?"—and, I infer from your remarks, you wish to know how far I have sued for criticism. By the question, I understand you to mean whether "criticism *can* be a libel."

Criticism means discriminating strictures on a book. It may, also, relate to other things. So long as these strictures relate solely to the subject of the criticism, there can obviously be no libel.—A *book* cannot sue for character. But if a criticism on a book contains calumnies on its author, whether these calumnies relate to the immediate book under discussion or not, I make no doubt it is libelous, and the imputation must be justified, in the usual manner, by showing the truth of the charge. When a criticism, or a pretended criticism, on a book, contains a calumny on its writer that is *not* connected with the book under review, it is not only a libel, but a libel of an aggravated nature. It is as if a clergyman should use the pulpit for the purposes of private malignancy and detraction. I would sue sooner for such a libel than for any other; and this I would do in the interest of Literature and the *real* Liberty of the Press.

I conceive that our Supreme Court holds that a review is, in no sense, a privileged communication. It has never decided the point directly; but it has indirectly given strong indications of its opinion, in the case of Cooper *vs.* Stone, on demurrer. All the difficulty connected with this point has, in my judgment, arisen from the English case of Carr *vs.* Hood. But that case decides nothing, in the first place. It is a mere opinion of a Judge given at NICI PRIUS, and given under this awkward dilema, viz:—

By the common law, in criminal proceedings, it is held that, the greater the truth the greater the libel. In civil proceedings the law in England is as it is in this State; (New York)—the truth is a complete justification. Now, under the first dogma, there arises this difficulty; a man writes a silly or a wicked book. The critic holds him up to merited ridicule or odium, personally, and in connection with this book. The author chooses to indict his reviewer, and then the more he deserved the castigation, personal as it was, the greater is the offence of the criminal. We have provided against this absurd consequence in the Constitution, which says: "the truth, with good motives, shall be a justification in the criminal proceedings." In other words, if a writer deserves the personal castigation, the defendant has only to prove it.

My answer in brief, is this: so long as critical strictures are confined to the book, they are not libelous, since the book cannot sue for character, but when criticism assails the man instead of his work, then it becomes libelous.

Thus, A, says a certain book, known by all to be written by B, is blasphemous. This is not a libel, since the remark applies strictly to the book and does not *necessarily* involve the character of the writer. Books often contain mistakes—men frequently write error innocently, &c.; but to charge B with being a blasphemer, and then to allude to a work generally in proof of the accusation, would be slander, as well as a libel. The justification would be, to show that the book contained blasphemy, written under such circumstances as fairly to bear the personal imputations.

I have never *sued* for any libel connected at all with criticism, except in the action brought against Mr. Stone. Mr. Webb is *indicted* also for a libel contained in a pretended review. In the case of Mr. Stone, the libels were contained in a review of the Naval History. They went very far *beyond* the book in many particulars; but there was one libel connected *with* the book, that clearly shows the distinction I mean. The critic—if critic he can be called—said that certain parts of the History were untrue. Had he stopped here, I had no remedy, unless it might have been to sue for especial damage, even allowing that the History was *true*, and the charge *false*. The character of the book alone was implicated, and the book could not be plaintiff in a libel suit. But the critic was not content to stop here. His context alleged substantially that the falsehoods were written with a base motive. This rendered the whole libellous, and reduced him to the necessity of showing first, that the History *was* false; second, that it had been falsely written, with the object declared. You will readily understand that a History may contain errors of fact, without necessarily effecting the moral character of the writer.

Had my reviewer been content to leave the matter there, although I subsequently showed that my History was *true*, and his criticism *false*, an action for a libel could not have been maintained. But a man is not to be called a liar, in connection with a book he may have written, more than in connection with any other subject.

This, I presume, is all you wish to know. I am constantly receiving newspapers sent to me from the extremes of the Union, denouncing my attempts to stifle the Liberty of the Press, and particularly deriding my supposed design to stop the mouths of my critics. I question if there is a living writer who cares less for criticism than myself. I seldom read it—never, I may almost say, when known to be friendly; and my intimate friends know it never disturbs me. This is not probably what you have been told; but those who know me, will corroborate it. I never had a thirst for criticism; but some twenty or thirty books have so hardened me, that I have some such dread of it now, as certain individuals have of insolvency.

If the editors of the papers I have mentioned, knew that they were circulating ridiculous falsehoods, they might understand how much I care for their strictures. One of these papers has just reached me, coming all the way from Illinois. It speaks of my having persecuted the "amiable and gentlemanly Horace Greely, Esquire," for criticism. Now, I never sued 'Squire Greely for any such thing. I sued him, some time since, for *calumny*, and beat him; and I have just sued him a second time for calumny, and depend upon it, sir, I shall beat him again; as I have every man I have sued, who has not retracted his libels.

I have never even sued for ridicule. Every action brought by me, has been brought for direct and palpable *calumny*. I have brought these suits because I am sick of being a Freeman in name only. The man is a slave who lives in dread of calumny, and I choose to struggle for my liberty.

As for money, not a human being who knows me, has the smallest idea, it, in any manner, influences my course. If *money* were the object, I own too much literary property, not to understand how important it is to my pockets, to make friends among the newspapers. I have lost a fortune by the hostile influence of the American press; but its power has never induced me to court it in any shape, or yield to it a single privilege. The calumny in connection with the battle of Lake Erie, has, of itself, cost me many thousands. It destroyed the sale of a work that ought, and otherwise would have put into my pocket a very large sum; whereas, I am now five or six thousand dollars poorer than if I had never written it. The injury is irreparable. I have refuted that calumny, but much of its moral effects will remain, long after I am dead; and, as for money, the loss once made, is made forever. This is a people that never yet repaired a wrong; bodies of men seldom do; the American people less than common. It will scarcely inforce justice as between man and man; much less will it, at its own cost.

To conclude, therefore, criticism *cannot* be a libel, while purely criticism. I have never sued for mere strictures on a book, and in only one case, that of Mr. Stones, for anything connected with a book.

I have never yet sued Mr. Webb, at all, though the papers have often affirmed the contrary; but he has been twice indicted for libels on me. Mr. Weed was sued five times. Four of the suits went to judgment, and the verdicts have been paid; the fifth libel was retracted, and the suit was dropped, defendant paying the costs. In the way of money, apart from the influence of the Press on the sale of my works, I do not believe the balance is fifty dollars in, or out of pocket. Several of the verdicts have not been paid at all, and never will be,—the bankrupt's sponge having been applied to them. In three cases I have had to pay my own costs, in whole, or in part. I may add that, all the clamor of the press, has no more influence on me than if it were the music of so many Jewsharps. The press must manifest more logic, more knowledge of law, more acquaintance with facts, and more love of truth, as a whole, before it could ever turn a man of ordinary intelligence and firmness from his course, in a matter like this. I fear my monument* will never be erected for want of funds. Its inscription was to have been "in

* It may be well to remark that, at the time Mr. Cooper was prosecuting his suits, various editors published it to the world that, the money Mr. Cooper obtained, by his suits for damages, was to be employed for the erection of a monument, in commemoration of his triumph over his critics. Of the truth of this, however, I know nothing.—*Hunt.*

honor of the triumph of the law, over Tyranny and oppression assuming the mask of Liberty."

The clamor which has been made about the recent decisions of Judges in my favor, is foolishness. These decisions have all been in perfect conformity with right, and practice. The best evidence of that is, that in only one case, has any appeal been made from them, and in that case (Mr. Barber's) the unanimous opinion of the Court above, sustained the Judge at Circuit. Nothing is less like the facts, than the newspaper accounts of these suits, that have been going the rounds. Take a late specimen of the falsehoods: Mr. Webb, in a recent article, denies some of my statements. Among other things, he flatly denies that he was under bonds to appear at Fonda, in 1841. "I was under bonds to appear at *Otsego*," he says, "but after the *venue* was removed to Montgomery, none was asked, &c." Now this is true, in one sense, and yet it conveys a deliberate falsehood, as the facts will show. The case was in the Oyer and Terminer. Mr. Webb applied to Chief Justice Nelson, to remove it to the Supreme Court, under the statute. Now this statute *commands*, as any one can see, who will take the trouble of turning to it—that the Judge, granting a *certiorari* to a *defendant*, in a criminal proceeding, *shall* take bail for his appearance above, in order to plead, if necessary, and to compel him to *render himself to judgment*, if found guilty. The *certiorari* cannot be granted, without this bail. The Chief Justice took this bail of Mr. Webb, having two sureties in addition to his own bond. So you see, Mr. Webb *was* under bonds to appear at Fonda, in 1841—his deliberate and prevaricating assertions to the contrary notwithstanding.

I merely mention this case, as a specimen of the manner in which falsehoods are early circulated, about these suits. I might go through all Mr. Webb's assertions just in the same way. He has not a distinctive truth in his whole article. He never has had an account of what has passed in Court, that approaches the truth.

Mr. Greely's account of the trial at Ballston, is a series of mistatements, both in fact and in argument. In the case of the inquest against Mr. Webb, I did *the very reverse* of that with which I was charged, and can prove it in open Court.

I will mention one fact, in order to show how the truth has been trifled with, in these matters. At Fonda, a lawyer in behalf of Mr. Weed, said he had a letter from Mr. Weed, stating that he was at the Railroad station, about to start, &c., when he was recalled to the bed-side of his sick daughter. Nothing was said why the counsel of Mr. Weed did not attend, you will remember. Well, Judge Willard told this lawyer that if he would make affidavit to the effect of his statement, and that he believed the account to be true, he would postpone the case. The *lawyer refused* to make this affidavit! Judge Willard mentioned this fact at the public table at Ballston, Judge Cushman, being one of his auditors, and I heard the facts to be as stated.

The question is simply this: Shall a combination of editors be let loose on a particular citizen, to endeavor to take away his character, or not?—Liberty cannot exist without protection of character, any more than it can exist without protection of person. Ordinary slander suits are usually contemptible things, but when a citizen meets a combination of editors, as I have done, every good man ought to wish him success, and every wise man, will see the importance of sustaining him to the fullest extent of the law.

Yours truly,

J. FENNIMORE COOPER.

The only thing I perceive in this letter which tends to make it objectionable, is his allusion that the American people never, or rarely, redress a wrong which they have been the means of inflicting. Galled and jaded, as Mr. Cooper then was, by the "envenomed shaft of calumny and retraction," we must exercise enough of charity to overlook the erroneous imputation, and which he puts forth with such unrestricted meaning.

With a fame extending to the outer bounds of civilization, Mr. Cooper has nothing to fear from a press, devoted in the main, to the diffusion of certain political principles and prejudices. Mr. Webb, Mr. Stone and Mr. Greely were Mr. Cooper's political opponents, and if the truth was made manifest, I am inclined to believe that their restrictions were meted out more to effect mere party purposes, than for the actual discovery of an untruth contained in any of his statements. In the highest degree sensitive, Mr. Cooper permitted his better judgment to be swayed by every unfavorable gale; and it served to embitter his tranquility, at a period when man—advanced as he was, far in the vale of life—needs the repose due to virtuous deeds. But peace and kindly forbearance follow him. His whole energies have been spent in a commendable pursuit; and before his eyes closed forever on this world of sudden and uncertain transitions, he experienced the proud satisfaction of having had the harmonious sound of praise to fill his ear, emanating both from the old and new hemisphere. A man, therefore, who sinks to his tomb, leaving behind him such an enduring monument of greatness, as Mr. Cooper, by his own industry and genius, has been the means of rearing, we who survive him, should feel in duty bound, to guard the same, unharmed against the encroachment of every Goth or Vandal, who dares to molest it. To this sentiment, gentlemen, I am confident of receiving your sanction and amen.

Faithfully, J. HUNT, JR.

Banks of the Ohio, Sept. 1851.

An unpublished letter from J. Hunt, Jr., to Dr. Francis, relating to the foregoing communication from James Fenimore Cooper. Cooper collection, Yale University Library.

Banks of the Ohio.
Chilo. Clermont Co. O. Nov. 6th 1851.

Doctor Francis,

Dear Sir:—permit me, though a stranger, to intrude for a moment on your leisure. I have just perused with feelings little short of idolitry [*sic*], your letter to Dr. Griswold, (and published in the Nov. No. of the *International*)[1] respecting the private character and literary genius of the late Fenimore Cooper. I am not a person who cherishes the disposition to flatter, but one thing is certain, and I am happy to place the same on record, that I have not, for years, read anything more touching and tender than are the remarks, contained in that communication. It is a Literary Gem, which,—(to make use of one of Mr. Cooper's own expressions) I shall "Keep with care and preserve with veneration."

I take pleasure, Dr. Francis, in sending you a *printed* copy of a letter, written to me by Mr. Cooper, a few years since, explanitory [*sic*] of those "Libel Suits," which at their date, made such a "noise in the world." This letter may, perhaps, prove of benefit to you, provided, at a future day, you feel called upon to defend his well-earned reputation against the Calumnies of certain bipeds, who style themselves "Critic's [*sic*]." There are many typographical errors contained in it, which your own observing eye will, at once correct.

A line from you, making mention of the recept [*sic*] of this, will be thankfully recd.

With sentiments in the highest degree respectful, I am, dear sir,

Yours, faithfully,

J. Hunt, Jr.

[1] *International Monthly*, IV (November, 1851), 453. This article is the same as the "Reminiscences of James Fenimore Cooper" published in the *Memorial of James Fenimore Cooper*.

An unpublished letter from James Fenimore Cooper to Peter Gansevoort, Counsellor at Law, Albany. New York Public Library.

Hall, Cooperstown, May 5th, 1841.

Dear Gansevoort,

I take the liberty, in a case of extremity, to enclose you some blank subpoenas, to enable me to meet Mr. Weed next Monday. I wish you to ascertain who was the foreman in Weed's printing office, in August, 1837, and to put his name in one of the tickets and have it served. I think one of the publishers would be a good witness. Our object is to prove the publication, unless Mr. Parnele [?] signs an admission that is now in his possession. I do not tell you how the subpoena and tickets are to be filled, as you know all that better than I do. Neither do I apologize for the trouble, well knowing you would not hesitate to ask a similar favor of me. We are thus late, in consequence of Stevenson's yearly migration to Philadelphia, where, if he goes for money, the Lord have mercy on his soul.

This summer, my dear Peter, you and Stevenson *must* come and see me. A week might be very pleasantly passed here, and we could all turn boys again. A few years hence, that exploit will be out of the question. Remember, I put my foot down for this concession, and about the beginning of July, you may expect to hear further on the subject.

Your answer, can be sent here, if mailed by Friday night—if not to Fonda, Montgomery county, where I propose to meet some of the enemy on Monday next. Stone did not appear, in person, or by attorney, and I might have walked over the course at our circuit, but prefer a match. At the proper hour he will be indicted.

Yours very truly

J. Fenimore Cooper.

Peter Gansevoort, Esquire.

[A postscript follows by Richard Cooper on the subject of fees. Another postscript by J. Fenimore Cooper asks for a file of the *Evening Journal* for the summer of 1837.]

An unpublished letter from James Fenimore Cooper to Theodore Sedgwick. Widener Library, Harvard University.

Hall, Cooperstown, June 1st 1839

My dear Sir,

I saw the article you mention,[1] and ascribed it, as a matter of course, to a friendly hand. It was substantially true, though it ascribed more virtue to my summing up than was merited. The judge, the law, and the facts were all with me, and I triumphed of necessity. I am willing, desirous even, of a new trial, but there is little probability that there ever will be one. Judge Willard knew what he was about, and his decision, I make no doubt, will be maintained. If there should be a new trial, I shall get double the damages. As it was, a portion of the jury felt it necessary to say that they were for a $1000. The manner in which a certain part of this community has worked to influence the verdict, *out of doors*, is astounding. Indeed, they produced a reaction by their high handed injustice and knavery. The change of opinion at Fonda in the course of a few hours, was prodigious; remarkable even for this changeable country.

The conflict between the press and myself is coming to a head. Webb will be found guilty beyond a doubt, on two indictments, one of which is not yet found, if not on four, for I am not yet decided whether to hold myself in reserve with two of them, or not. Of the result at Fonda I never entertained a doubt, nor do I feel any on the subject of Webb. I have Stone, Weed, Park Benjamin, a man by the name of Daniels, and one or two more in view. A few lessons of this nature will do more good than a dozen victories in the field. The Chenango Editor, who originally published the libel for which I have obtained a verdict, has no defence, and will suffer heavily. His own council told me he had not the head of a pin to stand on. Now, six months since, nay,

[1] See letter, Theodore Sedgwick, Jr., to Cooper, New York, May 28, 1839, *Correspondence of James Fenimore-Cooper*, I, 394-395.

two months since, both he and his Cooperstown associate were certain of victory. They swaggered about the liberty of the press, were evidently ignorant of what it meant, and trusted to a popular clamor. But when in court, matters, as I have always foreseen, took a very different appearance, and truth comes uppermost. The moral effect of this verdict is already as strong in this part of the country, as that on Dixon in yours. We shall bring the press, again, under the subjection of the law [?]. When one considers the characters, talents, motives and consistency of those who contrive it, as a body, he is lost in wonder that any community should have so long submitted to a tyranny so low and vulgar. When it is rebuked thoroughly, it may again become useful.

With much regard, yours very truly

J. FENIMORE COOPER

Theodore Sedgwick Esquire
(turn over)

Judge Willard laid down in his charge as law, that an allegation against the literary character of a literary man, if false and written in bad faith, which bad faith was to be inferred from the facts of the case, was as much a libel, as to say a tailor did not understand his trade. How many editors lie at my mercy!
I have not been in New York to pass any time, since last November. In going through town with my family, I merely went from boat to boat, had had barely time for that. I shall be at the Astor House however, in the course of this month, and should be there this week, but am compelled to wait here to *deliver an oration*, and to go before the Grand Jury.

A LIST
OF THE PUBLICATIONS AND MANUSCRIPTS USED AS SOURCES FOR THIS BOOK

Note: In Sections IV and V of this record, all periodicals are listed which are used in this book. The inclusive reference under any title records the numbers examined; particular numbers which have been cited or quoted are not indicated elsewhere than in the footnotes to the text. References to libraries tell what newspaper files were consulted.

I. Editions of Publications by James Fenimore Cooper Used in This Book.

Novels. Mohawk Edition, G. P. Putnam's Sons, New York, n. d.

The Pioneers. 2 volumes. New York, 1823.

The Pilot. 3 volumes. London, 1824.

Notions of the Americans: Picked up by a Travelling Bachelor. 2 volumes. London, 1828.

Paris, ou Le Livre des Cent-et-Un, IX, 221-250. Paris, 1832.

A Letter to His Countrymen. New York, 1834.

Sketches of Switzerland. 2 volumes. Philadelphia, 1836.

Sketches of Switzerland. Part second. 2 volumes. Philadelphia, 1836.

Gleanings in Europe: France. 2 volumes. Philadelphia, 1837.

Gleanings in Europe: England. 2 volumes. Philadelphia, 1837.

Gleanings in Europe: Italy. 2 volumes. Philadelphia, 1838.

The American Democrat. Cooperstown, New York, 1838.

Introduction to William Cooper, *A Guide in the Wilderness.* Rochester, 1897.

An Unpublished Letter, edited by W. K. Boyd, Trinity College, Durham, North Carolina, Historical Society, Historical Papers, Series 8, 1908-1909.

"Chronicles of Cooperstown" pp. 9-61 and 9-86 respectively in *A Centennial Offering,* edited by S. M. Shaw, *q.v.* and S. T. Livermore, *A Condensed History of Cooperstown, q.v.*

Correspondence of James Fenimore-Cooper, edited by James Fenimore Cooper [grandson of the novelist]. 2 volumes. New Haven, 1922.

New York, edited by Dixon Ryan Fox, New York, 1930.

II. Books by Other Authors

Alexander, De Alva S., *A Political History of the State of New York.* 3 volumes, New York, 1906-1909.

Barber, J. W., *Historical, Poetical, and Pictorial Scenes.* New Haven, 1851.

Beardsley, Levi, *Reminiscences.* New York, 1852.

Beers, Henry A., *Nathaniel Parker Willis.* Boston, 1885.

Bigelow, John, *William Cullen Bryant.* New York, 1890.

Boynton, Henry Walcott, *James Fenimore Cooper.* New York, 1931.

Bradsher, Earl L., *Mathew Carey, Editor, Author, and Publisher: a Study in American Literary Development.* New York, 1912.

Brainard, J. C., *Poems.* Hartford, 1847.

Brevoort, Henry, *Letters of Henry Brevoort to Washington Irving, together with Other Unpublished Brevoort Papers,* edited with an introduction by George S. Hellman. New York, 1918.

Bryant, William Cullen, "Discourse on the Life, Character, and Genius of James Fenimore Cooper," *Memorial of James Fenimore Cooper.* New York, 1852.

Cairns, William B., *British Criticisms of American Writings, 1813-1833. A Contribution to the Study of Anglo-American Relationships.* University of Wisconsin Studies in Language and Literature, 14. Madison, Wisconsin, 1922.

Clymer, William Branford Shubrick, *James Fenimore Cooper.* Beacon Biographies. Boston, 1900.

Coad, Oral Sumner, *William Dunlap: a Study of His Life and Works and of His Place in Contemporary Culture.* New York, 1917.

Cogewell, Frederick Hull, *James Gates Percival and His Friends.* New Haven, 1902.

Cooper, James Fenimore [grandson of the novelist], *Legends and Traditions of a Northern County.* New York, 1921.

Cooper, Susan Fenimore, "Small Family Memories," *Correspondence of James Fenimore-Cooper,* I.

Cooper, Susan Fenimore, *Pages and Pictures from the Writings of James F. Cooper with Notes.* New York, 1861.

Cooper, William, *A Guide in the Wilderness,* edited with an introduction by James Fenimore Cooper. Rochester, 1897.

Cowell, Joseph, *Thirty Years Passed among the Players in England and America.* New York, 1845.

Cushing, Caleb, *A Reply to the Letter of J. Fenimore Cooper.* By one of his countrymen. Boston, 1834.

De Kay, James E., M.D., Biography of Cooper, *National Portrait Gallery of Distinguished Americans,* I. Philadelphia, 1837.

Derby, J. C., *Fifty Years among Authors, Books, and Publishers.* New York, 1886.

Dewey, Mary E. (editor), *The Life and Letters of Catharine M. Sedgwick.* New York, 1871.

Dunlap, William, *Diary of William Dunlap.* 3 volumes. New York, 1930.

Dunlap, William, *A History of the American Theatre.* New York, 1832.

Dunlap, William, *A History of the Rise and Progress of the Arts of Design in the United States.* 3 volumes. Boston, 1918.

Emerson, Ralph Waldo, *Journals,* edited with annotations by Edward Waldo Emerson and Waldo Emerson Forbes. 10 volumes. New York, 1910.

Field, Maunsell B., *Memories of Many Men and of Some Women.* New York, 1874.

Fox, Dixon Ryan, *The Decline of Aristocracy in the Politics of New York.* New York, 1919.

Francis, John W., *Old New York: or, Reminiscences of the Past Sixty Years.* New York, 1865.

Francis, John W., "Reminiscences of Cooper," *Memorial of James Fenimore Cooper.* New York, 1852.

Godwin, Parke, *A Biography of William Cullen Bryant, with Extracts from His Private Correspondence.* 2 volumes. New York, 1883.

Goodrich, S. G., *Recollections of a Life-Time.* 2 volumes. New York, 1857.

Greeley, Horace, *Recollections of a Busy Life: including Reminiscences of American Politics and Politicians, from the opening of the Missouri Contest to the downfall of slavery.* New York, 1868.

Greene, G. W., "J. Fenimore Cooper," *Homes of American Authors.* New York, 1853.

Greene, G. W., *Biographical Studies.* New York, 1860.

Greenough, Horatio, "The Cooper Monument," *Memorial of Horatio Greenough,* edited by H. T. Tuckerman. New York, 1853.

Greenough, Horatio, *Letters of Horatio Greenough to His Brother, Henry Greenough. With Biographical Sketches and Some Contemporary Correspondence,* edited by Frances Boott Greenough. Boston, 1887.

Greenough, Horatio, *The Travels, Observations, and Experiences of a Yankee Stonecutter.* New York, 1852.

Griswold, Rufus [Wilmot], *Passages from the Correspondence and Other Papers of Rufus W. Griswold,* edited by W. M. Griswold. Cambridge, Massachusetts, 1898.

Griswold, Rufus Wilmot, *The Prose Writers of America. With a Survey of the Intellectual History, Conditions, and Prospects of the Country.* Philadelphia, 1847.

Hammond, Jabez D., *The History of Political Parties in the State of New-York, Including the Life of Silas Wright.* 3 volumes. Cooperstown, 1846-1847.

Herold, Amos L., *James Kirke Paulding, Versatile American.* New York, 1926.

Hone, Philip, *Diary of Philip Hone 1828-1851,* edited with an introduction by Allan Nevins. 2 volumes. New York, 1927.

Hudson, Frederick, *Journalism in the United States from 1690 to 1872.* New York, 1873.

Irving, Pierre M., *Life and Letters of Washington Irving.* 3 volumes. New York, 1883.

Irving, Washington, *Letters of Washington Irving to Henry Brevoort,* edited with an introduction by George S. Hellman. New York, 1918.

[Judah, S. B. H.], *Gotham and the Gothamites.* New York, 1823.

Lavisse, Ernest (editor), *Histoire de France Contemporaine.* 1921.

Lee, James Melvin, *History of American Journalism.* New York, 1923.

Livermore, S. T., *A Condensed History of Cooperstown, with a Biographical Sketch of J. Fenimore Cooper.* Albany, 1862.

Longfellow, Samuel, *Life of Henry Wadsworth Longfellow, with Extracts from His Journals and Correspondence.* Boston, 1896.

Lounsbury, Thomas R., *James Fenimore Cooper.* Boston, 1883.

Lowell, [James Russell], *A Fable for Critics.* New York, 1848.

Mathews, Anne, *Memoir of Charles Mathews, Comedian.* London, 1839.

Minnigerode, Meade, *Some Personal Letters of Herman Melville and a Bibliography.* New York, 1922.

Mitchell, Donald G., *American Lands and Letters.* New York, 1897.

Morse, Edward Lind, *Samuel F. B. Morse: His Letters and Journals.* 2 volumes. New York, 1914.

Mott, Frank Luther, *A History of American Magazines.* New York, 1930.

Neal, John, *Randolph.* 2 volumes. N.p., 1823.

Neal, John, *Wandering Recollections of a Somewhat Busy Life.* Boston, 1869.

Odell, George C. D., *Annals of the New York Stage.* 4 volumes. New York, 1928.

[Osborn, Laughton], *The Vision of Rubeta, an Epic Story of the Island of Manhattan.* Boston, 1838.

Outland, Ethel R., *The 'Effingham' Libels on Cooper,* University of Wisconsin Studies in Language and Literature, 28. Madison, 1929.

Payne, George Henry, *History of Journalism in the United States.* New York, 1920.

Phinney, Elihu, *Reminiscences of the Village of Cooperstown.* Cooperstown, 1891.

Pierce, E. L., *Memoir and Letters of Charles Sumner.* Boston, 1877.

Poe, Edgar Allan, *Works of Edgar Allan Poe.* Chicago, 1895.

Prime, Samuel Irenaeus, *The Life of Samuel F. B. Morse, LL.D., Inventor of the Electro-Magnetic Recording Telegraph.* New York, 1875.

Putnam, George Haven, *George Palmer Putnam: a Memoir.* New York, 1912.

Reilly, Joseph J., *James Russell Lowell as a Critic.* New York, 1915.

Scudder, Horace Elisha, *James Russell Lowell, a Biography.* 2 volumes. New York, 1901.

Shaw, S. M. (editor), *A Centennial Offering. Being a Brief History of Cooperstown.* Cooperstown, New York, 1886.

[Simms, W. G.], *Views and Reviews in American Literature, History, and Fiction.* New York, 1845.

Spiller, Robert E., *Fenimore Cooper, Critic of His Times.* New York, 1931.

Spiller, Robert E., Introduction to J. F. Cooper, *Gleanings in Europe: France.* Oxford, 1928.

Spiller, Robert E., Introduction to J. F. Cooper, *The Lake Gun.* New York, 1932.

Trent, William Peterfield, *William Gilmore Simms.* New York, 1892.

Tuckerman, Henry T., *America and Her Commentators, with a Critical Sketch of Travel in the United States.* New York, 1864.

Tuckerman, Henry T., *The Life of John Pendleton Kennedy.* New York, 1871.

Tuckerman, Henry T., *A Memorial of Horatio Greenough.* New York, 1853.

Ward, Julius, *Life and Letters of James Gates Percival.* Boston, 1886.

Weed, Thurlow, *Autobiography of Thurlow Weed*, edited by his daughter, Harriet A. Weed. Boston, 1884.

Williams, Stanley T., *The Life of Washington Irving.* New York, 1935.

Willis, N. Parker, *Complete Works.* New York, 1846.

Willis, N. Parker, *Hurry-Graphs, or, Sketches of Scenery, Celebrities, and Society Taken from Life.* New York, 1851.

Willis, N. Parker, *Pencillings by the Way.* 3 volumes. New York, 1833.

Willis, N. Parker, *Rural Letters.* New York, 1849.

Wilson, James Grant, *Bryant and His Friends, Some Reminiscences of the Knickerbocker Writers.* New York, 1886.

Wilson, James Grant, *The Life and Letters of Fitz-Greene Halleck.* New York, 1869.

Woodberry, George E., *The Life of Edgar Allan Poe, Personal and Literary, with His Chief Correspondence with Men of Letters.* 2 volumes. New York, 1909.

III. Essays Printed in American Magazines Since J. F. Cooper's Life-Time

Clark, L. G., "James Fenimore Cooper," *Lippincott's Magazine,* VIII (December, 1871), 625-629.

Cooke, J. E., "Cooper's Indians," *Appleton's Journal,* XII (August 29, 1874), 264-267.

Cooper, Susan F., "A Glance Backward," *Atlantic Monthly,* LIX (February, 1887), 199-206.

Cooper, Susan F., "A Second Glance Backward," *Atlantic Monthly,* LX (October, 1887), 474-486.

Greene, G. W., "James Fenimore Cooper," *New York Quarterly,* I (June, 1852), 215-228.

Hillard, G. S., "James Fenimore Cooper," *Atlantic Monthly,* IX (January, 1862), 52-68.

Howe, M. A. DeW., "James Fenimore Cooper," *Bookman,* V (March, 1897), 14.

Keese, G. Pomeroy, "James Fenimore Cooper," *Harper's Weekly,* XV (July 29, 1871, Supplement), 707-711.

Parkman, Francis, "The Works of James Fenimore Cooper," *North American Review,* LXXIV (January, 1852), 147-161.

Pattee, Fred Lewis, "James Fenimore Cooper," *American Mercury,* IV (March, 1925), 289-297.

Tassin, Algernon, "American Authors and Their Publishers," *Bookman,* XXXIX (May, 1914), 268-281.

Tuckerman, C. K., "James Fenimore Cooper on Secession and State Rights," *Continental Monthly,* VI (July, 1864), 79-83.

Tuckerman, H. T., "Cooper as a Novelist," *North American Review,* LXXXIX (October, 1859), 289.

Wilson, J. G., "Cooper Memorials and Memories," *Independent,* LIII (January 31, 1901), 251-253.

IV. Magazines Contemporary with James Fenimore Cooper

American Monthly Magazine (Willis). Boston. I (April, 1829)-III (July, 1831).

American Monthly Magazine. (Hoffman and Benjamin.) New York. I (March, 1833)-XII (September, 1838).

American Monthly Review. Cambridge. I (January, 1832)-IV (December, 1833).

American Quarterly Review. Philadelphia. I (March, 1827)-XXII (December, 1837).

Arcturus, a Journal of Books and Opinion. New York. I (January, 1841)-III (May, 1842).

Athenaeum. London. VIII (January 3, 1835).

Atheneum: or, Spirit of the English Magazines. Boston. VIII (October, 1820)-XVI (March, 1825).

Atlantic Magazine. I (May, 1824)-II (April, 1825).

Casket. Philadelphia. II (January, 1827)-XII (December, 1837); XVII (July-December, 1840). After 1840, *Graham's Lady's and Gentleman's Magazine.*

Christian Spectator. New Haven. VII (February, 1824).

Corsair, New York. I (May 25, June 1, 1839); (July 27, 1839).

Gentleman's Magazine. Philadelphia. I (July, 1837)-VII (December, 1840). After 1840, *Graham's Lady's and Gentleman's Magazine.*

Godey's Lady's Book. Philadelphia. II (January, 1831)-IX (December, 1834); XIV (January, 1837)-XXV (December, 1842).

Graham's Lady's and Gentleman's Magazine. Philadelphia. XVIII (January, 1841)-XXI (December, 1842).

Hartford Pearl and Literary Gazette. Hartford. IV (August 20, 1834).

Hesperian: or Western Monthly Magazine. Columbus. I (July, August, 1838).

Iris, or Literary Messenger. New York. I (November, 1840-October, 1841).

Knickerbocker, or New-York Monthly Magazine. New York. I (January, 1833)-XVIII (December, 1841).

Ladies' Companion. New York. X (November, 1838)-XVI (April, 1842).

Ladies' Magazine. Boston. I (January, 1828)-VIII (December, 1834).

Literary and Scientific Repository, and Critical Review. New York. I (July and October, 1820)-IV (January and May, 1822).

Literary Journal and Weekly Register of Science and the Arts. Providence. I (June, 1833-May, 1834).

Literary Port-Folio. Philadelphia. I (January 7-July 1, 1830).

Metropolitan Magazine. New Haven. I (January, 1833)-III (December, 1835).

Museum of Foreign Literature, Science, and Art. Philadelphia and New York. I (July, 1822)-XLIV (December, 1842).

New England Magazine. Boston. I (July, 1831)-IX (December, 1835).

New Havener. New Haven. III (July 15, 1837-July 28, 1838).

New York Mirror. New York. I (August 2, 1823)-II (July 23, 1825); IV (July 29, 1826)-XIX (December 25, 1841).
New York Review and Atheneum Magazine. New York. I (June, 1825)-II (May, 1826).
New York Review. New York. I (March, 1837)-X (April, 1842).
New Yorker. New York. Quarto: I (March 26, 1836)-XI (September 11, 1841).
New World. New York. I (July 11, 1840)-III (November 27, 1841).
Niles' Weekly Register. Baltimore, XXI n. s. (September, 1821)-XXXIV (August, 1828); XXXVII (September, 1829)-XLIV (August, 1834); XLVI (March, 1835)-LXII (August, 1842).
North American Magazine. Philadelphia. I (November, 1832)-III (April, 1834).
North American Review. Boston. II (July, 1820)-LVII (December, 1843).
Northern Light. Albany. I (April, 1841)-II (March, 1842).
Philadelphia Album. Philadelphia. I (September 6, 1826)-V (December 31, 1831); VII (January 19-June 22, 1833).
Philadelphia Monthly Magazine. Philadelphia. I (October, 1827)-II (September, 1828).
Port Folio. Philadelphia. IX series 4 (January, 1820)-II series 5 (December, 1827).
Portland Magazine. Portland, Maine. I (August 1, 1835).
Southern Literary Journal. Charleston. I (September, 1835)-II (August, 1836).
Southern Literary Messenger. Richmond. I (August, 1834)-VII (December, 1841).
Southern Review. Charleston. I (February, 1828)-VIII (February, 1832).
Southern Rose. Charleston. VI (September 2, 1837)-VII (August 3, 1839).
United States Literary Gazette. Boston. I (April, 1824)-IV (August, 1826).
United States Magazine and Democratic Review. Washington. I (October, 1837)-X (May, 1842).
Waldie's Select Circulating Library, Journal of Belles Lettres. I (1832)-III (1834); V (1835)-XIV (1839): XVI (1847).
Western Monthly Magazine and Literary Journal. Cincinnati. I (January, 1833)-V (December, 1836); I n. s. (February-June, 1837).
Western Monthly Review. Cincinnati. I (May, 1827)-III (June, 1830).
Yale Literary Magazine. New Haven. V (March, 1840).

V. Newspapers Contemporary with James Fenimore Cooper

Albany Evening Journal. Albany. May 30, 1839; November 22, December 11, 1841. Yale; Cooper collection.

Albion. New York. 1822-1840. Yale.

Atlas. New York. December 10, 1831. Yale.

Chenango Telegraph. Norwich, New York. October 4, 1837. Yale; Cooper collection.

Columbian Centinel. Boston. December, 1821-October, 1831. Yale.

Columbian Register. New Haven. November 13, 1821-December, 1830; January, 1839-December, 1840. Yale.

Commercial Chronicle and Daily Marylander. Baltimore. June 27, 1839. Yale; Cooper collection.

Connecticut Mirror. Hartford. February 4, March 4, 1822; November 7, 14, 1829. Yale.

Connecticut Observer. Hartford. March 1, 1825. Yale.

Daily Advertiser. Boston. January, 1832-December, 1841. Yale.

Evening Post. New York. December, 1821-December, 1841. New York Public Library.

Evening Signal. New York. March 19, 1840. Yale: Cooper collection.

Freeman's Journal. Cooperstown, New York. August 21, 28, 1837; July 1, 1839. Yale; Cooper collection.

Hartford Courant. Hartford. July 13, 1840. Yale.

Madison County Eagle. Cazenovia, New York. December 22, 1841. Yale; Cooper collection.

Morning Courier and New York Enquirer. New York. January-December, 1827. New York Historical Society. August, 1828-December, 1841. New York Public Library.

National Gazette. Philadelphia. October 22, 1839; May 15, August 21, 1840. Yale; Cooper collection.

New Haven Daily Herald. New Haven. November 26, 1840. Yale.

New York American. New York. Daily: December 21, 1821-August 8, 1831. Yale and Library of Congress. August, 1831-June, 1839. Library of Congress. Semi-weekly: July 2, 1839-August 27, 1841. Library of Congress.

New York Commercial Advertiser. New York. December 28, 1821-May 25, 1838. New York Public Library and New York Historical Society.

New York Daily Advertiser. New York. June 6, July 2, 1834. New York Public Library.

New York Spectator. New York. January 1, 1822-December 30, 1831. New York Public Library.

New York Tribune. New York. November 20, 30, 1841: December 12, 1842. Yale; Cooper collection.
Niagara Courier. Niagara Falls. June 26, July 17, 1839. Yale; Cooper collection.
Otsego Republican. Cooperstown. August 14, 1837. Yale; Cooper collection.
Philadelphia Weekly Ledger. Philadelphia. September 26, 1840. Yale; Cooper collection.
Plattsburg Whig. Plattsburg. October 14, 1837. Yale; Cooper collection.
Syracuse Morning Signal. Syracuse. May 28, 1840. Yale; Cooper collection.
Times. Oxford, New York. June 19, 1839. Yale; Cooper collection.
Wayne County Whig. August 11, 1841. Yale; Cooper collection.
Weekly Messenger. Philadelphia. January 30, 1839. Yale; Cooper collection.

VI. Unpublished Letters and Manuscripts in the Cooper Collection, Yale University Library

Anonymous and Unsigned Papers

Petition for the widow of Samuel Cromwell, signed by J. F. Cooper and others. [Written by Cooper?]
Copy of a letter, unsigned and undated, concerning A. S. Mackenzie.
Letter to Cooper, July 13, 1840.
"The Stranger" to Cooper, Honesdale, Pennsylvania, June 12, 1848.

Letters and Papers of Known Authorship

D. D. Barnard to Cooper, Albany, November 27, 1841.
D. D. Barnard to Cooper [Albany], June 20, 1842.
Anthony J. Bleecker to Cooper, New York, February 3, 1845.
Henri D. Brackette to Cooper, Kaskaskia, Illinois, August 5, 1842.
Luther Bradish to Cooper, New York, January 31, 1827.
H. C. Carey to Cooper, Philadelphia, April 21, 1835.
H. C. Carey to Cooper, Philadelphia, November 12, 1835.
H. C. Carey to Cooper, Philadelphia, April 29, 1836.
Carey and Lea to Cooper, Philadelphia, January 16, 1832.
Carey and Lea to Cooper, Philadelphia, October 21, 1831.
Carey and Lea to Cooper, Philadelphia, September 13, 1837.
Carey, Lea, and Carey to Cooper, Philadelphia, July 14, 1827.
Carey, Lea, and Carey to Cooper, Philadelphia, November, 1827.
Carey, Lea, and Carey to Cooper, Philadelphia, April 28, 1828.

Carey, Lea and Carey to Cooper, Philadelphia, July 17, 1828.
Carey, Lea, and Carey to Cooper, Philadelphia, September 8, 1828.
Carey, Lea, and Carey to Cooper, Philadelphia, December [?], 1828.
Carey, Lea, and Carey to Cooper, Philadelphia, January 14, 1833.
Carey, Lea, and Carey to Cooper, Philadelphia, June 26, 1837.
Carey, Lea, and Carey to Cooper, Philadelphia, August 18, 1838.
L. Gaylord Clark to Cooper, New York, n. d.
Charles P. Clinch to Cooper, New York, January 20, 1845.
Captain Conner to Cooper, Washington, November 22, 1841.
Ben Cooper to Cooper, February 11, 1821 [1822?].
Isaac Cooper to Cooper, New York, September 26, 1845.
James Fenimore Cooper, Journal, August 15, 1832.
James Fenimore Cooper, manuscript notes on *Gleanings in Europe: England.*
James Fenimore Cooper to Sturgis, Philadelphia, September 17, 1843.
James Fenimore Cooper to Susan Augusta Cooper, Cooperstown, June 26, 1834.
Richard Cooper to the editors of the *Otsego Republican,* Cooperstown, August 11, 1837.
Richard Cooper to A. M. Barber, July 16, 1840.
Susan Augusta [Mrs. James Fenimore] Cooper to her sister, Cooperstown, March 13, n. d.
Susan Augusta Cooper to her sister Martha De Lancey, Paris, April 20, n. d.
Susan Augusta Cooper to her sister Martha, Paris, April 27, 1827.
Susan Augusta Cooper to her sister, Miss De Lancey, London, May 1 [1828].
Susan Augusta Cooper to Susan Fenimore Cooper, London, May 15, 1828.
Susan Augusta Cooper to her daughter, Susan Fenimore Cooper, London, May 15, 1828.
Susan Augusta Cooper to Susan F. Cooper, London, May 19, 1828.
Susan Augusta Cooper to her sisters, Martha and Caroline De Lancey, Paris, November 29, 1830.
Susan Augusta Cooper to her sister Martha, Paris, August 29, 1831.
Susan Augusta Cooper to her sister Martha, Vevay, Switzerland, September 11, 1832.
Susan Augusta Cooper to her sister Martha, Paris, April 15, 1833.
Susan Augusta Cooper to her sister, Mrs. Pomeroy, New York, December 27, [1833].
Susan Augusta Cooper to Frederic, December 13, [1851].
Susan Fenimore Cooper to Susan Augusta Cooper, Paris, September 14, 1831.

Harriet Douglas Cruger to Mrs. Cooper, Ritchfield Springs, September 12, 1845.
Henry D. Cruger to Cooper, Great Western steam ship, December 4, 1838.
Auguste Danyan to Cooper, New York, April 4, 1840.
Auguste Danyan to Cooper, New York, March 27, 1841.
J. E. De Kay to Cooper, New York, April 8, 1831.
J. E. De Kay to Susan F. Cooper, Syosset, September 20, 1850.
William Dunlap to Cooper, New York, July 24, 1833.
J. D. Elliott to Cooper, Philadelphia, January 10, 1842.
L. Foot to Cooper, General Hospital, St. John's Bluff, Florida, August 10, 1841.
Manuscript of J. W. Francis, *Reminiscences of Cooper*, with corrections.
C. Gayarré to Cooper, New Orleans, February 5, 1841.
Horace Greenough to Cooper, Florence, Italy, December 20, 1830.
Horace Greenough to Cooper, Florence, June 21, 1831.
Horace Greenough to Cooper, Florence, December 17, 1831.
Horace Greenough to Cooper, Florence, August 22, 1832. Unpublished postscript. Letter published without this passage, *Correspondence of James Fenimore Cooper*, I, 284-285.
Horace Greenough to Cooper, December 18, 1832.
Horace Greenough to Cooper, October 8, 1839.
Horace Greenough to Susan Fenimore Cooper, Newport, August 11, [1851].
R. W. Griswold to Cooper, Philadelphia, August 6, 1842.
Robert Hare to Cooper, Portsmouth, Rhode Island, August 8, 1834.
Robert Hare to Cooper, Newport, August 17, 1840.
George S. Hillard to Cooper [1850].
J. R. Ingersoll to Cooper, Washington, July 22, 1846.
Peter A. Jay to Cooper, July 3, 1841.
William Jay to Susan Cooper, New York, April 15, 1854.
J. P. Kennedy to Cooper, Baltimore, May 15, 1846.
E. W. Laight to Charlotte Cooper, New York, August 30 [n. d.].
Lea and Blanchard to Cooper, Philadelphia, February 11, 1840.
Lea and Blanchard to Cooper, Philadelphia, February 9, 1841.
George Lippard to Cooper, Philadelphia, May 21, 1844.
W. R. McNally to Cooper, Paris, August 24, 1834.
Cornelius Matthews and Evert A. Duyckinck to Cooper, New York, December 4, 1841.
S. F. B. Morse to Cooper, New York, July 25, 1833.
Edward R. Myers to Cooper, Sailors' Snug Harbor, Staten Island, November 28, 1843.

John Neal to Cooper, Baltimore, October 18, 1822.
W. H. Norris, addressee unnamed, Baltimore, December 16, 1843.
J. L. O'Sullivan to Cooper, New York, June 22, 1842.
J. Oakley to Cooper, n. d. [1841?].
James De Peyster Ogden to Cooper, New York, June 10, 1839.
James De Peyster Ogden to Cooper, New York, June 20, 1839.
James De Peyster Ogden to Cooper, New York, August 24, 1839.
James De Peyster Ogden to Cooper, New York, November 7, 1839.
James De Peyster Ogden to Cooper, New York, June 10, 1840.
James De Peyster Ogden to Cooper, New York, August 4, 1840.
James De Peyster Ogden to Cooper, New York, March 23, 1841.
James De Peyster Ogden to Cooper, New York, August 15, 1845.
J. K. Paulding to Cooper, Washington, September 4, 1838.
J. K. Paulding to Cooper, Washington, May 20, 1839.
J. K. Paulding to Cooper, Washington, January 20, 1840.
W. Pell to Cooper, New York, August 29, 1839.
Thomas Randall to Cooper, Belmont, Florida, August 27, 1844.
W. C. Rives to Cooper, Paris, March 12, 1832.
Joseph Salkeld to Cooper, Naugatuck, November 13, 1846.
Charles A. Secor and others to Cooper, New York, August 31, 1844.
W. B. Shubrick to Cooper, New York, January 10, 1827.
W. B. Shubrick to Cooper, Baltimore, October 4, 1837.
W. B. Shubrick to Cooper, Newport, February 24, 1838.
W. B. Shubrick to Cooper, Newport, August 31, 1838.
W. B. Shubrick to Cooper, Navy Yard, Norfolk, Virginia, April 7, 1841.
W. B. Shubrick to Cooper, New York, September 9, 1842.
W. B. Shubrick to Cooper, Gosport, Virginia, January 6, 1843.
W. B. Shubrick to Cooper, Washington, November 23, 1843.
Benjamin Silliman to Cooper, New Haven, September 19, 1831.
William Gilmore Simms to Cooper, Charleston, South Carolina, September 27, n. d.
William Gilmore Simms to Cooper, Woodland, North Carolina, April 10, n. d.
Ashbel Smith to Cooper, New York, March 31, 1837.
I. W. Stevenson to Cooper, Albany, September 7, 1839.
W. M. Stewart to J. D. Elliott, Indiana, August 15, 1842.
Jacob Sutherland to Cooper, New York, March 13, 1822.
T. W. White to Cooper, Richmond, August 2, 1836.
John Willard to Cooper, Saratoga Springs, December 8, 1841.
Samuel Williams to Cooper, Waterloo, August 7, 1844.
G. A. Worth to Cooper, New York, September 14, 1838.
G. A. Worth to Cooper, New York, June 18, 1839.
G. A. Worth to Cooper, New York, July 11, 1839.

VII. Unpublished Letters and Manuscripts, in Various Collections

J. F. Cooper to the Bread and Cheese Club, Paris, November 18, 1826. New York Historical Society.

J. F. Cooper to Carey, Lea, and Carey, London, May 6, 1828. Aldis collection, Yale University Library.

J. F. Cooper to Captain Dobbin, Cooperstown, May 20, 1843. Buffalo Historical Society.

J. F. Cooper to the Editors of the Naval History, Yale University Library.

J. F. Cooper to J. G. Flügel, Cooperstown, June 15, 1844. Morgan Library, New York City.

J. F. Cooper to J. De P. Ogden, Cooperstown, June 11, 1839. Maine Historical Society, Portland, Maine.

J. F. Cooper to John Whipple, New York, January 14, 1834. Photostatic copy, Yale University Library.

Susan Fenimore Cooper to R. W. Griswold, Cooperstown, November 24, 1851. Boston Public Library.

Horace Greenough to W. C. Bryant, Boston, November 4, 1851. Penniman collection, Yale University Library.

S. F. B. Morse to Cooper, New York, February 21, 1833. Unpublished passage. Letter published without this passage, *Samuel F. B. Morse, His Letters and Journals*, II, 21 ff. Typewritten copy, Library of Congress.

S. F. B. Morse to Cooper, New York, July 16, 1833. Typewritten copy, Library of Congress.

J. K. Paulding to President Martin Van Buren, December 6, 1834. Van Buren correspondence, Library of Congress.

Alvan Stewart, Diary, July 5, 9, 12, 13. New York Historical Society.

Jacob Sutherland to President Martin Van Buren, Geneva, New York, April 12, 1837. Van Buren correspondence, Library of Congress.

INDEX